The Renewal of Civilization

Essays in Honor of Jacques Maritain

PUBLICATIONS OF THE

AMERICAN MARITAIN ASSOCIATION

General Editors:
Anthony O. Simon (1990 – 2004)
Michael Torre (2009-)

Jacques Maritain: The Man and His Metaphysics
Edited by John F.X. Kansas, 1988
ISBN 0-268-01205-9 (out of print)
Distributed by the University of Notre Dame Press

Freedom in the Modern World: Jacques Maritain, Yves R. Simon, Mortimer J. Adler
Edited by Michael D. Torre, 1989, Second Printing, 1990
ISBN 0-268-00978-3
Distributed by the University of Notre Dame Press

From Twilight to Dawn: The Cultural Vision of Jacques Maritain
Edited by Peter A. Redpath, 1990
ISBN 0-268-00979-1
Distributed by the University of Notre Dame Press

The Future of Thomism
Edited by Deal W. Hudson and Dennis Wm. Moran, 1992
ISBN 0-268-00986-4
Distributed by the University of Notre Dame Press

Jacques Maritain and the Jews
Edited by Robert Royal, 1994
ISBN 0-268-01193-1
Distributed by the University of Notre Dame Press

Freedom, Virtue, and the Common Good
Edited by Curtis L. Hancock and Anthony O. Simon, 1995
ISBN 0-268-00991-0
Distributed by the University of Notre Dame Press

Postmodernism and Christian Philosophy
Edited by Roman T. Ciapolo, 1997
ISBN 0-8132-0881-5
Distributed by the Catholic University of America Press

The Common Things: Essays on Thomism and Education
Edited by Daniel McInerny, 1999
ISBN 0-9669226-0-3
Distributed by the Catholic University of America Press

The Failure of Modernism: The Cartesian Legacy and Contemporary Pluralism
Edited by Brendan Sweetman, 1999
ISBN 0-9669226-1-1
Distributed by the Catholic University of America Press

Beauty, Art, and the Polis
Edited by Alice Ramos, 2000
ISBN 0-9669226-2-X
Distributed by the Catholic University of America Press

Reassessing the Liberal State: Reading Maritain's Man and State
Edited by Timothy Fuller and John P. Hittinger, 2001
ISBN 0-9669226-3-8
Distributed by the Catholic University of America Press

Faith, Scholarship, and Culture in the 21st Century
Edited by Alice Ramos, and Marie I. George, 2002
ISBN 0-9669226-5-4
Distributed by the Catholic University of America Press

Jacques Maritain and the Many Ways of Knowing
Edited by Douglas A. Ollivant, 2002
ISBN 0-9669226-4-6
Distributed by the Catholic University of America Press

Truth Matters: Essays in Honor of Jacques Maritain
Edited by John G. Trapani, Jr., 2004
ISBN 0-9669226-6-2
Distributed by the Catholic University of America Press

The Human Person and a Culture of Freedom
Edited by Peter A. Pagan Aguiar and Terese Auer, O.P., 2009
ISBN 978-0-9669226-7-7
Distributed by the Catholic University of America Press

Maritain and America
Edited by Christopher M. Cullen, S.J. and Joseph Allan Clair, 2009
ISBN 978-0-9669226-8-4
Distributed by the Catholic University of America Press

The Renewal of Civilization: Essays in Honor of Jacques Maritain
Edited by Gavin T. Colvert, 2010
ISBN 978-0-9669226-9-1
Distributed by the Catholic University of America Press

The Renewal of Civilization

Essays in Honor of Jacques Maritain

Edited by

Gavin T. Colvert

AMERICAN MARITAIN ASSOCIATION

Distributed by the Catholic University of America Press

Washington, D.C. 20064

Library of Congress Cataloging-in-Publication Data

The renewal of civilization : essays in honor of Jacques Maritain / edited by Gavin T. Colvert.
p. cm.
Includes bibliographical references and index.
ISBN 978-0-9669226-9-1 (alk. paper)
1. Maritain, Jacques, 1882-1973. 2. Civilization, Modern--Philosophy. 3. Catholic Church and philosophy. I. Maritain, Jacques, 1882-1973. II. Colvert, Gavin T., 1965-
B2430.M34R46 2010
306.01--dc22

2010036646

Manufactured in the United States of America

Distributed by the Catholic University of America Press
620 Michigan Avenue, N.E. /240 Leahy Hall
Washington, DC 20064

ACKNOWLEDGEMENTS

"Marriage has to perform in human hearts quite another work--an infinitely deeper and more mysterious, alchemical operation: I mean to say, it has to transmute romantic love, or what existed of it in the beginning, into real and indestructible human love, and really disinterested love which certainly does not exclude carnal passion and desire but which rises more and more above them, because in itself and by essence it is principally spiritual--a complete and irrevocable gift of one to the other, for the love of the other."

— Jacques Maritain, *Notebooks*, Chapter 7

With love and gratitude for the self-gift of those who cannot be repaid:

for
Danielle, Brendan, and Gabrielle

List of Abbreviations

CT - Compendium Theologiae.

DDN – Expositio super Dionysium De divinis nominibus.

DM – De Malo.

DV - De Veritate.

In Boeth. De Trin. – Expositio super librum Boethii De trinitate.

In Eth. – In Decem Libros Ethicorum Aristotelis ad Nicomachum Expositio.

In Pol. – In Libros Politicorum Aristotelis Expositio.

In Io – Lectura super Johannem Reportatio.

In Job – Expositio in Job ad litteram.

In Ps. - Postilla super Psalmos.

(I,II,III, IV) Sent. - Scriptum super libros Sententiarum.

SCG – Summa Contra Gentiles.

ST - Summa Theologiae.

Contents

PART II

CIVILIZATION AND THE ARTS

PART III

CIVILIZATION, CHRISTIAN MORALITY AND CHRISTIAN CULTURE

Introduction

If you give democratic peoples education and freedom and leave them alone... they will...make life daily more comfortable, smooth, and bland... But while man takes delight in this proper and legitimate quest for prosperity, there is a danger that in the end he may lose the use of his sublimest faculties and...at length degrade himself... In a democracy therefore it is ever the duty of lawgivers and of all upright educated men to raise up the souls of their fellow citizens and their attention toward heaven. There is a need...to make continual efforts to propagate throughout society a taste for the infinite, an appreciation of greatness, and a love of spiritual pleasures.[1]

In his magisterial study of American politics, Alexis de Tocqueville speaks of an inherent tension in modern life between the healthful progress of liberty and the cancerous growth of license. A democratic people that ceases to pursue human excellence, especially its spiritual dimension, is bound to degenerate. No mere expression of nostalgia for a bygone age, Tocqueville's warning is a serious reminder to those who embrace hope for progress in modern civilization not to lose sight of the transcendent and to be mindful of the pursuit of higher human virtues as a ground for moral and political action and theorizing. In spite of Tocqueville's warning, it appears that our politics is moving inexorably, since the past century, toward the very forgetfulness against which he warns.

Speaking of the particular version of liberal political theory that dominates contemporary American thought, Michael Sandel laments our form of discourse, because it insists that "government be neutral on moral and religious questions" and "that matters of public policy and law be debated and decided without reference to any particular conception of the good life."[2] This way of thinking and acting, Sandel

---

[1] Alexis de Tocqueville *Democracy in America*, 1st Perennial Library edition by J. P. Mayer (New York: Harper & Row, 1988).

[2] Michael J. Sandel, *Democracy's Discontent: America in Search of a Public Philosophy* (Cambridge, Massachusetts: Belknap Press of Harvard University Press, 1996), p. 24.

argues, "cannot contain the moral energies of a vital democratic life."[3] His own Communitarian alternative to contemporary Liberal political theory aims to recover, among other things, some sense of the commitments to formation of character and duty to the common good that animated pre-modern political thought. Sandel is not alone in his thinking. Numerous students of contemporary culture recognize that we are experiencing a crisis of "civilization at the crossroads" between Modernity and Post-Modernity, to adapt terminology used by Jacques Maritain. Modern life focuses increasingly upon the protection of individual rights, while at the same time losing a principled basis for that commitment. Governments become less responsive to individual citizens, precisely because they see themselves as "emancipated" from allegiance to traditional intermediate social institutions, such as the family and religious communities, which formerly gave them structures of representation and meaning.[4] The paradox of Modern times is therefore a tension between progress in our understanding of the dignity of each individual person, and a diminution of the individual's relationship to the mediating social institutions and ethical norms that provided the historical ground for this development. Slowly but surely, the Church and Catholic intellectuals have become increasingly aware of the need to respond to this civilizational crisis.

At the mid-point of the previous century, the Catholic Church promulgated the Pastoral Constitution *Gaudium et Spes*, toward the close of the Second Vatican Council. This document has shaped the Church's self-understanding of its responsibility toward the reform and renewal of modern life in the intervening half-century. Although imbued with a spirit of optimism about human progress characteristic of the time, the document evinces awareness of many of the cultural challenges that have become more apparent since its promulgation. Confidently, *Gaudium et Spes* "proclaims the rights of man" and "esteems the dynamic movements of today by which these rights are everywhere

---

[3] Ibid.

[4] For a helpful discussion of this point, see Pierre Manent, *Democracy without Nations?: The Fate of Self-Government in Europe* (Wilmington, Delaware: ISI Books, 2007).

fostered."[5] Yet, at the same time, it insists that "these movements must be penetrated by the spirit of the Gospel and protected against any kind of false autonomy."[6] As if to echo Tocqueville, the Pastoral Constitution goes on to warn that failure to recognize the place of transcendent goods in human life will lead to the destruction of human dignity, rather than to its preservation. Furthermore, it acknowledges the increasing urgency, due to the growth of skepticism and relativism, for more profound reflection: "Though mankind is stricken with wonder at its own discoveries and its power, it often raises anxious questions about the current trend of the world, about the place and role of man in the universe, about the meaning of its individual and collective strivings, and about the ultimate destiny of reality and of humanity."[7] *Gaudium et Spes* thus articulates a comprehensive challenge in moral and political theory for the contemporary Christian intellectual.

Jacques Maritain was an elder statesman and a leading Catholic intellectual of the twentieth century at the time *Gaudium et Spes* appeared in 1965. "Schema XIII," as he called it in the *Peasant of the Garonne*, promised to light a flame of renewal within the Church and set the blueprint for a new engagement with Modernity. Surveying this situation in *The Peasant,* Maritain understood with clarity that a true dialogue with the modern world could be neither facile nor conducted strictly in traditional terms. Old problems would need to be thought anew in the light of eternal truths. But this "aggiornamento," as Maritain described it, ought not to be a case of "kneeling before the world," either.[8] Merely un-insightful clinging to traditional sources would fail to engage Modernity's deep and accelerating problems, while uncritical acceptance of modern assumptions would fail to provide viable alternatives. Over forty years later, we continue the effort to navigate between that Scylla and Charybdis of modern life.

---

[5] *Gaudium Et Spes*, §41, "Pastoral Constitution on the Church in the Modern World," Promulgated by His Holiness, Pope Paul VI on December 7, 1965, http://www.vatican.va/archive/hist_councils/ii_vatican_council/documents/vat-ii_cons_19651207_gaudium-et-spes_en.html (accessed July 15, 2010).

[6] Ibid.

[7] Ibid., §3.

[8] Jacques Maritain, *The Peasant of the Garonne: An Old Layman Questions Himself About the Present Time* (New York: Holt, Rinehart and Winston, 1968), p. 53ff.

This collection of essays addresses the project of civilizational renewal from a variety of viewpoints, including its ethical, political, aesthetic and religious dimensions. The authors provide a variety of perspectives, both critical and hopeful, concerning such matters as the common good, moral truth, the virtues, human sociality, culture, art and the beautiful, Christian morality and metaphysics, and the vocation of a Christian intellectual. The essays draw upon traditional and contemporary philosophical and theological sources, including especially the work of Jacques Maritain. In the spirit of Maritain's Aristotelian-Thomism, perhaps it is best to begin with those considerations that lie at the end, namely both those that are addressed at the end of the volume, and those that concern the ultimate purpose of human life, especially the first principles that ought to guide our thinking. The third section of the book addresses this constellation of concerns, including moral first principles, the importance of a sound metaphysics and philosophical anthropology, and the task and authentic stance of Christian intellectuals toward being and truth.

With respect to these considerations, Maritain's *Peasant of the Garonne* provides a helpful starting point and some important guidance. He suggests that the task of the Christian philosopher is to engage Modernity in light of an understanding of permanent verities, in order to effect the transformation of the temporal world.[9] Perhaps, when some consider the active transformation of the temporal world, they imagine that Maritain is speaking exclusively of a sort of applied ethics and politics, or even of political activism, but this could not be further from the truth. To the contrary, he emphasizes the importance of "contemplation in the world" over against the misguided sense of a "messianic mission of the proletariat."[10] Two points merit consideration in light of this remark. First, Maritain's sarcasm shows that he is dubious of conceiving the temporal mission of the Christian person primarily or exclusively as the production of a heaven on earth through "social justice." He objects to this conception, in part, because it is utterly utopian and unrealistic. Christian humanism contemplates a more modest and realistic task than Marx, and therefore a more important one according to Maritain, because it is grounded in a

---

[9] See Ibid.

[10] Ibid., p. 199.

genuine philosophical anthropology, and because it is achievable.[11] The second and more important point to be considered is that the vision of a "messianic mission of the proletariat" fails to recognize the importance of "wisdom" itself and the idea of "contemplation in the world," which is very evidently an amalgam of the themes of action and contemplation. It is not only the Christian philosopher's task to contemplate what the temporal mission of the laity should be, but to be a witness to the importance of "contemplation in the world" as an essential component of that temporal mission itself.

Maritain suggests that we can begin to understand this concern by considering an essentially continuous line of thinking from Descartes to Marx. In Part VI of his *Discourse on Method*, Descartes announces that we are to achieve mastery of nature, while, for Marx, the work of the communist state is a kind of praxis that, as Maritain observes, will "give [man] full and complete mastery of the world and will make him, so to speak, the god of the world."[12] On the contrary, Maritain argues that we can never become masters of nature. We can only "intervene in the destiny of the world."[13] His point is not only that modern thought overestimates the capacity of human power to subdue the world, but also that it wrongly conceptualizes the relationship of human beings to the world, having lost the sense of the relationship between the Creator and creatures. Modern philosophy tempts us to misunderstand the call to transform our world through activity, because it fails to understand the theoretical and contemplative dimensions of life. Christian philosophy, on the other hand, must be an example of "contemplation in the world." The contemplative mindset is not only characterized by a certain type of activity, but also by a stance toward the world, which includes respect for an order of truth and goodness that transcends our manufacturing and demands a responsible posture. This view has important ethical and political implications, but it also requires significant epistemological and metaphysical premises. Maritain concludes that Christian philosophy is especially well suited to the task

---

[11] See Ibid., p. 204.

[12] Ibid., p. 200.

[13] Ibid., p. 201.

of renewal in the present circumstances, because it is disposed to metaphysical realism and recognition of transcendent truth.

In his recent book, *The Wisdom of the World*, the French thinker Rémi Brague makes essentially the same point. According to Brague, the traditions of Greek philosophy and Biblical faith, synthesized by Christian philosophers in the Middle Ages, understood the importance of what he calls, "the wisdom of the world."[14] The wisdom of which he speaks is not physicalism or *réal politique*, but an awareness of a transcendent objective reality and the sense of man's place in a cosmological order that has genuine ethical implications for human existence. The task of engaging Modernity contemplated by *Gaudium et Spes* thus necessitates a careful consideration of metaphysical and ethical first principles, as well as an appropriate reinvigoration of philosophical anthropology. Brague's use of the term "cosmology" does not imply a crude deduction of ethical and political norms from the stars and human nature, but a reflective understanding of the world in which an explanation of the meaning of human existence is of central importance. The Christian intellectual cannot simply revert to the ancient conception of the *cosmos* as a means of addressing this concern, but he or she must find a way back from the failure of reductionist and empirical conceptions of nature that dominate our contemporary conceptual landscape.

In his article "Christian Identity And Scholarly Vocation In A Secularized World," Carlos Casanova considers the plight of the contemporary Christian intellectual in the secular academy, including the increasingly secular ethos that pervades even religiously affiliated institutions in the United States. Post-Modern Liberalism's insistence upon bracketing transcendent principles from our public discourse, according to Casanova, exercises a coercive influence on the standards by which institutions train and measure their up-and-coming academics. He contends that this coercion contributes to a diminution of the quality of scholarly dialogue and teaching at Catholic institutions.

---

[14] Rémi Brague, *The Wisdom of the World: The Human Experience of the Universe in Western Thought* (Chicago: University of Chicago Press, 2003).

Denis Scrandis, in his article "Christian Morality: A Morality Of The Divine Good Supremely Loved According To Jacques Maritain And Pope John Paul II," makes the case for the importance of appealing to the transcendent first principles that Casanova laments are often lacking in the modern academy. Drawing upon the moral philosophy of Jacques Maritain and the theology of John Paul II, Scrandis argues that the Christian conception of the transcendent purpose of human life provides essential clarification of certain *aporiae* in Aristotle's classical attempt to articulate human happiness in terms of the natural end of man. In particular, Scrandis points to the Christian understanding of self-giving love as an essential aspect of a satisfactory account of the moral life.

Patrick Lee also takes up this very theme in his essay "St. Thomas On Love Of Self And Love Of Others." It has been said by some influential historical and contemporary commentators that Aquinas' moral philosophy is necessarily a form of moral egoism, because his account of *eudaimonia,* or human happiness, presupposes that the highest end is one's own beatitude. Contrary to this supposition, Lee argues that Aquinas' account of friendship and human excellence depends upon an inherently social conception of human nature. St. Thomas is not an egoist, according to Lee, because for him genuine self-love is inseparable from the love of God and love of neighbor.

James Hanink's essay "Analogy: Mischief, Malice And Metaphysics" picks up the question of the importance of a realist metaphysics and philosophical anthropology as a sound basis for moral philosophy. He applies his insight that a sound metaphysics is essential to the practical questions of one very important form of human friendship—marriage. Hanink makes the provocative argument that clarification of the metaphysical and ontological issues at stake provides reason for defending the distinctive character of the institution of traditional marriage.

Finally, Joseph Califano argues in his article "Truth And Suffering" that coming to terms with the most important, fundamental and comprehensive first principles or truths of human existence requires some experience of human suffering, and that such suffering can for that very reason be a great gift.

The essays in the first section of the volume depend upon the foregoing metaphysical and anthropological foundations discussed by authors in the third section, while taking up questions concerning the relationship between individual persons and the common good from a variety of perspectives. A central concern of a number of these essays is the relationship between the progress of individual rights in Western culture and the defense of a conception of moral absolutes and the common good, especially as these relate to the American political context.

"There is no peace without justice," Pope John Paul II often said.[15] Many of our contemporaries, although fond of this expression, strenuously disagree with the stands John Paul took on such fundamental matters as abortion, contraception, and the nature of marital life. Citizens of Western liberal democracies agree about the general principle that social justice requires the protection of fundamental rights, but they disagree with equal vigor concerning who counts as a person, and about the extent and limitations of human rights. What is the source of this simultaneous agreement and difference of opinion? It is a product of the evolution of the doctrine of human rights and the concepts of the dignity and autonomy of persons, upon which the doctrine is based. While we all profess respect for personal dignity and individual autonomy, the theoretical underpinnings of this surface consensus are deeply disputed. The dispute is an inevitable result of the fact that "rights" discourse was intended by many of its early proponents to repudiate traditional concepts of nature, justice and the common good. We ignore this fact at our peril, since it makes us fail to appreciate the difficulty of achieving consensus regarding the necessity of grounding rights in a substantive theory of the human good.

Undoubtedly, acknowledgement of the inalienable dignity of individual persons is of practical value in advancing the cause of freedom. The United Nations adopted a Universal Declaration of Human Rights in 1948. Jacques Maritain was instrumental in the

[15] See, e.g, "Message of His Holiness Pope John Paul II for the Celebration Of The World Day Of Peace," January 2002, URL: http://www.vatican.va/holy_father/john_paul_ii/messages/peace/documents/hf_jp-ii_mes_20011211_xxxv-world-day-for-peace_en.html.

creation of this document. His support for the cause of human rights continued the ground-breaking work in Catholic social thought inaugurated by Leo XIII's encyclical letter *Rerum Novarum*. As a result, Catholic social teaching since Vatican II has placed heavy emphasis upon the rights and dignity of the human person. At the same time, however, what constitutes a "human right" and who counts as an entity worthy of respect has been a point of increasing dispute. What is remarkable is that this should come as a surprise to any Catholic social theorist. Maritain recognized that talk about natural or human rights involves an agreement to disagree about the theoretical underpinnings of a theory of justice. In the wake of various challenges to the natural law tradition in the early modern period, thinkers postulated the existence of certain inalienable natural rights. Thanks in part to the work of Immanuel Kant, we have come to understand these rights in terms of a theory of autonomy. But Kant divorced the concept of personal autonomy from a substantive conception of human nature as ordered to a final end. Those who have followed in Kant's wake have taken this doctrine further, conceptualizing human rights as "unencumbered" properties belonging to persons regardless of any particular substantive vision of human nature or the moral good.

This raises a serious question as to whether the modern language of "rights" can be domesticated by the efforts of Catholic social theorists, including Maritain, in order to render it compatible with traditional accounts of the natural law and justice. The empirical evidence of growing disagreement about how to define and limit contemporary rights claims renders this prospect increasingly doubtful. Maritain's work in this area is especially seminal, because he represents one of the best-known efforts to straddle the divide between the older natural law tradition and the contemporary discourse of human rights. His work also appears to contain various successful and failed strategies. For instance, his personalistic account of human dignity may allow him to avoid many of the pitfalls of the modern "unencumbered" conception of the self, because it recognizes the necessity of rooting human dignity in a substantive conception of human nature and the human good. Furthermore, Maritain's "personalist" as opposed to "individualist" view of persons insists upon a relational account of the person and society and asserts an important difference between genuine liberty under law and mere license. On the other hand, some scholars have suggested that Maritain's "integral humanism" goes too far in the direction of accommodating modern Liberalism's understanding of individual freedom and pluralism.

The source of Maritain's putative difficulties in this area may have originated with the emergence of the rights doctrine as a form of discourse in Catholic social teaching during the nineteenth century. The language of rights, especially natural rights, became a familiar part of the vocabulary of Papal teaching with the publication of Leo XIII's encyclical letter *Rerum Novarum* in May of 1891. As Ernest Fortin points out in his study of the encyclical, Pius IX had condemned the errors of Modernism as late as 1864 and had resisted the intrusion of Liberalism into the Church's teaching at that time.[16] Leo XIII, on the other hand, embraced the doctrine of natural rights as a means of providing the Church's response to social concerns arising out of the struggles between labor and capital in the 19th century. Leo did not implement the rights doctrine uncritically in his encyclical. He was careful to combine the language of rights in the document with that of duty.[17] In addition, the foundation for his doctrine of rights was the Thomistic conception of natural law and its corresponding teleological account of human nature.[18] Modern doctrines, on the other hand, tend to treat rights as benefits or moral powers belonging to an agent, not duties arising from the order of law and justice.[19] Some critics maintain that this development in Catholic social teaching is unprecedented, and that it constitutes a dangerous opening to radical individualism and moral subjectivism.[20]

---

[16] See Ernest L. Fortin, "Sacred and Inviolable: Rerum Novarum and Natural Rights," in Ernest L. Fortin and J. Brian Benestad, *Human Rights, Virtue, and the Common Good: Untimely Meditations on Religion and Politics* (Lanham, Maryland: Rowman & Littlefield, 1996).

[17] See, for example, *Rerum Novarum*, §12-13, which speaks of the "rights and duties" of the state and the family.

[18] See, for example, Rerum Novarum, §9.

[19] See Fortin, "Sacred and Inviolable," pp. 202-05.

[20] See, for example, Robert P. Kraynak, *Christian Faith and Modern Democracy: God and Politics in the Fallen World* (Notre Dame, Indiana: University of Notre Dame Press, 2001).

The extent to which Pope Leo's endorsement of rights language represents a problematic departure in thinking depends significantly upon how we understand medieval theology's relationship to the rights doctrine. Opinions on the subject vary. John Finnis, for example, argues that Thomas Aquinas had a conception of natural rights, even if he did not have the terminology to express it.[21] On the other hand, scholars such as Ernest Fortin and Robert Kraynak argue that Aquinas never had anything like a modern concept of rights, nor indeed the political ideology that underlies them. The core of their argument is that medieval thinkers emphasized virtue and duty towards the common good as primary, whereas the modern language of rights in Locke and Hobbes emphasizes the priority of the atomistic individual and claims made upon the social order.[22] Fortin offers a compelling illustration of this point in his discussion of *Rerum Novarum*. Pope Leo asserted in §7 that "Man precedes the state, and possesses, prior to the formation of any state, the right of providing for the substance of his body."[23] Pointing to Aristotle and Aquinas' view that the state is prior in nature to the individual, Fortin suggests that Leo's departure from the classical terminology constitutes, in essence, an embrace of the contractarian notion of a state of nature in place of the Aristotelian-Thomistic concept of the naturalness of the community and the priority of the common good. The embrace of the natural rights tradition in *Rerum Novarum* thus constitutes an important departure from the tradition.

---

[21] See John Finnis, *Aquinas: Moral, Political, and Legal Theory* (New York: Oxford University Press, 1998).

[22] See, Fortin, "Sacred and Inviolable," pp. 201-07; p. 21: "The passage from natural law to natural rights and later (once 'nature' had fallen into disrepute) to 'human' rights represents a major shift, indeed the paradigm shift in our understanding of justice and moral phenomena generally. Prior to that time, the emphasis was on virtue and duty, that is to say, on what human beings owe to other human beings or to society at large rather on what they can claim from them."

[23] Ibid., pp. 202 and 206. For a similar claim about the priority of the possession of natural rights to the state, see *Rerum Novarum*, §12-13: "Hence we have the family...a society very small, one must admit, but none the less a true society, and one older than any state"; "...the family must necessarily have rights and duties which are prior to those of the community, and founded more immediately in nature."

In response to this line of argumentation, it must be granted that modern rights theories often pit the rights of the individual against duty, the moral law and the common good. There is an obvious sense in which the language of "right" or "rights" has been transformed by atomistic conceptions of the individual and the rejection of natural teleology, which specifies the priority of the political community. These terminological transformations have important implications that cannot be ignored. The remaining question is whether these obvious and important differences in terminology and concepts create a gap that cannot be bridged between the language of natural law and that of natural rights, or whether there is a way to preserve the tradition while engaging the modern world in its own terms. In other words, is there a way of speaking the Kantian language of the dignity of the person without failing to recognize the priority of duty, law, virtue and nature?

An important line of thinking concerning this question, which is addressed by several essays in the volume, is that Maritain's philosophical personalism provides a means of achieving that goal. He lays down the key tenet of his personalist philosophy, the distinction between "personality" and "individuality" in *The Person and the Common Good.*[24] According to Maritain, contemporary political regimes, including the United States, stray from their appropriate foundations when they embrace a radically individualistic conception of persons over against a relational conception of citizens as both free and simultaneously obligated to a community. This relational conception allows him to speak of the inherent dignity of the individual, and to be comfortable with the language of rights. But his conception of personal dignity is grounded in our status as creatures made in the image and likeness of God, who are ordered to natural and supernatural fulfillment. Personalism thus provides Maritain with a vehicle to affirm a coherent framework from which to defend both liberty and moral obligation to the common good.

In a sense, the conception of the person for which he wishes to argue is a retrieval of an earlier, pre-modern view, since it recognizes a

---

[24] Jacques Maritain, *The Person and the Common Good*, translated by John J. Fitzgerald (Notre Dame, Indiana: University of Notre Dame Press, 1966).

transcendent dimension of human personality as ordered to a final end specified by our nature.[25] On the other hand, it is clear from Maritain's argument that our full awareness of the political role of personality is distinctively modern, in part because it is a deliberate reaction to radical individualism, and in part because the distinctively modern awareness of human subjectivity is new.[26] Maritain does not therefore regard the modern turn toward the "self" and interiority as unqualifiedly bad. It is unhealthy when we lose sight of the fact that individual human beings' value is firmly rooted in their transcendent dignity as creatures made in the image and likeness of the Creator. The modern preoccupation with "human dignity" is therefore not misplaced when the source of that dignity is properly understood. Maritain can then endorse the value of concepts such as "autonomy" and "individual freedom," provided they are placed in the proper context.

For Maritain, materialistic philosophies of human life, on the other hand, share some key deficiencies, whether they are individualistic or collectivist. The individual is treated as an "atomic" component of the state.[27] Both extremes repudiate the idea of a natural or "organic" harmony between individual and communal goods.[28] Common ethical norms are therefore imposed against the will. More significantly, materialism denies the intrinsic ordination of the person to a transcendent good, toward which the common good of the state must be "indirectly" subordinated.[29] Maritain notes that modern liberal democracies fail to overcome these difficulties, just like their totalitarian and communist counterparts, although for them the stakes are ultimately higher. Neither the Third Reich nor Stalinist repression could contain the aspirations for liberty of the millions they oppressed and killed. But McDonald's and the Internet are a great deal more seductive. In the final analysis, Maritain proposes that liberal democracy will survive and flourish only if it repossesses a sense of its

[25] See Ibid., pp. 11 and 13.

[26] See Ibid., p. 12.

[27] Ibid., p. 101.

[28] Ibid., p. 101.

[29] Ibid., p. 103.

subordination to a spiritual quest that cannot be its own particular goal, but must, in a plurality of ways, be the goal of its citizens.[30]

In discussing his own view, Maritain stresses that there is no single doctrine of "personalism" as such.[31] It is not a particular thesis or school of thought. If there is a family resemblance among these views, it is that the concept of "person" provides a suitable focal point for a critique of nineteenth century individualism and its antithesis, collectivism. Maritain draws upon his personality/individuality distinction in order to argue that, whereas individuals are strictly incommunicable, persons are inherently social and capable of self-giving.[32] Of course, for St. Thomas, incommunicability is an essential feature of personality.[33] But Maritain is aiming at a point on which he and St. Thomas can find common cause. The individuality or distinction that marks material substances divides them from the rest of reality, whereas personality, both in the case of the Trinity and also of human persons, indicates "subsistence" or "interiority to oneself" and simultaneously community.[34] Personality suggests a kind of wholeness or unity that is not contrary to being a part of something else.[35] Liberal individualism conceives of human beings as atomic wholes that cannot easily be joined to one another, while communist and totalitarian collectivism must reject the integrity of the individual in order to reduce him or her to being a part of the whole. Maritain sees in the shift from "individuality" to "personality" a healthy middle course to follow, between individualism and collectivism.

Some may think of the concept of "personality" as an expression of self-interest and power, like Callicles in Plato's *Gorgias*, who advocates *pleonexia* or constant over-reaching toward self-gratification.[36] Maritain calls the reader's attention, on the other hand, to the "personality" we

---

[30] See Ibid., p. 105.

[31] See Ibid., p.12.

[32] See Ibid., p. 39.

[33] See ST I 30.4c.

[34] Maritain, *The Person and the Common Good*, p. 41

[35] See Ibid., pp. 56-58.

[36] Ibid., p. 31.

associate with heroism, generosity and self-sacrifice. He makes sense of these incompatible characterizations of personality by identifying a "material" and "spiritual pole" in human nature.[37] The material dimension of nature is the source of our separation from all other things—our individuality. The spiritual dimension of nature is the source of an agency that goes out from the person to other beings—our personality. Persons are therefore centers of action who are capable of self-giving in spite of their material separation and incommunicability.[38] Focusing exclusively upon material individuality leads us away from the community of other persons, toward physical self-gratification, and it fails to recognize the higher calling of human personal life.[39] This, in turn, leads to distorted political theories that stress radical individualism or the subordination of the individual to the collective. The metaphysical conception of persons as unities of matter and spirit ordained to the transcendent good of friendship with God and one another thus provides Maritain with a powerful tool for analyzing and offering a corrective to the pitfalls of nineteenth and twentieth century political ideologies.

Contemporary Liberalism views the common good as the maximal concomitant liberty of each material or "unencumbered" individual.[40] The rights of the individual are characterized as being apart from and prior to any substantive conception of the human good. Maritain's personalist conception, on the other hand, recognizes the ordination of the political community to a good for each person that transcends the material dimension of individuality. For the sake of this good, which is genuinely a good for each, and for the common good of society, some material liberties to dispose of ourselves and others as we wish are limited. This point is the basis for Maritain's claim that the secular political state, while it must admit religious pluralism and other forms of diversity, should simultaneously have an uncompromising commitment to objective principles of the natural law and to a deeper sense of the transcendent value of human life. Since the political

---

[37] Ibid., p. 33.

[38] See Ibid., p. 39.

[39] See Ibid., p. 45.

[40] See Ibid., p. 50.

common good must respect the transcendent vocation of human persons, Maritain's conception of liberty and the protection of rights is very different from that of contemporary Liberalism. We do not respect the dignity of persons merely by removing any and all barriers to the satisfaction of personal preferences. Although a pluralistic society such as the United States cannot make the deeper purpose of human life its direct objective, it must secure the pursuit of that higher purpose for its members. This includes those who claim that pursuit as their birthright, as well as those who do not, and also the defenseless, who cannot claim it. Genuine respect for persons thus includes the political community's commitment to principles of the natural law and human fulfillment.[41] Genuine liberty is therefore inherently social, and it can only be preserved through the acknowledgement of objective truths about the transcendent good of human persons.

The essays in the first section of the volume address the foregoing concerns relating to the individual and the common good, the necessity of grounding a concept of rights in substantive moral first principles concerning the human end, and human beings' natural sociality. They draw upon a variety of sources from within the Catholic intellectual tradition, including Maritain, Aquinas and Aristotle, among others. Particular attention is given to the question of whether Maritain's personalism is able to provide him with the tools necessary to balance individual rights against duties of justice, virtue, and the common good. Peter Simpson's essay "We Are Bruised Souls: Maritain's America Fifty Years On" takes up these questions by offering a careful consideration of how Americans can say that out of the many we form one body politic. Simpson compares Jacques Maritain's and Karol Wojtyła's philosophical personalism as two distinct but related ways of accounting for genuine political community. He takes the personalistic notion of human beings as centers of interiority and self-gift as a way of describing what constitutes the community, and he applies this concept to Maritain's observation that American optimism is explained by the historical narrative of immigrants who have come to our shores in order to re-invent themselves "hopefully" as members of a new political community. John Trapani discusses one important source of our American hope and optimism, the set of first principles articulated

---

[41] See Ibid., p. 63.

in the *Declaration of Independence*, which formulates the propositions that constitute our national identity. His essay, "We Hold These Truths: Objective Truth, Reasoned Conviction, And The Survival Of Democracy," offers a meditation upon the opening words of the *Declaration*. The abiding concern of Trapani's essay, however, is whether we as Americans have lost the deeper meaning of the truth of our ideals. Trapani worries that the principles articulated by the Framers of our political regime have become, in essence, mere words that we repeat out of a sense of loyalty to our traditions, and he contends that unless we repossess a living grasp of the meanings that undergird those words, our way of life will thereby be endangered.

Fr. Joseph de Torre's essay, "The Common Good And The Good Society: The Genesis Of A Concept And Its Consequences," provides a helpful overview of the genesis of the concept of the common good within the Western and Catholic intellectual traditions. As de Torre observes, at the core of the evolution of Western thinking concerning this concept there is a fruitful tension between increasing respect for individual rights on the one hand, and preservation of duties to the community on the other. Having articulated the concept of the body politic and explored some of the essential features of political communities' shared commitments to moral truth and the common good, James Jacobs offers an interesting and provocative argument concerning the concrete implications of these concepts. Contrary to the prevailing academic fashion of procedural political theory, his essay, "Moral Absolutes, Moral Relativism, And Political Representation," sets out to defend two bold conclusions: first, that contemporary efforts to exclude "one's moral vision" from his or her stand on matters of public policy must ultimately reduce to a form of moral relativism, and second, that Christian political candidates who bracket their personal beliefs about the morality of abortion are unsuited for political office. Jacob's conclusions rest upon a fairly straightforward argument, with premises that he admits are highly controversial. The bulk of the essay consists in an examination and defense of his three central premises: 1) that relativists hold each person "competently defines the good for himself," 2) the primary responsibility of government is to legislate for the common good, and 3) that the relativist cannot endorse legislation for the common good, since he or she necessarily is agnostic about any particular "vision of the good."

Arguably one of the most important contemporary Catholic intellectuals to address the question of the relationship between one's deeply held religious and moral beliefs and life in the public square, John Courtney Murray, is the subject of Michael Torre's essay, "Murray After Fifty Years: Reflecting On America And Its Proposition." Torre offers a thoughtful analysis of Murray's own thinking and various reactions to it by Protestant and Jewish intellectuals over time. Torre's central thesis is that Murray was correct to assert the need for Americans to repossess the intellectual foundations of their belief in certain moral first principles, by acknowledging and embracing a common commitment to the natural law tradition. Similar to Jacobs and other authors in the volume, however, Torre criticizes what he sees as Murray's underestimation of the corrosive influence of secular individualist culture upon American's ability to recognize and accept the common foundation of natural law principles. Fr. James Schall, S.J., in his essay "The Real Alternatives To Just War," takes up what may constitute a primary example of the distorting effects of contemporary culture upon Americans' understanding of traditional moral principles. Far from being a "war hawk" or an advocate of moral Machiavellianism, Fr. Schall's thesis is that it is vitally necessary to make the rational case for some uses of force in our modern world. Schall's argument rests upon his agreement with St. Augustine that we cannot escape the reality of our fallen human condition. Contemporary culture often tends toward the utopian idea that our institutions have permitted us to evolve beyond war, that "war is not the answer." Schall reminds the reader that the forgetfulness of our principles associated with this utopian illusion can lead us to fail to protect the very order of peace and justice, and the institutions of liberty, equality, and dignity, that allow us to contemplate such a utopian idea.

A recurring theme in Alice Ramos' essay, "Toward A Recovery Of The Moral Sense," is the need for recollecting moral first principles, especially those relating to the transcendent meaning and purpose of human life, which Aquinas argues are contained in the natural *habitus* of *synderesis*. Ramos takes as her point of departure a dialogue between the secular humanist Umberto Eco and Carlo Maria Cardinal Montini. While sympathetic to Eco's notion of a natural ethics that neither presupposes transcendent premises nor is incompatible with them, Ramos observes that "nature wounded by sin does not do all the good that it would have done in the state of original justice." Her contention is that Christian scholars should do more to cultivate the inherent openness of *synderesis* and conscience to the infinite good, which is contained at least implicitly in every operation of conscience. The final essay in the first section of the volume, "Aquinas On Trust And Our Social Nature," by Marie George, considers Aquinas' teachings concerning natural human sociality. Like the preceding essays that concentrate upon the human personal capacity for self-gift, George argues that the forms of trust appropriate to various kinds of friendship provide an essential ingredient for the maintenance of human society. Her account shows that a presumption of trust, with certain qualifications, is necessary. Trust speaks both to the moral goodness of the person who trusts, and also to the possibility for him or her to attain happiness through friendship. George thus shares with Patrick Lee a similar account of the priority of friendship and community in the attainment of human happiness.

The three essays in the middle section of the volume address the relationship between the arts and artistic activity on the one hand and civilization and the human good on the other. To say that this relationship is the most complicated topic considered in the volume's reflection upon the renewal of civilization is almost an understatement. As Jacques Maritain observed on numerous occasions, the relationship between art and morality is complex and multi-faceted. One must avoid the twin dangers of reducing art to morality and of falling into a kind of nihilistic aestheticism. As in his relationship to the modern discourse concerning rights, Maritain was sympathetic both to the classical understanding of beauty, and to the authentic value in numerous contemporary forms of artistic creativity.

In this respect, he differed from some of his religious contemporaries, who were inclined to dismiss various modern aesthetic perspectives as illegitimate. Maritain also differed with those contemporaries who were inclined to reduce artistic expression to a didactic or specifically moral and religious purpose. Here, again, it was necessary to find a path between two extremes. On the one hand, he had to oppose a set of moralizing tendencies that would threaten to diminish the intrinsic value of the artist's aesthetic conscience. On the other hand, Maritain was profoundly concerned about the tendency among some modern schools of art to ignore or even repudiate the moral responsibility of the artist, as a person and as a creator of art, to oneself and to his or her community. Similar to his personalist solution to the shortcomings of modern individualism, Maritain's response to the modern artistic challenge was to embrace a forthright dialogue with modernity in light of classical principles.

In *Art and Scholasticism,* for example, Maritain lays down the basic contours of his definition of "art" in classical Aristotelian terms. Art involves a kind of practical intelligence (art itself is an intellectual virtue), but it differs from morality as "making" differs from "doing."[42] While "doing" is the proper sphere of ethical action, and concerns the virtue of prudence and the good of human persons, art is not, strictly speaking, as an activity or an intellectual habit, concerned with the human good. Considered precisely in terms of its own object, Maritain argues, art "stands therefore outside the human sphere; it has an end, rules, values, which are not those of man, but those of the work to be produced."[43] For this reason, he observes, artistic excellence does not always presuppose rectitude of the will with respect to the human good.[44] In a short work entitled *The Responsibility of Artist,* Maritain cites the artistic genius of Wagner, which was incidentally inspired by an illicit attraction to a woman other than his wife, as an example of this phenomenon. [45]

This way of speaking is, however, open to at least two important forms of misinterpretation. First, we must distinguish the internal demands of artistic excellence, which are governed by the aesthetic requirements of the particular form of artistic activity engaged in by the artist, from the artist's activity as a human person. Maritain is quick to point out that *qua artist*, the activity of the human person enters into the realm of morality: "But for the man working, the work-

---

[42] See Jacques Maritain, *Art and Scholasticism, and the Frontiers of Poetry* (New York: Scribner, 1962), chapter 2.

[43] Ibid.

[44] See Maritain, *Art and Scholasticism and the Frontiers of Poetry*, chapter 4.

[45] See Jacques Maritain, *Scholasticism and Politics* (Garden City, New York: Image Books, 1960).

to-be-made enters—itself—into the line of morality...If the artist took the end of his art or the beauty of the work for the ultimate end of his operation and therefore for beatitude, he would be but an idolater."[46] Maritain's point here is that artists engage in their craft as a form of self-determination and choice. As such, their artistic actions are directed to the attainment of their own final ends, and they also have consequences for others that may contribute to the common good or violate the order of justice. Given that this is so, artists must not fail to appreciate the moral implications of artistic activity. Furthermore, they must not engage in the moral failure of imagining that artistic activity has no moral dimensions or implications.

These concern are addressed in different ways by Cornelia Tsakiridou's essay, "When Art Fails Humanity: Jacques Maritain: On Jean Cocteau, Modernism And The Crisis Of European Civilization" and Jorge Garcia's essay "White Nights Of The Soul: Christopher Nolan's Insomnia And The Renewal Of Moral Reflection." Tsakiridou discusses Jacques Maritain's very personal involvement in the life of the contemporary artist Jean Cocteau, who briefly converted to Catholicism under the influence of the Maritains. Cocteau's conversion was evidently not to last very long, in part because of his own personal moral struggles, but also in part because of his artistic sensibilities. A central consideration of her paper is Cocteau's modernist aestheticism, which tended to treat the moral quality of artistic activity—if not the whole of life—superficially. Tsakiridou sees in Cocteau an instance of what Maritain recognized more generally as the crisis of Western civilization's growing inability to grasp "vital forms of beauty" and value.

More hopefully, Jorge Garcia discusses Christopher Nolan's film *Insomnia* as an instance of popular artistic culture that demonstrates the possibility of a renewal of ethical reflection. To be sure, Maritain would have been sympathetic to Garcia's effort, since he did not despair of all things modern—especially modern art. Indeed, Maritain was at pains to clarify both the moral responsibility of the artist, against Post-Modern aestheticism, and the intrinsic responsibility of the artist to his or her work. Maritain opposed what he saw as the

[46] See Maritain, *Art and Scholasticism, and the Frontiers of Poetry*, chapter 9.

temptation of some of his co-religionists to favor an excessively traditional representational and moralizing aesthetic.

The claim that art, in itself, considered as an intellectual virtue, is not concerned with the human good, is also open to a second, more subtle, form of misinterpretation, which happens to be the central subject of the other essay found in this middle section of the volume, Monsignor Robert Sokolowski's essay, "Visual Intelligence in Painting."

While the standards of beauty that govern the excellence of a particular artwork may be intrinsic to it, and distinct from moral considerations as such, the subject matter of that work may be the human good itself. As Fr. Sokolowski suggests, the best way to understand a work of art, such as a "portrait" at its highest level, which differs from a mere "likeness," is as a "depiction of an essay at beatitude." Just as spoken or written language can be analyzed in terms of levels of meaning relating to the grammatical components of human speech, so a painting can be analyzed in terms of elements such as color, line, and placement. Ultimately, though, speech is intended to convey a holistic meaning, such as a thought or even a complete argument. Similarly, portraiture and other forms of visual artwork may be described as giving an account of an instance of a life—an attempt at happiness. In this way, also, the artist through his or her artwork is intimately involved in the work of civilization, even though responsibility to his or her activity—the work of art itself—may be governed by a set of standards that are not strictly speaking about the good of the person, but about the good of the thing made.

Given that there are any number of ways in which artistic activity can be said to have ethical implications, one may wonder why Maritain goes to some lengths to show that a classically inspired aesthetic can reserve room for the place of art as an intellectual virtue distinct from moral understanding and judgment. It would appear that this can be explained precisely by his concern to account for what is genuine in the modern repudiation of a moralizing conception of artistic activity, without giving into the assertion that art and the artist ought to have nothing to do with morality. Maritain's constant concern is always to engage in a dialogue with modern life and thought on its own terms, and yet to elevate it with the help of principles drawn from the Catholic and Western intellectual traditions. We may applaud the success or criticize the failure of his various attempts to walk this fine line between contemporary thought and the tradition. But, in every case, his work serves as a seminal example of how Christian intellectuals may take up the challenge of the renewal of civilization. The essays in this volume honor Maritain's life and work by attempting to continue that conversation, drawing from Maritain surely, but also engaging freely and forthrightly with classical, medieval and contemporary sources.

Gavin T. Colvert
Associate Professor of Philosophy and
Director of the Ecumenical Institute at Assumption College.

PART I

Civilization and the Common Good

"We Are Bruised Souls":

Maritain's America Fifty Years On

Peter L. P. Simpson

1. Introduction

The title quotation above comes from the heading of a chapter in Maritain's *Reflections on America.*[1] Maritain first wrote those reflections over fifty years ago now, for a series of seminars he gave at the University of Chicago in 1956. He released them in book form two years later. They constitute, as it were, his hymn of thanks and even his paean of praise for the country that he visited often, where he lived for many years, including the painful war years, and with which he came to fall in love. His love for America was the love of a man from 'Old Europe', a man who had grown up in and been informed by the history, mores, and thinking habits of that centuries-old civilization. America caught him almost off-guard. It certainly fascinated him with its vibrancy, its charm, and its very un-European newness.

This author can speak with some confidence on this point, not only because I am following Maritain's own remarks (especially Chapter IV), but also because I am an immigrant from 'Old Europe', like Maritain, who has gone through some of the same experiences. Admittedly my native country is Britain, not France, and that is no small difference. Still, it leaves us with a lot in common as well. As I read Maritain on America, both for the first time and again recently, I was struck by how often I found myself spontaneously agreeing with him. There is something tired and world-weary about 'Old Europe' that jaundices the way Europeans who have never been here look upon America and Americans. And there is something exasperating about trying to tell such Europeans, when one returns thither after long exposure to American life, that their opinions about America are as faulty as they are old.

---

[1] Jacques Maritain, *Reflections on America* (New York: Scribner, 1958), p. 83.

Let me, in fact, by way of illustration, relate a personal experience from a few years ago at a conference in Germany. One of the presenters was arguing against American foreign policy in Afghanistan (the invasion of Iraq had not yet happened). She wanted to trace such policy to the philosophical ideas of the German thinker Carl Schmitt, who was noted for his authoritarian and anti-liberal political views. Her argument was that George W. Bush was a latter day Schmittian, who needed to be exposed and resisted as such. But in fact whatever similarities there may have been at the level of effects between Bush's policies and Schmitt's statism, there were no such similarities at the level of political thinking. Bush was straightforwardly and even simply a Jeffersonian, like many Americans. He held that all men are created equal; that they have fundamental rights; that to take away these rights is only what tyrants do, and that tyrants should be resisted by all freedom-loving peoples. Bush likely knew little about Carl Schmitt and would, in any event, have rejected his totalitarian doctrines. But it was impossible to tell this to my colleague at the conference. She was convinced that a man who had started a war in Afghanistan and wanted to start another in Iraq could be nothing but a war-mongering statist. To suppose that Bush might have been motivated, however mistakenly, by love of freedom, and by the desire, however misdirected, to preserve freedom where it already existed and to bring it to victims of tyranny where it did not, was a manifest falsehood. Most of the other presenters shared a similar opinion, and some even professed ignorance of Jefferson's thought.

Anecdotes, such as this are, of course, merely anecdotal and can hide as much as they reveal. In particular, one must concede in this case that there are many Americans who held opinions of President Bush like the participants at the European conference. Few of these would be inclined to credit Bush with sufficient intelligence to know about or understand Carl Schmitt, nor would they be inclined to regard his Jeffersonian rhetoric of freedom as sincere. Still, they would admit that his rhetoric, for all its insincerity, was Jeffersonian and not Schmittian, and that only a Jeffersonian rhetoric could sell in America. The scholars at the aforementioned European conference, by contrast, were not able to reach a similar conclusion.

I repeat this story, not to build very much on it, but to signal my fundamental sympathy with Maritain's *Reflections on America* and to illustrate the contrast, or one of the contrasts, that he sees between the American and the European mentalities, or between the idealism of the first viewpoint and the world-weariness of the second. Consider the following statement made by Maritain:

> ...people [in America] need...to know more unquestionably, either through better established rational convictions, or through the testimony of their fellow men, that they are right, especially as regards their idealistic incentives and their faith in the power of good will and generosity.
>
> As a corollary, I would say that the unjust European (and Asian) refusal to recognize the good intentions of this country, while trying to offer for the immense effort of American good will any kind of cheap cynical explanation, is of a nature to cause damage to the American soul itself.[2]

I am not as fearful as Maritain on this point, but he is right about the idealism and good intentions that motivate, if not all American policy, then certainly the American people's support for such policy. We will return to this point later. For the present, however, it is important to raise a more directly philosophical or rather metaphysical question. Maritain does not discuss it in *Reflections*, although he does raise it elsewhere. The question concerns what it is that makes a book like *Reflections on America* metaphysically possible in the first place. What is the being of America, or indeed of any nation, such that we are justified in attributing to it characteristics, like optimism, that would seem proper only to individuals? Is such talk when predicated of nations literal, or metaphorical, or analogical, or something else? While this question is interesting in its own right, it also permits one to thematize an important feature about America that Maritain recognized and that bears repeated emphasis.

2. Collectives and Individuals

Let us begin to answer this question by quoting and summarizing some passages from Maritain's *Man and the State*. In that book he says a great deal that is relevant, in particular by drawing distinctions among the terms "nation," "society," "body politic," and "state." By a nation,

---

[2] Ibid., pp. 46-47.

Maritain understands a certain sort of *community*, and by a community he means something whose:

> ...object is a fact which precedes the determinations of human intelligence and will, and which acts independently of them to create a common unconscious psyche, common feelings and psychological structures, and common mores.[3]

It is thus distinct from a *society* where, by contrast, the object:

> ...is a *task* to be done or an *end* to be aimed at, which depends on the determination of human intelligence and will and is preceded by the activity—either decision or, at least, consent—of the reason of individuals.[4]

He says further about community that it is "a product of instinct and heredity in given circumstances and historical frameworks"[5], and that hence in a community, as opposed to a society:

> ...the collective patterns of feeling...have the upper hand over personal consciousness, and man appears as a product of the social group.[6]

Communities thus typically precede societies in time, but they may also follow them, since a society, in addition to its existence as a conscious and free creation around a common aim, will throw up a community and community feelings within itself. The spontaneous and instinctive operate as much in society as out of it and produce similar effects in both cases. The specific community that is a nation is described by Maritain as:

> ...a community of people who become aware of themselves as history has made them, who treasure their own past, and who love themselves as they know or imagine themselves to be, with a kind of inevitable introversion...The Nation has a historic calling, which is...a historical and contingent particularization of

---

[3] Jacques Maritain, *Man and the State* (Washington, D.C.: Catholic University of America Press, 1998), p. 3.

[4] Ibid.; italics in original.

[5] Ibid., pp. 3-4.

[6] Ibid., p. 4.

> man's calling to the unfolding and manifestation of his own multifarious potentialities.[7]

By the *body politic* or *political society*, on the other hand, Maritain means the most perfect of societies—in contrast to the lesser societies of families, business firms, labor unions, or scientific associations. It is, of course, like a community, a body of men and so is possessed of flesh and blood, instincts, passions, reflexes, and unconscious psychological structures and dynamisms, but:

> ...all of these subjected, if necessary by legal coercion, to the command of an Idea and to rational decisions. Justice is a primary condition for the existence of the body politic, but Friendship is its very life-giving form. It lives on the devotion of the human persons and their gift of themselves.[8]

The body politic is thus very close to the idea of the nation and in given cases the two might be practically synonymous or the same in their extension, though differing still in their intension or their fundamental meaning. Indeed the two may so feed into each other that a national community of a higher human degree can spontaneously take shape on the basis and by virtue of the very existence of the body politic.

> Nothing matters more, in the order of material causality, to the life and preservation of the body politic than the accumulated energy and historical continuity of that national community which it has itself caused to exist. This means chiefly a heritage of accepted and unquestionable structures, fixed customs and deep-rooted common feelings which bring into social life itself something of the determined physical data of nature...[9]

Maritain expressly mentions America (along with France) in this connection, thus indicating what sort of phenomenon he takes America

---

[7] Ibid., pp. 5-6.

[8] Ibid., p. 10.

[9] Ibid., pp. 10-11.

to be: a nation formed by and forming its own political reality, its own body politic.[10]

Still, the body politic, for all its political reality, is not the same as the *state*. Rather it is related to the state as a whole is related to its part, or to its topmost part. The state is identified by Maritain with the governing part of the body politic or the part that is:

> ...especially concerned with the maintenance of law, the promotion of the common welfare and public order, and the administration of public affairs.[11]

Maritain's accounts of "community," "nation," "society," "body politic," and "state," which I have merely summarized here, are pregnant with significance for the understanding of human life and action, as *Man and the State* in particular goes on to show. In fact, by way of an aside, it is worth remarking that John Rawls' political thought, which is currently so dominant in academic circles, would have been much improved and have had more salutary effects, both in theory and in practice, if it had paid proper attention to Maritain's work. Still, that is not our present concern. Nor is our concern the state, whether the American or any other state. For it is clear that in his *Reflections on America* Maritain was not focusing on the American state. On the contrary, as he himself says, there is no allusion to politics to be found in that work. It is "by peoples, not by governments"[12] that his attention is captivated, and, further specifying this, he says:

> ...our appreciation of a country or a people has to do with the knowledge of...that immense collective personality which is a people with its history, its mores, its common psyche, its dreams, its vocation.[13]

These words clearly echo what Maritain says about the nation in *Man and the State*, so we may readily conclude that it is America as a nation in the way previously explained which is his object in *Reflections*.

---

[10] Ibid., pp. 8-9.

[11] Ibid., p. 12.

[12] Maritain, *Reflections on America*, p. 11.

[13] Ibid., p. 16.

Recall, nevertheless, that the American nation is there explained by reference also to the American body politic. The American nation is not a merely biological or ethnic phenomenon, as might be some ancient tribe of Mongols or Goths. It is, like many another nation, a *political* growth. This is a point to which we will return again below.

When we put together Maritain's remarks in *Man and the State* with those in *Reflections on America*, we can therefore fairly say that he has properly isolated and explicated what he is taking as his subject matter. But while Maritain has isolated the phenomenal fact of the collective identity of a nation, it is not clear that he has fully penetrated the constitution of the fact. That is, he has yet to give an account of what it is about individuals that enables them, while remaining individuals with all the rights and privileges and dignity of individuals, to take on collective characteristics or even a collective individuality and personality. How do the many become a one? In a footnote to *Man and the State*, Maritain says the following:

> The notion of moral or collective personality—in which "personality" has a *proper analogical* value—applies to the people as a whole in a genuine manner: because the *people* as a whole (a *natural whole*) are an ensemble of real individual persons and because their unity as a social whole derives from a common will to live together which originates in these real persons. Accordingly, the notion of moral or collective personality applies in a genuine manner to the *body politic*, which is the organic whole, composed of the people...[14]

In the same footnote Maritain denies that the state is a moral personality, except metaphorically, because, he says, it is not a whole but an agency of the body politic that it serves in some sense to represent.

Maritain is correct that the state is not a moral personality as the people are, but this statement must be qualified. For while the state is not a proper political whole, nevertheless, insofar as it is in fact constituted by and in given individuals (those vested with the authority of the body politic), these individuals can very well, and often do, form

---

[14] Maritain, *Man and the State*, p.16, footnote #11; italics in original.

a whole and possess a collective personality in exactly the same way as the individuals who constitute the body politic can. The European critic of American foreign policy in Afghanistan mentioned above, for example, was attributing to the Bush administration such a collective personality. To that extent, indeed, she may well have been right, and may well have been correct also in attributing to the Bush administration something of a Schmittian personality. Men in power are easily tempted, and sometimes by the best of motives, into amoral *realpolitik.*

Insofar as those who actually wield political power form a collective personality and arrogate to themselves the rights of the body politic, they are committing injustice, the injustice, as Maritain himself points out, of tyranny. But then what we should say is not that the state *is not* a moral personality but that it *ought not* to be, or that, to the extent it does, in a given case, come incidentally to form one, it possesses no rights. Its function is rather to represent and foster the rights of the body politic. Maritain, to be sure, would not object to this emendation or rather clarification of his remarks, since it would seem to express what he really intended. Still it does, when made explicit, require us to return to and reflect more deeply on the phenomenon of collective personality—not, indeed, as to the fact, for that is plain to see, but as to the reason for the fact. Thus, we repeat the question, how do the many form a one?

The previously mentioned footnote from Maritain quoted above points the reader in the correct direction. It speaks of the collective personality of the body politic as deriving from a *common will* that originates in the real persons who are the body politic. But this just throws the question further back, for how do many individual persons come to form a common will sufficient to create a single personality? To repeat, the question is not whether people can do this. For it is manifest they can. The important question is *how* they do it, or what are the psychic mechanisms of this process.

In order to answer this question, we may turn to another of Maritain's writings, his *Person and the Common Good.* In that work he distinguishes between what he calls individuality and personality. He says of the former that it is the material pole of man and of the latter that it is the spiritual pole. Individuality refers to man as he is an actually existing entity, a concrete composite of body and soul that stands out both from nothing and from all other things. In short, it refers to man as he is a primary substance. Personality belongs in the same category but is very differently focused. Maritain understands it principally through what a man, already constituted as this individual, can do, namely to love another human being. Love in turn he understands as self-gift, or the capacity we have both to give our own self and to receive back as a gift the self of another. Love may thus be the act, as opposed to the substance, of a person, but it comes from and goes to the very essence of the person and not merely from or to qualities and accidents.

> Personality bears witness in us to the generosity or expansiveness of being...which constitutes, in the secret depths of our ontological structure, a source of dynamic unity and unification from within. Personality, therefore, signifies interiority to self...[which], of its essence, asks for a dialogue in which souls really communicate.[15]

It is clear that what Maritain means by individuality and personality are not the same as what is meant by body and soul. An individual is already, he says, the substantial unity of body and soul, but he is not yet, or not yet understood as, a person. A person is also an interior and self-possessed unity capable of self-gift, or at least that is how I would express Maritain's intention. Maritain himself, however, seems to be struggling to find the right words to say what he wants. Perhaps he is operating with distinctions that are too limited for his meaning. The distinctions in question are those of body and soul and of substance and accident. Maritain clearly wants personality to belong to the category of substance and not to that of accident, even though he comes to it, and describes it, through something that does belong to the category of accident, namely the act of love. On the other hand, he does not want to identify personality with soul, even though soul does belong in the category of substance, because soul does not express what is distinctive of personality, namely self-gift, and, further, because soul, along with body, already constitutes what he means by individuality. So in effect,

---

[15] Joseph W. Evans and Leo R. Ward, *The Social and Political Philosophy of Jacques Maritain: Selected Readings* (Garden City, New York: Image Books, 1965), p. 8.

he says and does not say that personality is and is not substance and accident. What Maritain really wants, or at any rate needs, is to break out of the categories of substance and accident and body and soul and adopt some other way of speaking about the phenomenon of personality that he has in mind.

At the same time that Maritain was trying and failing to find the right terms to use in speaking about the person, a young man was trying and succeeding at the same endeavor. The young man, who was an admirer of scholasticism just like Maritain, was Karol Wojtyła, later to become Pope John Paul II. While accepting and using scholastic categories, Wojtyła added to them the categories (though he did not call them that) of *lived experience* and of the *self*. These categories were not new things introduced to supplement or to replace old things, nor were they new dimensions, never before noticed, of old things. Rather they were new ways of looking at or thematizing old things. They were, to speak in the terms of the history of philosophy, phenomenological ways of doing scholastic things. For that is what, in the last resort, Wojtyła was: a phenomenological scholastic, or a scholastic phenomenologist.

This can be illustrated with a few quotations from Wojtyła, supplemented by some explanatory remarks made previously by this author. First, Wojtyła wrote:

> The self is nothing other than the concrete suppositum humanum which, when given to itself by consciousness...in the lived experience of action, is identical with...self-possession and self-governance...The lived experience of our personal subjectivity is simply the full actualization of all that is contained virtually in our metaphysical subjectivity (suppositum humanum)... The suppositum humanum and the human self are but two poles of one and the same experience of the human being.[16]

Notice here how Wojtyła, almost in verbal echo of Maritain, speaks of two poles. Maritain spoke of the two poles of *man*, which he

[16] Karol Wojtyła, *Person and Community*, translated by Theresa Sandok (New York: Peter Lang Publishing, 1998), pp. 231-32.

identified as the material and the spiritual poles, and as individuality and personality. Wojtyła, by contrast, speaks of the two poles of *experience*, which he identifies as *suppositum* and self. Maritain, in other words, is doing ontology or metaphysics and so he speaks of the being that man is, while Wojtyła is doing phenomenology, and so speaks of the experience that man has. This difference is crucial. For whereas Maritain has difficulty saying what he means without falling into scholastic difficulties, Wojtyła, whose intention and even meaning are really the same as Maritain's, has no such trouble. To quote my own comments on Wojtyła on this point:

> [T]he concept of the suppositum, taken precisely as such (that is, as a *metaphysical* subject), does not yet bring to light the full richness of the being of that suppositum, namely that it is a *personal self.* Only in lived experience, in reflexive consciousness and deliberate action, does the self both come to light and, in a sense, also come to be. The self after all, says Wojtyła, "is constituted through the mediation of consciousness in the suppositum." The self, we may say, is none other than the suppositum come to itself through a sort of re-creation of itself in its own self-conscious activity. Such a reality can, of course, be reduced to the metaphysical categories of substance and accident. But before one does that one can pause at it and take it for what it is in its own dimension as lived experience.[17]

In other words, when we look at the person, not through the scholastic categories of substance and accident or body and soul, but as it manifests itself to us in the category of lived experience, what we find is the self, and this self is neither mere *suppositum* nor some accident superadded to *suppositum*, but *suppositum* consciously possessed and consciously determined. It is Maritain's free self-giving person expressed in non-Maritainian and non-scholastic ways.

This point needs some further elaboration. Elsewhere, Wojtyła speaks of what he is doing as "pausing at the irreducible" in man.[18] He does not mean, of course, pausing at the metaphysically irreducible, for man is manifestly reducible in this way (namely to the being of body

---

[17] Peter Simpson, *On Karol Wojtyła* (Belmont, California: Wadsworth, 2001), p. 17.

[18] Wojtyła, *Person and Community*, p. 213.

and soul and of substance and accident). He means pausing at the experientially irreducible. For our subjective being as concrete selves or self-experiencing subjects is indeed irreducible as a lived experience. It cannot be expressed or explicated in metaphysical or scholastic terms but only, as Wojtyła puts it, in *personalistic* ones. This does not mean abandoning metaphysics or scholasticism (Wojtyła is insistent that there is no opposition here but rather complementarity). It only means abandoning metaphysical or scholastic terms that are arguably the source of Maritain's embarrassment and confusion. He wants to do with one set of terms, those of scholastic metaphysics, something that can only be done with another set of terms, those of personalist phenomenology.

But let us not be unduly harsh on Maritain. For, despite the inadequacy of his categories and his vocabulary, he succeeded in isolating what is distinctive of the person, namely the self-possession of self-gift. Moreover, he used this idea, though not these words, to shed light on many matters, political and moral and theoretical and practical. His *Man and the State*, as I have already remarked, not to mention others of his writings, was outdoing Rawls even before Rawls put pen to paper, and he himself, through his service at the UN, was outdoing rights activists before rights activism had come of age. Moreover, and more to the point of the present analysis, his ideas, as re-expressed in the terminology of Wojtyła, can be used to answer the initial question posed above: namely how can the many persons in a nation and a body politic become the one that is that nation and body politic and take on the corresponding characteristics?

The answer can be articulated by appealing to the aforementioned concept of self-gift, which is common to both Maritain and Wojtyła. For it is by and because of self-gift that several persons can come together and form a single whole or a community. Still, we need to know precisely what is meant by self-gift, or how it is that persons can give themselves to each other and thereby become a one from many. In a previous treatment of this subject this author noted:

> ...participation is the acting together of two or more persons who, through such joint action, are constituting, as it were, a joint self. Each is thus energizing his personal freedom (which only the person himself controls) in the service of the other's

> energizing his personal freedom. This amounts to self-gift in the sense that the self that is constituted through that action...is given to the other so that both may, as regards their realization in that action at least, be one joint self and be jointly realized and fulfilled in that one self. The one is being constituted in the other as the other is being constituted in that one.[19]

The key concept expressed here is that a community, or at least a deliberately formed community, is the self-determination by several individuals of their individual freedom in the realizing of a common activity, and thereby the formation, by those same individuals, of a self that is many—because formed in many individuals—and one—because formed by one activity. For if the self, as Wojtyła explains, is the self-determined activity lived by and in the *suppositum humanum*, then any self-determining of this *suppositum* is creative of the self, and a self-determining activity of the *suppositum* that is at the same time the self-determining activity of other *supposita* is creative of a self that is the self of many *supposita* at once. This resulting joint self is genuinely many because it is realized at the same time in many *supposita*, and genuinely one because it is one activity done at the same time by these many. This activity could not, for instance, exist, at least not as this activity, if only one of the many was in fact acting, since the activity is, *ex hypothesi*, common and not single. Such a reality, despite its conceptual complexity, is exceedingly common. Two or three people willingly pushing a car up a hill together are, on this account, constituting a joint self for themselves in that joint action. The creation of a joint self through the self-gift of many is thus as ordinary as the day.

If we understand the one that is a nation along these lines, we will be able to say both how a nation is a genuine reality and not, for example, a mere being of reason formed by an act of mental aggregation. We can also explain how a nation can have characteristics that are personal and conscious. For it will be a reality constituted in acts of which many supposita are equally the self-determining agents.

However, there is more that needs to be said. For Maritain is insistent, and correctly so, that there is something biological and even

---

[19] Simpson, *On Karol Wojtyła*, p. 56.

automatic about the being of nations, something that is sub-conscious or pre-conscious in their make-up. A nation, unlike a body politic, is not in every respect a deliberately formed self. There are elements in it that happen to its members and that its members do not choose or do. Now Wojtyła is himself insistent on this difference between what happens to or in us and what we do. It is the latter and not the former that makes us to be the selves that we are. Nevertheless, what happens to or in us cannot simply be dismissed. On the contrary, it is a real part of what we are. Moreover, where possible, it supplies matter to be taken up by self-determination and consciously integrated into the selves we are making. For whatever belongs to us in some way, whether physically or psychologically or emotionally, is going to be caught up, if only unconsciously, into the self that we are creating through our acts of self-determination. That we are male or female, for instance, black or white, tall or short, even hairy or bald will have some effect on the whole that we are whether we want it to or not. The whole realm of the bodily, and consequently the whole realm of spatial and temporal determinations, is of this sort. There is no doubt that we do not have to pay express attention to all or even much of this most of the time. We can let it be as part of the mass of contingent material that always conditions our environment and that pretty much takes care of itself. But we can pay attention to it and any of it can, at particular times and places, become something we should pay attention to. So, the fact that we are bald or balding may require us, in very hot or cold weather, to wear some protection and thus baldness will become matter for conscious self-determination as regards headgear.

Such matters are perhaps relatively minor, but other bodily parts and certainly our passions and feelings are not so. They are in particular need of conscious integration if we are to be fully harmonious wholes. The same holds also for the features that Maritain notes as proper to the formation of nations. While these, in a sense, just happen to us, they can become consciously chosen or even consciously rejected. Our native language and our particular accent as well as our mannerisms are of this kind. Of course we can, at least when we come of age, consciously embrace them or consciously go about changing them. Admittedly, we cannot do much to change our color or our height. But we can do something to change our bodily shape and mannerisms so as to conform to those of another nation or class. We can certainly subject ourselves willingly to the unconscious processes that form languages and accents and mannerisms by living among those who have and display those characteristics.

Emigration and immigration are, in fact, among the archetypal processes whereby we do this, and, at least in the case of America, the phenomenon of immigration is of the greatest significance. For America, both North and South, is, almost solely, a creation of immigrants. True, there are descendants still among us of the pre-Columbian peoples, but these have been reduced to minuscule proportions or are now, through intermarriage, merged and mixed into the general mass. What stands out as the overwhelming fact and feature of America is immigration.

3. Immigration and Bruised Souls

An immigrant is that strange creature who, having abandoned the nation or people he happened to be born into, has made a self-determined choice to join another nation or people. He is someone who has chosen to turn what, for others, is happenstance into a self-conscious creation. Why anyone should do that; why anyone should leave his ancestral hearth and home and embrace what was never his and become what he never was, is an interesting question. But let us not downplay its metaphysical peculiarity. For an immigrant is the closest a human being can normally come to remaking himself from scratch, or to making the happenstance in him to be as much a matter of personal choice as the deliberately chosen. He is the closest to being a self-made man. Immigration can happen for many reasons, including those of force and compulsion. But the immigration that formed, and still daily forms, America is voluntary immigration. Typically, it is the voluntariness of both regret and hope: regret that leaving hearth and home was necessary and hope that arrival would make the leaving worthwhile.

Such regret and hope return me to the title of my talk and to Maritain's chapter in his *Reflections* on "bruised souls." He heard the words "We are bruised souls" from an American friend and they struck him, he said, in an "indelible" manner.

> They alluded to the wounds and sorrows of ancestors, and that memory of the sufferings caused by persecution and

prejudice which they left to their progeny as a spiritual patrimony...Each day, each year brings to the shores of America a flux of men and women who come from every part of the world and every cultural tradition, nearly broken by the moral persecutions, moral distress or physical poverty suffered in the Old World.

They come over to commit all their remaining forces to the common task of the land of promise which receives them. Their children will be told of their sufferings and keep them in memory, but they will share in the youthful force, hope, and activity of their new national community. They will embark on the pursuit of happiness...Here lies, in my opinion, a distinctive privilege of this country, and a deep human mystery concealed behind its power and prosperity. The tears and sufferings of the persecuted and unfortunate are transmuted into a personal effort to improve human destiny and to make life bearable...

But what is the objective meaning of that transmutation of the sufferings of the poor and the wounded into a new strength and a new hope—if not a Christian meaning projected into the sphere of temporal, social and political existence? Except under the shade of the Gospel such a phenomenon could neither take place nor make sense in human history.[20]

Picking up on this theme in the last chapter of the book, entitled "America is Promise," Maritain says:

There is one thing that America knows well, and that she teaches as a great and precious lesson to those who come in contact with her astounding adventure: it is the value and dignity of the common man, the value and dignity of the people...America knows that the common man has a right to the 'pursuit of happiness'; the pursuit of the elementary conditions and possessions which are the prerequisites of a free life and the denial of which, suffered by such multitudes, is a horrible wound in the flesh of humanity...[21]

---

[20] Maritain, *Reflections on America*, pp. 83-85.

[21] Ibid., p. 195.

Of course we are all aware, and Maritain is aware, of how America has denied this truth, beginning with the treatment of Blacks and Native Americans. But it is peculiar also how America, or the idea of America, was what kept America aware of the truth that she was at the same time denying. Those ringing words from Thomas Jefferson's *Declaration of Independence*, that all men are created equal and are endowed by their Creator with certain inalienable rights, have never ceased to accuse Americans within their own consciences and thus have never ceased to motivate them, sometimes at the expense of their treasure and their lives, to make that truth real, not only for all Americans, but also for all men.

We should not, of course, be starry-eyed about any of this. As Maritain is not slow to remind us, America, for all its gospel roots, is a human construction, not a divine one, and is as flawed and will be as temporary as any other human construction. Nevertheless, even human constructions are suffused with the divine and we should always ask about any one of them where and what the divine within them is. In America's case, the divine is the assertion of the equal dignity of all men from the greatest to the least. Moreover, the worldwide recognition, within public rhetoric at least, of such dignity is due almost entirely to the fact and success of the American experiment. The French experiment of equality, liberty, and fraternity, which followed closely on the heels of the American Revolution, has, as a matter of historical fact, been nowhere near as decisive. France never managed to form itself, or any other people, into a nation according to those ideals.

In America things have, for the most part, developed differently, despite the drive that has kept on manifesting itself in US history to imitate European oligarchy at home and European imperialism abroad—on which points, by the way, Mark Twain's exposés remain incomparable (as in his "To the Person Sitting in Darkness" and "Banquet for a Senator"). The reasons are still those that Maritain identified, namely that immigrants in pursuit of a more fully human life flock here because only here do they hope to find it. As a young man explained, just after becoming a citizen, in answer to the question why he had chosen to come to America, "here everyone has a chance." That is perhaps still not as true as it should be, but it is truer here than almost anywhere else. In too much of the rest of the world, birth into the wrong family or religion or class or place condemns one to a lifetime of inferiority. If this is ceasing to be as true in any particular place, as in parts of Europe, it is because of the increasing number of immigrants going there. In America, while there are social divisions, as there are elsewhere, these divisions are not fixed, or not in the sense that movement from one to another is hard or impossible. On the contrary, movement is fluid and rapid, and, as Maritain noted, he who is famous and rich one day may be forgotten and poor the next and the reverse again the day after.[22] That is why Maritain said America was a classless society and had no bourgeois—not because there were no extreme differences in wealth and privilege but because no such differences were static or fixed and no class mentality could accordingly develop.

The point at issue here might be put like this. In America, the human capacity to create one's own self through one's own self-determination, and not under the ineluctable pressure of fixed structures and traditions, is at its freest. Less is determined for people in advance and more is left for them to determine for themselves. The national character, unconscious as well as conscious, is to let the self determine the self. The national self, the joint product of many selves acting freely together, is that the self should be a free creation of each. To use Maritain's terms, the common object about which this human society has formed itself is personalist and pluralist[23]; or, to use Wojtyła's words, America has made self-determination the object of its own self-determination. It is the deliberate creation of the conditions for the fullness of self-determination for all, and so the deliberate creation of the conditions for the recognition, actual and concrete, of the human dignity of each. Although there are many for whom this is not true, there are many more for whom it is.

Self-determination is, to be sure, not some rudderless liberalism or individualism that is so adrift it cannot hold a course for human solidarity or responsible choice. There is no social indifference or moral relativism lurking beneath the surface here. That would be to deny the presence of truth in the American national character and in the idea of

---

[22] Ibid., p. 177.

[23] Ibid., p. 179.

self-determination. That all men are created equal and are endowed with rights is not an opinion, or an ethnic preference, or a historical quirk of mind; it is a self-evident truth. Our elites may want to forget or deny this, for example our trendy intellectuals, or our fevered hedonists, or even self-righteous secularists. But immigrants seldom do. Still, one might well wonder why the immigrants' intuition of what America really stands for—as opposed to what the elites say it does or should stand for—does not occupy a firmer place in the expression of public opinion or in the pronouncements of public figures. The foreigner has to dig out for himself the actual practice of America and the real experience of Americans. He can feel it, perhaps, as soon as he arrives; indeed, he has already felt something of it at home in imported movies, or music, or machines. But he lacks an adequate name for it. He knows the name of freedom, to be sure, but what content is he to give it here? What more does it mean in the concrete beyond what names like McDonald's and Microsoft and Marlboro mean? Indeed, what do even these names mean; that is, what human and metaphysical reality do they express? For there are many who cannot get beyond the names of McDonald's and Microsoft and Marlboro, or who, if they do, see in them only a reality that, while of some material advantage, is spiritually sinister.

Maritain took note of this problem:

> You are advancing in the night, bearing torches toward which mankind would be glad to turn; but you leave them enveloped in the fog of a merely experiential approach and mere practical conceptualization, with no universal ideas to communicate. For lack of adequate ideology, your lights cannot be seen. I think it is too much modesty.[24]

It is interesting that Maritain spoke of a lack of *adequate* ideology and not a lack of ideology simply. For we have had, in the public realm, quite a bit of very powerful ideology over the years. In more recent years, unfortunately, the ideology has been that of a relativist liberalism trying desperately to justify to itself the freedom, amongst other things, to kill babies in the womb and old people in their beds, and to export the same freedom throughout the World.

---

[24] Ibid., p. 118.

Now, it is not enough to protest this ideology or to oppose these deeds. A better ideology and better deeds must be put in their place. Such an ideology, or at least its fundamental ideas, has been present in America from the beginning, in those words from the *Declaration of Independence* quoted just above. What is needed, though, is not merely to repeat these words, for the true depth of their meaning is rarely penetrated. What is needed is to articulate them, as Maritain said, in an adequate ideology. Maritain can give us a lot of that ideology, but he cannot give us the whole thing. Moreover, he cannot give it to us in a powerful and distinctively contemporary form. He pointed the way forward; however, that way leads ultimately to the other author previously mentioned, namely Karol Wojtyła. Wojtyła's articulation of Jefferson's words and of Maritain's development is arguably the adequate ideology that Maritain wanted. This point was discussed previously, but it can be further illustrated by the words that Karol Wojtyła, or rather John Paul II, delivered in Saint Louis on his last visit to America in 1999:

> America first proclaimed its independence on the basis of self-evident moral truths. America will remain a beacon of freedom for the world as long as it stands by those moral truths which are the very heart of its historical experience. And so America: If you want peace, work for justice. If you want justice, defend life. If you want life, embrace the truth – the truth revealed by God.[25]
>
> At the same time I know that you will hear my plea to open wide your hearts to the ever increasing plight and urgent needs of our less fortunate brothers and sisters throughout the world. This too – the spirit of compassion, concern and generous sharing – must be part of the "*Spirit of St. Louis*". Even more, it must be the renewed spirit of this "one nation, under God, with liberty and justice for all." God bless you all! God bless America![26]

Much has changed since Maritain composed his reflections on America and much has remained the same. Most importantly, the idea

---

[25] John Paul II, "Homily at Vespers," January 28, 1999, Cathedral Basilica, St. Louis (*L'Osservatore Romano*, February 3, 1999).

[26] John Paul II, Arrival Speech, St. Louis Airport, January 26, 1999.

of America, as Maritain identified it, has remained the same. It is under attack, to be sure, as it was many times in the past, both at home and abroad. But many immigrants, Maritain's bruised souls, still know it and still embrace it. John Paul II also knew and embraced the American idea. He knew how to articulate it, to give it its adequate ideology, not only for the bruised souls, but also for the elites. Maritain's America fifty years on, if it is to continue true to itself, must be Karol Wojtyła's America.

We Hold These Truths:

Objective Truth, Reasoned Conviction, and the Survival of Democracy

John G. Trapani, Jr.

1. Introduction

The full title of this essay is, perhaps, even more contrived than the one that appears above; it is: "We (well, some of us) ... Hold (well, sort of) ... These Truths (well, at least ostensibly)." In order to justify this contrivance on these famous words from the Declaration of Independence, the first section of this paper explores the general significance of language used in human verbal communication. The second section ponders the interpretations and complications that result when these insights about language are applied to the expression: "We Hold These Truths." The conclusion of this paper reflects upon Jacques Maritain's essay, "The Philosopher in Society," and the practical significance of his words for the present world situation.

2. Words and Human Linguistic Communication

All human linguistic communication has at least three elements or "moments:" 1) what is meant by the one who speaks or writes, 2) what is said or written—the words used to convey that meaning, and 3) what is read or heard by the one who receives these words. These three components may or may not coincide—such are the delicacies and perils of human linguistic communication.

In the first "moment," the expression "what is meant," refers to the meaning or understanding of something that the speaker or writer has in mind when he or she desires to communicate.

In the second moment, this thought, meaning or insight, needs to be expressed in "adequate" language—those chosen words and expressions which the speaker or writer intends to capture and convey that meaning. It is interesting to note, however, as Suzanne Langer points out in *Philosophy In A New Key*, *meaning* is often like the clothes we wear—layered and all at once. The "*language*" we use to express that meaning, however, is like those same clothes strung out consecutively on a clothesline—they are then something noticeably different than when we wore them.[1] Moreover, as Ludwig Wittgenstein has observed, our words do not have "meaning" *per* se, but rather a "use" in a context.[2] Thus, the difficulties of human linguistic communication are often found not only in the poverty of our vocabulary and poor word choices, but also in the way in which we *use* language to express ourselves. Surprisingly, this difficulty comes from the richness of the words and symbols themselves. That is, since the connotation of a word or term refers to all of the attendant meanings that are connected to it, we sometimes end up "saying" even *more* or *less* than we intended. Additionally, is it not also true that we are sometimes obscure even to ourselves? We know "what we think we want to say," but we still may not be completely sure or clear about the words and expressions that we should employ in order to best capture that meaning. We may know we "haven't gotten *it* quite right;" or sometimes we may even experience that someone else standing nearby expresses more aptly the thoughts that *we* have in our mind!

Finally, as if this process of human linguistic communication were not already fragile enough, then comes the reception of these words by "the Other," this human person, in the vast depth of richness that constitutes his or her own historical, intellectual, and spiritual self. For beyond the sameness of the potentialities of our human nature are all of the nurtural differences of an individual's environment, upbringing, past experiences, and material/genetic makeup, including our predispositions, formed predilections, tastes, opinions, affections, prejudices, etc. Thus, not uncommonly, what someone *hears* (#3), in what was *said* (#2), may be different from what was *meant* (#1)!

With all of these delicacies of human linguistic communication in mind, we may now apply these insights to the expression "We Hold

---

[1] Suzanne K. Langer, *Philosophy In A New Key* (New York: The New American Library, 1951), p. 77.

[2] Ludwig Wittgenstein, *Philosophical Investigations* (Oxford: Basil Blackwell, 1967), p. 20.

These Truths" and ask: first, what are we to understand by the word, "We?" What might the Framers have meant by it? How do we understand it today, and in what ways, if any, has that meaning shifted from when it was first penned? Secondly, what is meant by the word "Hold?" Is there any significance to be found in the writer's choice of that term? Thirdly, what of the term "Truth" or "Truths?" Isn't it possible that, especially today, different people may hear that term to mean different things? And finally, we should ask, what bearing do these considerations have on the meaning of the expression as a whole, and for our understanding of democracy, both our own and others, in the world today?

3. "We," "Hold," and "Truths"

Question: "Who are "*We*?" Answer: "...the people." But who are "*the people*?" Answer: the body politic; the citizens of the nation. This definition, though simple, can have several interpretations. For example, first, in the broadest sense, "the people" refers to all of the inhabitants who have citizenship by birthright or by legal bestowal. Secondly, in a more restrictive sense, "the people" might refer only to those who are active *participants* in the process of government. A third sense (one worthy of mention but beyond the scope of this paper) may be implied when these terms are used rhetorically by the officers of government to obscure the line between the second sense and their own decisions. For example, on September 1, 2004, at the Republican National Convention, Vice President Dick Cheney used the expression, "*We* will decide," in a series of rhetorically effective ways that concealed a subtle shift of meaning and an intentional ambiguity: in one usage, his expression meant: "we, *the people of the United States* will decide;" but on a different occasion, he used it in such a way that it obscured a reference to a unilateral, purely executive decision: "we, *the President and I,* will decide."

In any case, in the first sense of the uses just mentioned, all citizens, including children, minors, the mentally disabled, and those who are not registered voters, are included; in the second sense, they are not. The second sense refers to those who, in Lincoln's celebrated expression, constitute a democratic government "*of* the people, *by* the people," while the first sense would refer to and include those excluded in the second sense, when it refers to a government that is "*for* the people."

Historically, this notion of "the people" has changed since the country's early beginnings. Then, African Americans were counted as only a percentage of a "whole man" (for census-taking and population representation), and they and women did not have the right to vote nor could they actively participate in government. Both of these groups were originally part of "the people" in the first sense, although not in the second. Although the Emancipation Proclamation and the Thirteenth and Nineteenth Amendments would officially or technically right these wrongs, it would still take many decades for these freedoms to be available in fact. In addition, ignorance, apathy, political pessimism, and a lack of will also keep a large percentage of "the people" from registering to vote and/or from exercising their privilege and responsibility. Moreover, language barriers, poverty, and illiteracy also contribute to the lack of participation by many citizens in their own governmental self-determination. These forms of self-disenfranchisement keep vast numbers of people from moving themselves from the broad sense of "we, the people" to the narrow, more restrictive sense. As a result, democratic government today appears to be more like a government "of *some* of the people, by *some* of the people, for *all* of the people." As we shall see, the voluntary (and sometimes involuntary) lack of participation and involvement will play a considerable part in threatening the very foundation of democracy itself.

The understanding of the second term, "Hold," is simpler to explore. On the one hand, a physical holding of something means to grasp it, to support it, to have in one's possession. By extension, when one "holds" something as a truth, it too becomes something that one grasps, supports and embraces. However, given the disparity between the first two senses of the word "people" or "We," and given the pluralistic nature of our current multicultural democracy, it is often times quite difficult to assess and understand the degree of intellectual conviction that "hold" signifies in the expression "We *Hold* These Truths."

The last term, "Truths" (or "Truth" in general), is the term most fraught with confusion and misunderstanding today; it is also the most important. On the surface, it, too, appears quite simple: the Framers had in mind certain values or ideals, which they understood to be essential for the foundation and sustenance of the new democratic government they sought to establish through the principles of the Constitution. These principles or ideals include not only life, liberty, and the pursuit of happiness, but imbedded in both the Declaration and the Constitution are the assumed or implied values that, as Jacques Maritain says, are the "moral tenants...on which democracy presupposes common consent."[3] What is interesting to observe in this discussion is the word that the Framers used to refer to these "moral tenants." They did not say "We Hold These *Values*," or "We Hold These *Ideals*," but "We Hold These *Truths*." Of course, they could not have known what a source of contention the word "truth" would occasion in a post-modern world! Had they used the terms "values" or "ideals," there likely would be no problem today, since, for most people, these terms have a kind of moral, metaphysical, or epistemological ambiguity. There are indeed all kinds of values and ideals that one might embrace today, and judgments about them are, generally, considered to be "value-neutral." Not so with the word of choice: truth; truth-claims imply that any opposing or contrary value or ideal must be *false*. The Framers *did* use the word "truth" and, by it, we can legitimately conclude that they *did* intend the objective validity of these truths. These are the "moral tenants" without which, Maritain warns, "democracy cannot survive."[4]

But what if it is the case that, today, these so-called "truths" receive only patriotic lip service and become occasions for flag-waving celebrations where the citizenry display, as Maritain says, a "deep-seated devotion to...values in which their intellect has ceased to believe?"[5] What if there should come a time when the vast majority of a democracy's citizens are "at a loss to find any rational justification"[6] for democracy's founding ideals? Has that time come? What if these ideals should lose their objective truth and unconditional value? Has that

---

[3] Jacques Maritain, "The Philosopher in Society," in *On The Uses Of Philosophy* (Princeton, New Jersey: Princeton University Press, 1961), p. 12.

[4] Ibid.

[5] Ibid., p. 11.

[6] Ibid., p. 12.

moment in history arrived? And if so, what, we might speculate, are the practical implications of this collective amnesia for the survival of democracy?

4. Objective Truth, Reasoned Conviction and The Survival of Democracy

When we reflect on the life of most Americans today (especially when contrasted with life in the many other troubled regions of the world), it is all too easy for us to take our abundant blessings for granted and to lose sight of the philosophical underpinnings of the Declaration of Independence and the U.S. Constitution, those principles upon which this nation was built, and which ought not to be overlooked or forgotten. As Maritain's essay challenges us to consider, what if a time should come when citizens of a nation such as ours today should "suffer a cleavage"[7] between the philosophical foundations of their ideals (what he refers to as "the inner cast of mind"[8]) and the ideals themselves? Then, might we not continue to *talk* about such things as rights and freedoms all the while that we have no idea about the true meaning (i.e., the philosophical underpinnings) of these foundational values and principles? If this indeed were to become the case, we then might continue to embrace the appearance of these ideals out of the habit of inherited tradition (what Maritain calls "the memory of past experiences"[9]) even though we may be "at a loss to find any rational justification for" them. "These things," Maritain stresses, would "no longer have for [our] minds any objective and unconditional value."[10] Is there a danger in this? Maritain certainly thinks so:

> There are a certain number of moral [and metaphysical] tenets—about the dignity of the human person, human rights, human equality, freedom, law, mutual respect and tolerance, the unity of mankind and the ideal of peace among men—on which democracy presupposes common consent; without a general,

[7] Ibid., p. 11.

[8] Ibid.

[9] Ibid.

[10] Ibid., p. 12.

> firm, and *reasoned-out* conviction concerning such tenets, *democracy cannot survive.*[11]

Maritain's practical challenge is as real and serious today as it was when he first wrote down these thoughts in the early fifties; perhaps, even more so. Given present-day current events, is it not the case that the partisan patriotism concerning our present military engagements in Iraq and Afghanistan is reminiscent of that team-spirit brouhaha that accompanies the send up to, and then the contest itself, found in rival athletic competitions? Do we really comprehend the gravity of our actions? Or, do we party-loving Americans wave our flags, enjoy our Memorial Day barbeques and 4th of July fireworks, all the while that, as a nation, we have lost any real sense of the true meaning of these ideals and hence may easily tire of some steady stream of bad news and body counts? Is our conviction based upon a commitment to realistic and meaningful principles, or do we too easily become weary through a lack of true conviction? In the enjoyment of the benefits that accompany the varying degrees of our economic prosperity, have we lost the intellectual understanding of the truth of those ideals that undergird the government's role and responsibility in helping its constituents to make a good life for themselves? These ideals include: the inherent dignity and sanctity of the human person, mutual tolerance and respect, human rights, equality, and freedom, respect for the rule of law, and the unity and peace of all humankind. Without these, Maritain's admonition remains clear, provocative, and disquietingly ominous; and as such, it bears repeating: "without a general, firm, and reasoned-out conviction concerning [these] tenets," he warns, "democracy cannot survive."[12]

---

[11] Ibid.; emphasis added.

[12] Ibid.

The Common Good And The Good Society:

The Genesis of a Concept and its Consequences

Joseph M. de Torre

The idea of the common good as the goal of the just society is a key feature of the Catholic intellectual tradition, and, more broadly, Judeo-Christian culture. It can be traced to the teachings of the Bible from the beginning of "salvation history" with the divine creation of the first man and the first woman formed out of the earth and quickened by a divine spirit. It is a part of the three great monotheistic religions claiming descent from Abraham, "the father of all peoples," as this name means in the Hebrew language.

The creation of Adam ("from the earth") and Eve ("mother of the living"), "both in the image and likeness of God" implies both a *community* of nature and a unique and unrepeatable *individuality* of each person, oriented to the infinite being of the Creator.

It seems evident from this teaching that in a good society there cannot be any incompatibility between the individual good of each person and the good of the entire community. However, if we look at the idea of the common good in historical perspective, we cannot deny this apparent conflict. In the Catholic intellectual tradition, we can trace the presence of this concept in major sources, from Augustine's *City of God,* to Aquinas's *bonum commune,* greatly elaborated by Francisco de Vitoria in the 16th century, and all the way to Paul VI's "integral *good* of the *whole* man and *every* man," developed further by John Paul II's central concept of *solidarity.*

If we relate the Catholic intellectual tradition to other schools of thought in the history of ideas, we observe a continuous debate regarding the concept of the common good and the nature of the individual and his rights. For example, we may be inclined to think in a Hegelian fashion of an antithetical or dialectical opposition or contradiction between individual and society.

Our purpose here is to make an historical review and reflection of the trajectory of the *common good* based on the Catholic intellectual tradition and to compare it to other traditions.

1. Historical Perspective

The concept of person as an autonomous image of a personal God was already in the mind of some of the earliest human beings on earth, as the findings of modern anthropology have suggested.[1] After those primitive societies, later civilizations—India, Persia, Assyria, Egypt, China, Greece—embraced pantheism and polytheism. With the exception of the Hebrews, many lost sight of the concept of person, and lapsed into political absolutism and a slavery-based economy. The ancient Hebrew nation, however, preserved the belief in a personal God to whom every man and woman is responsive and responsible.[2]

The great Greek thinkers, led by Socrates, under his motto "know thyself," focused once again on the uniqueness of the human being, open to infinity through *logos* (reason) and *eros* (love), *dynamis* (power) and *aretê* (virtue). The Romans, in their turn, through their legal and juridical genius, and enriched by Greek culture, arrived at a concept of *persona* approaching the Biblical view, with their stress on freedom and responsibility, liability and accountability before the law.

2. Toward a perfect definition

Boethius, in the 6th century of the Christian era, synthesized the best insights of Greco-Roman culture into the sublime view of the human person found in the Judeo-Christian tradition. His classic definition of "person" was a "*rationalis naturæ individua substantia,*" i.e., an "individual substance of rational nature." Key elements of his concept include:

(a) "individual," as opposed to abstract and universal, stands for what is undivided in itself and divided from anything else, implying a relative or

---

[1] Cf. Wilhelm Schmidt, *Der Ursprung der Gottesidee* (Münster, 1912-1952), 12 volumes.

[2] Cf. Ronda Chervin and Eugene Kevane, *Love of Wisdom: An Introduction to Christian Philosophy* (San Francisco: Ignatius Press, 1988).

absolute autonomy and independence, as well as existential actuality;

(b) "substance," as opposed to accident, stands for a being that exists by itself (subsistent) and may be the subject of accidents or beings that exist in another and perfect it, unless it is the perfection of being itself, which therefore does not need any accidents;

(c) "rational" stands for radical and unlimited openness to reality by means of understanding or intelligence, i.e., grasping in a non-material way what is essential in everything (what it is) in the context of existential reality;[3]

(d) "nature" stands for the essence of a substance as principle of operations specific to that substance, in this case the human nature, characterized by rationality and free decision.[4]

This is a classical, logically perfect, definition, inasmuch as it puts forward the proximate genus (individual substance) whereby the human person is classified as an animal, and the specific difference (of a rational nature) whereby the human person is neatly distinguished from other animals, and is in turn defined as a rational or political (i.e. social or other-oriented) animal.

The metaphysical make-up of the human person is thus constituted by an organic and symbiotic composition of:

(a) physical or material elements, with a potential but passive infinite divisibility which he or she shares with all the bodies of the cosmos;

(b) an active principle of life or immanent self-motion and self-production, which he or she shares with all plants;

(c) a consciousness of the outside world, indefinitely expanding his or her presence in it, which he or she shares with all animals by means of the sensory system and its consequent emotional system of responses; and

(d) an intelligence or reason, opened toward infinity by trans-sensible

---

[3] Aquinas widened this Aristotelian concept of rationality *(logos)* to include openness to divine revelation, whereby reason is brought to its full illumination.

[4] Cf. the author's *Christian Philosophy* (Manila: Vera-Reyes, 1980), 13 b; 16 d and e; 17 a, b and d; 23 b; 24 a; 25 f; 32; 33 f; 37 b, d and e; 40 f; 42 a.

knowledge and love, thus transcending or going infinitely beyond the limits of (a), (b) and (c).

3. The Total Picture of the Person

This wondrous reality of the human person, astride the physical and the metaphysical, the visible and the invisible, the quantifiable and the qualifiable, the earthly and the heavenly, the temporal and the eternal, moved Aquinas to remark that the person is the most perfect thing in the whole universe.[5]

That is why God, the most perfect being, cannot be a non-person, i.e. an impersonal force at work in the universe, but the most perfect Person. This is not an anthropomorphic scaling down of God to our level, but a scaling up of ourselves to His level.

The person thus stands out in the cosmos as clearly and essentially distinguished from

(a) mere machines or systems of transmission of motions, whether existing in nature or artificially made by human ingenuity: the human person certainly has mechanical aspects, but it would be a metaphysical blunder of the first magnitude to reduce the human being to them (this is the error of Cartesian mechanism);[6]

(b) mere vegetables and animals: obviously he or she has elements of such, but it would also be metaphysically inappropriate to reduce the human being to them (this is the error of biologism or organicism).[7]

4. Person, World and Community

The 20th century has witnessed atrocious occurrences of such metaphysical blunders in the name of misguided ideologies attacking

---

[5] See the author's Being Is Person: *Personalism and Human Transcendence in Socio-Economic and Political Philosophy* (Manila: University of Asia and the Pacific, 2005), ch. VII.

[6] Cf. the author's *The Humanism of Modern Philosophy* (Manila: SEASFI, 1989), ch. IV, p. 5.

[7] Cf. Stanley L. Jaki, *The Relevance of Physics* (Chicago: University of Chicago Press, 1966), ch. 1, 2 and 7.

the person and his or her surpassing dignity. In view of modern man's inhumanity to man, one ought to shudder at the frequently recurring utterances and judgments reducing persons to machines or animals.

The individual dignity of the human person gives him or her a value transcending the entire physical universe. It renders each person unique and unrepeatable. But that each person is also essentially other-oriented exhibits the social nature of human beings. Human beings are not mere individuals, but also "political animals," as Aristotle said. The person constitutes his or her individual identity in and through association with other persons. Society is for the person, and not the person for society, but the person is not for himself or herself, but for others.

The common good, or good common to each and every person, must be the infinite good, for only this can satisfy the infinite desire of the human person for knowledge and love. But this common good can only be attained in and through society.

5. The Image of God

The good or happiness of a human person can only be an infinite good, since such a good alone can satisfy the infinite desire of his or her will for love, as well as his or her capacity for truth, i.e., for the appropriation of reality through knowledge. This ultimate end of the human person can be no less than infinite being, perfect unity, absolute truth, supreme good and the most sublime beauty.[8] This is the *transcendent* common good of man, which human reason, when unclouded by any preconception, identifies as the personal salvific Creator of all things from nothing, the infinitely just, infinitely merciful, infinitely lovable, Father and lover of mankind, with whom every person can communicate directly by prayer of adoration, thanksgiving, reparation and petition.[9]

---

[8] Cf. the author's *Christian Philosophy,* 21; and the *Roots of Society,* 2nd ed., (Manila: Sinag-tala, 1984), ch. I.

[9] Cf. the astonishing discoveries of anthropologist Edward Horace Mann in *The Aboriginal Inhabitants of the Andaman Islands* (London: Royal Anthropological Institute, 1885).

For Christians, this one and only God has revealed Himself fully to mankind in his Son, the Messiah or Christ, Jesus, Son of Mary, and in the Church founded by Him.[10]

Since every man and woman has the capacity to attain to that transcendent common good, he or she has:

(a) the moral obligation to search for it to the best of his or her ability, an obligation which, given the social nature of man, extends also to society; and

(b) the right to search for, to accept and to profess freely his or her religious faith, without any external coercion, as long as he or she does not disturb public order.

Hence, the insistence of the Catholic Church, especially since the 1965 Declaration on Religious Freedom (*Dignatis Humanae)* of the Second Vatican Council, on the right to religious liberty or freedom of conscience, understood in the sense of (a) and (b), as one of the most fundamental of human rights, and therefore as an indispensable condition for peace and progress. Pope John Paul II put this very forcibly in his celebrated speech to the United Nations of October 2, 1979.

The infinite good of every human person can already be somehow enjoyed in this life through earthly society, but it can only be securely possessed after this life. In this earthly life, man does not have a sufficiently clear vision of that supreme good, because of the condition of the body, as Plato suggested in his famous myth of the cave. The human person's soul or principle of life, however, through the faculties of intelligence and free will, can transcend these bodily conditions, both in space and in time. It can plunge into the unknown without horizons, as the history of philosophy and culture, science and art, proclaim, and as the co-relative and symmetrical human capacity for evil likewise indicates throughout the length of human history. [11]

---

[10] Cf. Manuel Piñon, O. P., *Religion and "Religions"* (Manila: RTP Foundation, 1980).

[11] Cf. the author's *Christian Philosophy*, 31 and 45 b and c.

Unlike matter, the human soul is incorruptible or deathless, and so it enters into eternity as soon as it leaves the body, an eternity of infinite happiness if its final choice remained the infinite good, or of infinite pain if its final choice was its own self: the radical and irrevocable frustration of human nature, made for the infinite.[12]

The path to attaining the supreme good passes through earthly society, which, therefore, has its own value. The good of earthly society or the immanent common good, as distinct from the transcendent common good which is God, must be that which makes earthly society a suitable means for each person to attain his or her own good. Society must become good, so that man can be good. The person and the community thus interact in the creation of good for each other.[13]

6. The Good of Society

That the good of society remains within society and does not transcend it shows that the immanent common good is not absolutely good but only relatively so. In other words, while the good of society is for the sake of the good of the person, the good the of person is found ultimately in loving wholeheartedly the supreme good, Who is the Creator. But this also entails loving all His creatures with order and justice. This is the ultimate metaphysical foundation of social ethics.[14]

It is also the metaphysical foundation for the distinction between Church and State.[15] The latter is mainly concerned with the immanent common good, while the former is directly concerned, so to speak *ex officio,* with the transcendent common good. Both of them are interrelated and they even overlap, but they must be clearly distinguished.

Human activity is not, of course, confined to political activity, nor is political activity confined to economic activity, since the human person transcends both matter and society. Political activity is basically

---

[12] Cf. Ibid., 29 d; 38 e; 39 e.

[13] Cf. the author's *The Roots of Society,* ch. III and IV.

[14] Cf. *Christian Philosophy*, 38 d.

[15] Cf. the author's *Politics and the Church* (Manila: Vera-Reyes, 1987), ch. 10, and *The Church and Temporal Realities* (Manila: SEASFI, 1988), ch. 2.

ethical, as ordained to the common good, both immanent and transcendent. It is not just a technique, or the machine of government, or economic activity regardless of morals.

The role of government in civil society is the temporal or immanent common good, as we have argued. But, the temporal common good is ultimately both material and spiritual. "Temporal" should not be identified exclusively with "material," just as "spiritual" is not equivalent to "eternal." The "spiritual" is anything in which the human person is involved, whether in this life (temporal) or in the next (eternal). It is with the latter that the Church is concerned as its own proper domain.

There should thus be continuity and harmony between the temporal common good (which is the primary concern of the State) and the eternal common good (which is the primary responsibility of the Church), although they are distinct. Strictly speaking, they should not be "separated," since there are common areas of responsibility, i.e., all that has to do with morality or what leads persons to their ultimate good or last end. But they should indeed be distinguished, since:

(a) they have exclusive areas of their own competence (e.g., for the State the system of government or the fiscal laws; for the Church the administration of the sacraments and the appointment of ministers); and,

(b) their respective authorities are different in nature, although both come from God: one is "natural" and arguably "democratic" (people power—of the State), and the other "supernatural" and "hierarchical" (sacred power—of the Church).[16]

In other words, it is the ethical or moral aspect of temporal matters with which the Church is properly concerned, not the technical aspects. This is why the Church ought not to ally herself with any particular economic or political ideology or party.

In what is strictly temporal, the Church can only give orientation as to the moral principles involved, not as to the prudential choices to be made, since temporal considerations are by their nature changing and multiple. And, in what is strictly supernatural, the State has no

---

[16] Cf. the author's *The Church and Temporal Realities*, ch. 2 and 4.

competence. However, taking into account the subordination of the immanent common good to the transcendent common good, the State should both:

(a) protect and facilitate public morals, as related to the eternal; and

(b) favor and facilitate the worship of God, in accordance with the dignity of the human person.[17]

[17] Cf. the author's *Work, Culture, Liberation* (Manila: Vera-Reyes, 1985), ch. 10, and "The Roots of International Law and the Teachings of Francisco de Vitoria," *Ave Maria Law Review* (2004: 2): 123-51.

Moral Absolutes, Moral Relativism, and Political Representation

James M. Jacobs

1. Moral relativism

In recent years, every election cycle presents Christian voters with the unfortunate dilemma of voting on candidates who claim to believe strongly in the Christian moral worldview, but who nevertheless feel constrained not to support legislation to further that moral position. These candidates evidently believe that in order to protect the separation of Church and State they must maintain a strict separation of purely personal morality from public policy.

It is an obvious fact, however, that, for public policy to further the common good, policy-makers must take a stand on certain moral issues related to the welfare of individuals and groups. For example, public policy has come to hold as uncontroversial social goods such moral views as that: slavery is bad, fair wages are good, and children require special protections. If a candidate insists upon completely isolating policy from morality, he would not be able to fulfill the duties of his office, which include guiding the nation to some concrete realization of the common good.

Since it is impossible for office-holders not to legislate *some* vision of the common good, legislative choices not based on a coherent moral vision of the common good would be merely arbitrary preferences for the claims of one group over another. This paper contends that the operative principle behind an absolute refusal to legislate on the basis of one's moral vision is ultimately a type of moral relativism. That is, while the candidate personally acknowledges an act to be evil, the candidate also insists that act cannot be prohibited lest the prohibition infringe upon the right of each person to decide moral values for himself. My purpose is to show that a complete exclusion of morality from public policy decisions is indicative of moral relativism and, further, that moral relativism prevents a politician from fulfilling the duty to enact with integrity policies for the sake of the common good. As a means of exploring this topic, the paper will employ as its primary example the case of a candidate for political office who personally believes abortion is wrong, but who nonetheless refuses to oppose legalized abortion as a matter of public policy. Thus, the Christian candidate who supports abortion rights will be argued to be unfit for office.[1]

2. The moral relativist as a representative

The question of whether a moral relativist can hold office may seem to be an unrealistic concern in that it is unlikely moral relativism has ever prevented anyone from holding office. But it ought to be of concern, since the practice of moral relativism would necessarily shape one's approach to public policy. The fundamental problem is that a consistent moral relativist, who should be unwilling to impose his personal beliefs on others, would be unable to support a government's purpose of directing a nation to the common good. The argument for this contention is very brief. The remainder of this paper will aim to clarify and defend the problematic premises in the argument. The argument runs as follows:

1. Definition of a moral relativist: A moral relativist is one who holds that every person competently defines the good for himself.

2. The duty of the government: The primary duty of the government is to legislate for the sake of the common good of a country.

3. A moral relativist cannot direct the country to a common good: Since the moral relativist necessarily remains agnostic about the objective nature of any perceived good, he cannot legislate any one vision of the good on behalf of the citizens. At best, he could encourage every person to pursue his own individual idea of the good, but this amounts to anarchy.

4. Thus, a moral relativist cannot properly fulfill the function of president or legislator. It follows, also, that no citizen who embraces

---

[1] The author acknowledges that there are Christian denominations that do not take a consistently pro-life stand. However, he writes specifically from the Roman Catholic perspective, where the role of the Magisterium makes the issue much less ambiguous for Catholic voters.

the moral objectivity inherent in a substantive notion of the common good should ever vote for a moral relativist.

While I think this argument is cogent, it is also true that the premises are far from uncontroversial. In particular, objections might arise against the assertion that the government's duty is to guide the nation to a common good, and also against the presumption that the common good must be something other than the sum of individual goods. Both of these points can be defended by showing that they are interdependent and that, consequently, the attainment of the common good is inconsistent with moral relativism in a national leader.

3. Government and the common good

First, it must be argued that that the common good cannot be simply the sum of individual goods, but is an end over and above the individual good. Then, because the common good is not simply the sum of individual goods, we can argue that the executive branch must legislate the substantive moral standards necessitated by that vision of the common good. The interdependence of these points is important; for, if the common good were the sum of individual goods, then an executive could be a relativist, for his duty would be to maximize individual goods as defined by each person, no matter how incommensurate those goods might be among themselves. However, if there is a specifiable common good which takes precedence over any individual good, the government would have to recognize this common good as the objective end of its activity. But if there is a specifiable common good over and above the sum of individual goods, then a moral relativist would clearly have to be excluded from office.

This line of argument explains why the paper uses abortion as a primary example of the conflict between religious belief and public policy legislation. Abortion is an issue that sheds valuable light on the two main points above. To make this example probative, we need also to show that the candidate who asserts that abortion is merely a matter of individual conscience is a moral relativist.

Obviously, persons have many beliefs that simply reflect individual taste, and all would agree that these personal preferences ought not to be legislated as constituents of the common good. For example, there are vegetarians who oppose meat eating, but few would expect them to order all the steakhouses closed. Similarly, there are people who oppose the consumption of alcohol, but there would be credible objections against the reintroduction of Prohibition. Likewise, many people find smoking tobacco to be repulsive and unhealthy. Nevertheless, despite the increasing marginalization of smokers, few would endorse an absolute ban on smoking. In all of these instances, we would expect the candidate to say, "I personally do not smoke (or drink or eat meat), but I believe people have the right to decide for themselves whether they will do so." Is there any reason why abortion should not also be considered a matter of purely personal belief?

Despite the aforementioned examples, it is nevertheless the case that some behaviors ought not to be evaluated with similar agnosticism. For example, to say that one personally is opposed to rape, but that there ought not to be a public prohibition, since it is up to the individual, strikes one as evidently wrong. It is also implausible to claim personally to abhor racism, but to allow people to practice it according to their own doctrines. Similarly, to oppose torture or terrorism, but complacently to accept its occurrence as merely an expression of individual conscience is to manifest a moral obtuseness so evident as to make that person unfit for office.

Clearly, then, there are issues that are crucial to the common good that must not be relegated by official agnosticism to the realm of subjective opinion. For a government to refuse to take a stand on these issues is to admit implicitly to an unacceptable dichotomy between personal morality and the public good, and so to sanction a radical form of relativism.

Abortion provides a compelling illustration of this situation precisely because pro-life advocates see it as being like the second set of issues in that it is objectively wrong, and so worthy of universal prohibition, while abortion supporters see it as a matter of personal conscience, and so exempt from government interference in the exercise of personal freedom.

We must, therefore, analyze this issue to demonstrate why it is a fundamental matter for the common good, thereby making the candidate in question a moral relativist in refusing to legislate against it. In order to do this, though, we must first return to the notion of the common good, for this will give us a criterion by which to evaluate specific acts in relation to public policy. Thus, it is in light of the government's duty to pursue the common good that we can evaluate the so-called right to choose. In short, if abortion can be shown to be directly contrary to the human good, it is objectively wrong and so must be prohibited. To believe then that it is contrary to the common good and yet not prohibit it, to leave it as a matter of conscience and personal freedom, is a clear indication of moral relativism, since the candidate is then condoning behavior he admits to be contrary to the common good.

We therefore must first establish what is required for the common good. In the process, we shall also defend our two original points: that the common good is not simply the sum of individual goods and that the government must take determinate positions on moral issues.

Before entering that debate, however, let us first acknowledge that the primary role of the government is concretely to advance the common good. While most philosophers from Plato to Rawls would agree that governments are instituted for the sake of coordinating efforts of the populace so as to best realize what is good for the country as a whole (leaving open for now what that good is), Thrasymachus or Machiavelli, or their modern day counterparts, would not accept this premise. The basic question here is the nature of justice: is justice an objective moral order, or is it merely a conventional standard subject to change and distortion?

While this problem is beyond the scope of this paper, my argument rests on the natural law tradition in which there is an objective order of justice.[2] To reject this principle would be to doom the nation to a voluntaristic positivism in which rights are merely arbitrarily asserted and denied.[3] Presupposing the objective moral order of justice,

---

[2] See Thomas Aquinas, *ST* II-II 57.1. All references to the *Summa Theologiae* are to the translation by the Fathers of the English Dominican Province in 5 vols. (New York: Benzinger, 1948; reprint, Allen, TX: Christian Classics, 1981).

[3] For some extended arguments along these lines, see Heinrich Rommen, *The Natural Law: A Study in Legal and Social History and Philosophy*, translated by Thomas R. Hanley, O.S.B. (Indianapolis: Liberty Fund, 1998); John Finnis, *Natural Law and Natural Right* (Oxford: Clarendon Press, 1980); and John Rist

government legislation must be judged according to the standard of that objective order. Consequently, the role of the government is to legislate so as to encourage justice as a civic virtue[4] and the concomitant friendship which, by forming a natural community, furthers the common good that is the standard for public laws.[5] In order to do this, the legislative and executive branches of government must determine prudentially the social order so as to guarantee the common good of its citizens.[6] In turn, citizens are bound in allegiance to the government that justly serves their needs.[7] If a law fails to protect the common good, it is not just, and so it is not a true law.[8] But any government that refuses to protect the common good is a tyrannical government not worthy of obedience.[9] Thus, the common good, which is the very *raison d'etre* for a government's action,[10] is at the very heart of the notion of justice, and ought to be the standard by

---

Real Ethics: Rethinking the Foundations of Morality (Cambridge: Cambridge University Press, 2002).

[4] *ST* I-II 92.1.c.: "Consequently it is evident that the proper effect of law is to lead its subjects to their proper virtue: and since virtue is 'that which makes its subject good,' it follows that the proper effect of law is to make those to whom it is given, good, either simply or in some particular respect. For if the intention of the lawgiver is fixed on true good, which is the common good regulated according to Divine justice, it follows that the effect of the law is to make men good simply."

[5] See *ST* I-II 96.1, 2, and 3.

[6] *ST* II-II 50.1.

[7] *ST* II-II 26.2: "Each kind of friendship regards chiefly the subject in which we chiefly find the good on the fellowship of which that friendship is based: thus civil friendship regards chiefly the ruler of the state, on whom the entire common good of the state depends; hence to him before all, the citizens owe fidelity and obedience."

[8] *ST* I-II 95.2.

[9] *ST* II-II 42.2 ad 3: "A tyrannical government is not just, because it is directed, not to the common good, but to the private good of the ruler.... Consequently there is no sedition in disturbing a government of this kind."

[10] As Aquinas says, the common good is the final cause or end of all law: *ST* I-II 90.2; thus, human laws are passed for the sake of the community, the common good of the people: *ST* I-II 96.1.

which governments are evaluated by their citizens and by history. Those who hold government office, then, are required to act for the common good.

4. The common good

While this argument supports the notion that the government is meant to act for the common good, we have not yet explored what that common good is. The works of Yves Simon and Jacques Maritain articulate a notion of the common good that points us toward a solution to the problem of moral relativism and the limits of legislation.[11] Crucial to their idea of the common good is a hylomorphic anthropology that distinguishes human individuality, which is grounded in our material constitution, from human personality, which is based upon our spiritual nature (or form) and which defines our essence.

In considering man as a composite of individuating matter and defining form, we must recognize that, following the general metaphysical principle that the lower exists for the higher and the less perfect for the more perfect, the body exists for the sake of the soul and its operations; the soul does not exist for the sake of the body.[12] It follows, then, that the end of human existence lies in those operations of the soul which we all have in common due to our formal nature; it is not in our individual material existence. In other words, our individuality is for the sake of our personality, and we act as individuals

---

[11] My argument follows those presented in Yves R. Simon, *A General Theory of Authority*, introduction by Vukan Kuic (Notre Dame, Indiana: University of Notre Dame Press, 1962) and Jacques Maritain, *The Person and the Common Good*, translated by John J. Fitzgerald (Notre Dame, Indiana: University of Notre Dame Press, 1966). My argument draws from both these works without attempting to be either a comprehensive summary of their positions, or a comparative analysis of their unique insights.

[12] See *ST* I 105.5.c.: "For the less perfect is always for the sake of the more perfect: and consequently as the matter is for the sake of the form, so the form which is the first act, is for the sake of its operation, which is the second act; and thus operation is the end of the creature." See also *SCG* III 20.5, in which Aquinas argues that matter exists and is good only in relation to its reception of form.

for the perfection of ourselves (and others) as persons, an end that is common to all persons. More specifically, the common good must be understood primarily in terms of the pursuit and communication of virtue and truth, those activities by which persons perfect their rational nature.

It is at this point that we immediately recognize the necessity of social order for the achievement of this end, since the development of virtue and knowledge is naturally contingent upon well-ordered social interaction. Thus, the common good is attained by ordering society to enable the perfection of the spiritual nature we all share as unique persons. This perfection is realized in acts of knowing and loving, both of which imply cooperative social relations. It follows that the common good cannot be achieved merely by supplying for the material deficiencies of atomistic individuals. Indeed, these materialistic needs, being rooted in the principle by which we are distinguished from others, are necessarily self-interested. On the contrary, the point of common action is for the sake of the communication of common principles which perfect each person subsisting in relation to society by making knowledge and virtue possible.[13]

Given that common action is not done to meet material needs but to enable the perfection of the higher principle, we are faced with a new issue. The rationality we aim to perfect also underlies human freedom.[14] Because freedom is concomitant with rationality, there are many possible ways to perfect our personal, or spiritual, nature. From this fact we draw two significant conclusions. First, since people are free, there must be some authoritative direction of the individuals so that they might act with common purpose, for this unity is necessary for the development of knowledge and virtue. Second, since the purpose of that common action is the perfection of our spiritual nature, the authority who directs the community must take substantive

---

[13] This is clearly elucidated in Russell Hittinger's comment: "The word *communicatio* simply means making something common, one rational agent participating in the life of another. Society, for Thomas, is not a thing, but an activity." Russell Hittinger, *The First Grace: Rediscovering the Natural Law in the Post-Christian World* (Wilmington: ISI Books, 2003), p. 271.

[14] *ST* I.83.1.

positions on moral issues as worthy of pursuit or as contradictory to that end. A society directed to the common good will benefit the persons whose communion constitutes the perfection of man in his spiritual nature. Since humans cannot enjoy perfection without a society well-directed to the common good, any authority within society has both a right and a duty to command or prohibit specific behaviors in light of the common good of personal relations.

It is clear now that the government must take substantive moral positions; as a result, we can understand better why the common good is not simply about the aggregate welfare of individuals, but about a community of persons whose perfection depends on relations and common ends. This obviously refutes the popular utilitarian notion that the common good is simply the sum of individual goods.

Common to both the utilitarian principle and contemporary bourgeois liberalism is the belief that the common good is merely the aggregate of pleasures experienced. The duty of society to the common good, therefore, would be to make available the consumption of pleasure, primarily in terms of material "creature comforts" as ends in themselves and not merely as necessary preconditions for spiritual development. As Mary Ann Glendon has argued, this pursuit of materialistic ends has been absolutized by taking on the language of rights: "[T]he new rhetoric of rights is less about human dignity and freedom than about insistent, unending desires."[15] This misleading idea of the common good has utterly destructive consequences, for, according to it, authority can only act to satisfy the material desires of individuals; authority loses all power to shape society to meet our true spiritual ends. As a result, the state must become agnostic with respect to those spiritual ends it is in reality meant to inculcate.[16]

---

[15] Mary Ann Glendon, *Rights Talk: The Impoverishment of Political Discourse* (New York: The Free Press, 1991), p. 171.

[16] Russell Hittinger again diagnoses this defect: "The postmodern state... is far less sure of its powers. It claims to be axiologically blind and deferent to individual conceptions of the good" (*First Grace*, p. 137). Appropriate here also is Jacques Maritain's remark that "The mistake of bourgeois liberalism has been to conceive democratic society to be a kind of list or arena in which all the conceptions of the bases of common life, even those most destructive

Let us clarify this point succinctly: as material individuals, we pursue ends that are strictly our own; as spiritual persons, on the other hand, we pursue ends that are necessarily communal—knowledge and virtue. While the common good does consider the material individual as a part of the community and so insures that basic material needs are met, those material needs are never in themselves the end of government action; rather, those public acts are for the sake of persons, the inter-relational, spiritual wholes which merit consideration over the disintegrative self-interest of the material individual. The government's pursuit of the common good, then, can never give preference to our individual material needs, for then it would contradict the very point of common action. In Maritain's words, to make the mistake of assuming that the common good is the sum of individual goods "would dissolve society as such to the advantage of the parts, and would amount to either a frankly anarchistic conception, or the old disguised anarchistic conception of individualistic materialism in which the whole function of the city is to safeguard the liberty of each."[17]

This assumption of moral authority by the executive branch in no way denies the value of democracy, since democracy, as a method of encouraging individuals to work together toward a common end, is an invaluable tool to guarantee the adequacy of the chosen end. However, it is important to remember that democracy, as a method, is merely a

---

to freedom and law, meet with no more than the pure and simple indifference of the body politic, while they compete before public opinion in a kind of free market of the mother-ideas, healthy or poisoned, of political life.... Just as it had no real *common good,* it had no real *common thought.*" Jacques Maritain, *Man and the State* (Washington, D. C.: Catholic University of America Press, 1998; licensed by University of Chicago Press, 1951), pp. 109-10.

[17] Maritain, *Person and the Common Good*, p. 50. In a more prophetic voice, Maritain makes the argument this way: "By being concerned for truth, and by grasping it, the spirit transcends time. To make the things of the spirit pass under the law of the ephemeral—which is the law of matter and the purely biological—to act as if the spirit were subject to the lord of the flies, is the first sign, the first symptom of the sickness denounced by St. Paul." Jacques Maritain, *The Peasant of the Garonne,* translated by Michael Cuddihy and Elizabeth Hughes (New York: Holt, Rinehart, and Winston, 1968), p. 14.

means and not the end itself.[18] If democracy were an end, the result would be a relativization of values to cater to base desires; this would destroy all hope of achieving the end for which democracy was instituted, the moral perfection of persons engaged in communal activity.[19] The democratic/utilitarian accumulation of individual goods would perpetually leave the higher urges of humanity unfulfilled, since its basis in self-centered material desires would militate against the sacrifice necessary for common action. In other words, the destiny of the human race is not each individual for himself, but a moral and relational community, since persons are necessarily relational moral beings who transcend the self-interested acquisitiveness of individuality.[20] But this transcendent end can only be realized by ordering sacrifices and duties within society, thereby implicitly demanding the acceptance of the dictates of authority which subordinate individual desires to the common good. As Simon concludes, "Thus we are led to understand that the principal act of social life is immanent in the souls of men. It is a communion in some belief, love, or aversion."[21] This is illustrative of the fact that, as the ancients recognized, politics and ethics are continuous, and that virtue

---

[18] The consequences of this point are brought out by Robert P. Kraynak, *Christian Faith and Modern Democracy: God and Politics in the Fallen World* (Notre Dame, Indiana: University of Notre Dame Press, 2001).

[19] This point is made in different ways by Maritain, *Man and the State*, p. 61; and by Rist, *Real Ethics*, pp. 111-12 and 248.

[20] For an insightful discussion about the nature of the human as relational, see W. Norris Clarke, S.J., *Person and Being* (Milwaukee: Marquette University Press, 1993); see also Rist's analysis of the Platonic and Aristotelian principle that the *polis* is an essential component of the good life, in *Real Ethics*, pp. 205-22.

[21] Simon, *A General Theory of Authority*, p. 125. Thus Maritain's definition of the common good: The common good "is the maximum possible development, here and now, of the persons making up the united multitude to the end of forming a people, organized not by force alone, but by justice"(*The Person and the Common Good*, pp. 53-54).

is only accomplished in the context of a society dedicated to the common good of men as persons pursuing truth and goodness.[22]

5. Conclusion

We conclude, then, that the aim of common action is not the satisfaction of individual desires, not the mere establishment of an aggregation of atomistic consumers; rather, it is the founding of a just community capable of informing people of the common good. This explains why the government must take substantive positions on moral issues. Political authority in this community has the duty to institute practical laws so as to guarantee the continued moral flourishing of this community. Because the common good is not simply the sum of individual goods; and because it can only be achieved by the moral leadership of a government directing common action, it follows that a moral relativist would be unable to fulfill the duties of leadership.

These conclusions might seem to be at odds with the great Liberal tradition, which holds that governments must prescind from moral or metaphysical opinions so as to guarantee absolute freedom of individual conscience.[23] We may respond to this concern first by noting that both Simon and Maritain make devastating critiques of this particular notion of Liberalism.[24]

---

[22] John Rist well describes the turn away from this notion of the good life to our modern predicament: "With such ideas [emphasizing individualism] important steps have been taken towards the thesis that the principal function of the state is to protect its members against one another (and presumably also against itself) rather than enable them together to work for a richer whole for all of its members than anything they could achieve individually" (*Real Ethics*, p. 208).

[23] A good illustration of this ideology is found in the Supreme Court's decision in *Planned Parenthood of Southeastern Pennsylvania v. Casey, Governor of Pennsylvania, et al.*, June 29, 1992, which, as Robert Bork recently commented, makes each person his own sovereign nation.

[24] See in particular, Simon, *A General Theory of Authority*, pp. 104-31; and Maritain, *The Person and the Common Good*, pp. 90-105.

In addition, we may recall Chesterton's criticism in *Heretics*.[25] Chesterton points out the widespread modern phenomenon of insisting that, while details can be matters of discussion, larger metaphysical or moral principles should simply be ignored as utterly subjective. As he puts it: " Everything matters—except everything." But, as he goes on to argue, this attitude is antithetical to man's rational spirit for, in our search for truth, it is precisely the larger matters that matter most because they give context to and make sense of all the details. This is pertinent here: government, in order to secure the common good, must take a stand on metaphysical and moral matters, for without them we cannot realize our vocation as rational persons. Lacking that larger metaphysical and moral framework, any particular freedom is without context and loses its sense of ultimate purpose, since there is no cohesive common goal uniting society.[26]

Furthermore, the piecemeal approach to behavior inculcates a preference for individual goods over the rational and communal common goods of persons. Therefore, since the nature of the common good demands an authoritative direction to substantive moral goals that necessarily override freedom of individual conscience (at least with respect to issues essential for the common good), it is once again clear that a moral relativist cannot exercise the duties associated with government office, even under the aegis of the great liberal tradition.

It might be objected at this point that just because someone maintains that certain evil acts ought not to be legally prohibited does not make that person to be a moral relativist. Indeed, even Aquinas recognizes that the law is meant neither to repress all vices,[27] nor to

---

[25] Gilbert K. Chesterton, *Heretics* (New York: John Lane, 1909), in the "Introductory Remarks," especially pp. 12-15.

[26] This has been recognized as the great crisis of contemporary democracy: if there is no moral standard, there is no way to discriminate legitimate claims from illegitimate ones, so the government has no real reason to support some and not others. Rocco Buttiglione discusses this with respect to the social thought of Karol Wojtyła in *Karol Wojtyła: The Thought of the Man Who Became Pope John Paul II*, translated by Paolo Guietti and Francesca Murphy (Grand Rapids: Eerdman's, 1997), pp. 377-78.

[27] *ST* I-II 96.2.

inculcate all virtues.[28] This would seem to open the door for politicians to hold moral principles privately and yet not to legislate those moral principles as public policy. In these same statements, however, Aquinas does specify that the law must forbid the more grievous vices that make social harmony impossible, and it must encourage those virtues necessary for the common good. As a result, we need to delineate the minimum of virtue which is necessary for a society to function. Once we understand that minimum of virtue, we can distinguish the true moral relativist from those who exercise the correct prudential decision to not use laws to enforce morality.

If a politician were to see that an act is utterly contrary to the common good and not legislate against it for fear of infringing upon freedom of choice, he is abandoning the very idea of the common good as the end of government in favor of disintegrative individualism. He consequently would be a moral relativist, for he would act as if moral values could not be publicly endorsed even for the common good. By insisting that private choice supersedes the common good, the politician is abandoning the very idea of a common good as necessary for personal perfection. In fact, because this personal perfection is the end of all private choice, the citizens rely on the politician to guide our choices toward the common good.

Having established the criterion the common good sets out as a means to evaluate legislative positions, we can now consider whether a prohibition of abortion is an essential component of the common good. If it is essential to the common good, then a candidate who leaves it to personal choice must be a moral relativist. If, on the other hand, it is not essential, it is best left as a matter of individual preference because the common good insists on the legitimate exercise of personal freedom as necessary for the perfection of the rational being. From what has been argued above, this matter can be settled by the articulation of the following general legislative principles.

With respect to goods related to our material individuality, since these are merely means to the common good and are not essential to the common good in themselves, the government has a right and duty to control them (by taxation, restrictions on use, or intervening for

---

[28] *ST* I-II 96.3.

fairer distribution of wealth and property) for the sake of empowering each person's attainment of the common good.[29] But, since these goods are not essential to the common good, there can be neither an absolute right nor an absolute prohibition concerning them. Consequently, material individuals freely decide the use of these goods. It follows, then, that a politician is neither required to, nor able to, implement his own conscientious opinion as public policy in this area. This explains how abortion differs from smoking, drinking, or vegetarianism. These behaviors, as acts associated with our material individuality, do not directly concern the person as the spiritual, relational end of society. Rather, as material indulgences, they represent one's individuality: as such, while the government has a right to regulate these activities, it cannot issue an absolute prohibition or compulsion since they are not essential to the common good. Thus, in these areas, protection of the freedom for personal choice and conscience ought to be the ultimate aim of government legislation.[30] However, as merely material ends, the

---

[29] For example, while the government must insure that its citizens have a proper amount of food for personal development, it also has the right to limit its food distributions to nutritious foods, as the current WIC program attempts to do.

[30] This is not to say that there is *no* moral quality to these acts whatsoever; indeed, few acts are so unambiguous. Rather, it is only to say that the moral issue is not essential to the common good. As non-essential, it is within our rights as rational persons to exercise freedom of choice with respect to these activities. Two comments follow from this: First, there are indeed "true believers" in the vegetarian and anti-smoking camps who believe that prohibiting such things is essential to the common good. However, it can be doubted whether they can justify this belief, and certainly not on the basis articulated in this paper, since bodily health must be put in the larger context of spiritual perfection, which requires free choice about material means. Second, as non-essential, the government can restrict and coerce behavior within society for the sake of the common good of persons; hence, there can rightly be limitations or taxes imposed upon these behaviors, even while leaving them as objects of free choice. Even here, though, these acts are normally ordered to the common good in terms of health costs—that is, in terms of our material individuality, and not in terms of spiritual personality. That is why they can be so ordered.

government can levy taxes or implement other regulations so as lead the material individual toward his proper fulfillment as a person.[31]

Those goods that are related to the spiritual ends of persons, on the other hand, are essential to the common good. Therefore, the government must protect or prohibit them absolutely, since the common good is impossible without that protection or prohibition. Moreover, a government must not control these activities by taxation or regulation, since that in itself would be an impediment to personal perfection. As a result, no politician can vary from his personal conscience in these areas, since the very purpose of government is to further the common good in its essential ends (and not just by material means). Thus, education, inquiry,[32] and especially life must be protected. Of these, life itself is the foundation for all personal goods, and so it deserves priority in the protection of absolute rights.

Given this distinction, any believer who insists on legislating absolute rights about merely material ends would be transgressing the correct limits to legislation and so would be imprudent. On the other hand, the believer who legislates to protect the spiritual and personal nature of the citizens would in fact be protecting the common good. Failing to legislate in order to protect the common good would demonstrate negligence of duty in his role as a government official. It is important to note here that this is based upon a philosophical consideration of the person and so it is not an imposition of religious doctrine.

Part of our contemporary problem with respect to legislating for the common good is the unwieldy use of the notion of "religion" as a topic to be excluded from public debate. Many problems can be clarified if we

---

[31] This would indicate why condom distribution in high schools is essentially unjust. It encourages behavior that satisfies human material individuality with absolutely no context about the meaning of that act for the human person. Again, we see that it is the lack of a moral context that vitiates what would otherwise be a resolvable problem.

[32] Inquiry is important since, according to this thesis, freedom of inquiry is essential to personal development and so merits protection; freedom of speech, on the other hand, is a material *means* to inquiry and, as such, can be controlled to the extent that it violates the spirit of the common good.

consider religion as only those beliefs grounded in revelation, as opposed to those of natural theology or natural law. Thus, all those metaphysical ideas that Aquinas refers to as "preambles" of the faith—such as the existence of God, His unicity, etc., as well as metaphysical notions of the soul and ethical doctrines of natural law—cannot be excluded from public debate, since they are legitimate objects of rational inquiry apart from revelation. Indeed, it is precisely these metaphysical notions which are universally necessary for the establishment of the common good and the growth of knowledge and virtue in society.

We can now turn this argument to the issue of abortion. The main criterion for legislation with respect to the common good, as we have seen, is that it must further our interests as persons, that is, as rational beings capable of transcendent spiritual communion in terms of knowledge and virtue. Any activity that negates this is contrary to the common good, and so can be prohibited; any that is essential to it must be protected. From this perspective, we can now detect the problem with the right to abortion: it reduces personality to individuality.[33] It is helpful at this point to return to the metaphysical basis of this argument: that the lesser is always for the sake of the greater. As Aquinas points out, not only is matter for the sake of form, but the substance exists for the sake of its operations.[34]

A human person's form, then, is for the sake of all its operations, and first among these is life. In other words, life is the essential basis of all the higher operations of personal perfection. Life is, therefore, an end in itself for the person; it cannot be seen simply as a means to an end. Here is where the anti-life politician errs: he seems to conceive of life as a material good, and so a means to some further end; as a mere means, he believes it is an object of free choice. But life, the *sine qua non* of all goods and the necessary foundation of the common good, is the primary (the first, though not the final) end in itself. It thus cannot be an object of personal choice. Indeed, without protecting life as the very basis of personhood and the foundation of the common good, there

---

[33] To confuse these, as Maritain points out, leads to the slavery of the person to the mere individual; see *The Person and the Common Good*, p. 77.

[34] See footnote #2, *supra*.

would be no protection for those very acts of freedom by which the person is brought to perfection. In the end, we must recognize that there can be no legally protected choice that ever runs contrary to the personal nature of the common good. Clearly, then, there must be an absolute legal protection of life as an end in itself.[35]

This would render the candidate who is personally opposed to abortion but publicly "pro-choice" a moral relativist. In being opposed to abortion personally, he recognizes it as inimical to the common good; however, in not legislating in accord with his conscience, he implicitly acts so as to cast his notion of the common good into doubt. An important result of this analysis is that the relativist who opposes abortion personally, but allows it as a public policy, is actually in a more untenable position than the candidate who is frankly pro-abortion. This is because the former falls into an inconsistency with respect to his notion of the common good and the protection of persons; the latter is at least consistent if he denies the personhood of the unborn child.

This, of course, does not mean the latter candidate is preferable. It is simply a fact that the argument against him would entail a metaphysical discussion of personhood. Insofar as the notion of "person" is the critical defining point for the common good, this is an important, albeit neglected, discussion in its own right, a neglect that is related to our society's enforced silence on metaphysics in general.[36]

---

[35] See Maritain, *Man and the State*, pp. 167-68. I believe that this same reasoning can be applied with respect to sexual morality: the only form of sexual expression that is necessary for the common good is that within the context of a monogamous heterosexual marriage, for only in that is true unitive friendship and procreative fruitfulness possible. To allow all other expressions of sexuality, including contraception, fornication, homosexuality, etc., is degrading personality to mere individual pursuit of physical pleasure and so misconstrues the true gift of human sexuality.

[36] For those who think the definition of a person is a purely religious issue (which is certainly not the case, unless one reduces metaphysics to religion), we should note that, on the basis of my argument, society cannot eliminate religious perspectives from consideration, for this would deny the person's transcendent good and reduce man to a mere individual and so beg the question of personality to begin with.

The evidence is clear that societies with inadequate understandings of personhood—as exemplified by slavery, genocide, labor camps, etc.—have virtually defined the morally evil society.

Thus, we may conclude that, because of the nature of the common good, it is necessary that governments address the goods of humans as persons, and not merely as material individuals. This focus on persons necessitates absolute prohibitions or freedoms. The moral relativist, in accepting moral absolutes concerning personhood for himself, but allowing others to form variant opinions, is unable to defend coherently the objective good of the person or the common good of a society. He therefore is also unable to legislate coherently so as to direct a nation to its proper end. Thus, the Christian who refuses to prohibit abortion because he believes it to be merely a private opinion becomes a moral relativist. As a consequence, he cannot rightfully represent the common good of the people and should not hold public office.[37]

---

[37] Maritain points out this deep inconsistency between Christian faith and relativism: "It is impossible for a Christian to be a relativist. Those who make the attempt have no chance of succeeding" (*The Peasant of the Garonne*, p. 89).

Murray after Fifty Years:

Reflecting on America and its Proposition[1]

Michael D. Torre

1. Introduction

I will attempt to do three things in this paper: first, give the salient lines of Murray's argument in his richly textured classic *We Hold These Truths*;[2] second, note how that argument was immediately received by thoughtful Protestant thinkers; third, ask how we ought to view his project today: is it merely unfinished or flawed, and, if so, how deeply?

One can begin with Murray's conscious embrace of American pluralism, and religious pluralism in particular. It had ever been a part of the American experiment, was fundamental to its self-identity, and was here to stay. He naturally deplores the Christian division behind the pluralism—"religious pluralism is against the will of God" (23)—but he accepts the civil reality: "The United States...is a civil community, whose unity is purely political, consisting in 'agreement on the good of man at the level of performance without the necessity of agreement on ultimates,' to adopt a phrase from the 1945 Harvard Report on General Education in a Free Society" (54). He further argues that a Catholic can and should defend the civil right to religious freedom America supposes and defends (63): a position that he and others helped ensure

---

[1] For Father Joseph D. Fessio, S.J.—who hired me to teach at the University of San Francisco—for Father John Lo Schiavo, S.J.—who offered me a tenure-track position there—and for Father John P. Schlegel, S.J.—who then granted me tenure: in gratitude.

[2] John Courtney Murray, S.J., *We Hold These Truths: Catholic Reflections On The American Proposition* (New York: Sheed and Ward, 1960). Hereafter, all page references in the text are taken from this work. All of its chapters—save the two on the "public consensus" (2 and 3)—had been previously published as articles, between 1950 and 1960: see the selection of Murray's writings made by J. Leon Harpers, S.J., in *Bridging The Sacred and The Secular* (Washington, D.C.: Georgetown University Press, 1994), p. 350.

became part of the Church's express doctrine in Vatican II's Declaration on Religious Freedom.[3] If the Church had opposed 19th century democracy (e.g. in France), this was due to its particular form and hostility to the Church, and not to democracy or pluralism *per se* (68).

Yet every plurality poses a challenge to civil discourse. Were the country to splinter into an irreducible cacophony of opposing voices, then there could be no society. A commitment to a common constitution and law is essential. This allows the pluralism to be (at least potentially) a conversation, rather than a verbal war. Now, every conversation supposes its parties hold truths in *common*; otherwise there is no basis to conduct the conversation or the quarrel (4). This common basis is what Murray, following Lincoln, calls its "Proposition" (vii). America, he argues, has been and necessarily must be committed to a series of truths, upon which all its civil discourse is based and which also guide its undertakings (viii); for the truths at stake (e.g. that "all men are created equal") mandate *civil action*, that they might be rendered meaningful in the fabric of American institutions and life (e.g. so that its citizens might enjoy the *fruits* of equality).

2. Murray's analysis

Murray thus argues that the *implicit* basis of the American Proposition is a commitment to the natural law tradition. He means something specific by this, but also something very general. Specifically, he argues that the American Founders were committed to *discernible truths*. Here is a typical passage: "our Fathers...thought the life of man in society under government is founded on truths, on a certain body of objective truth, universal in its import, accessible to the reason of man, definable, defensible. If the assertion is denied, the

---

[3] Murray's involvement in Vatican II's *Declaration on Religious Freedom* (*Dignitatis Humanae*) is of course well known. He spent the few years left to him after the Council chiefly explaining and defending its doctrine on the civil right of religious freedom. See his *The Problem of Religious Freedom* (Westminster, Maryland.: Newman, 1965) and "The Vatican Declaration on Religious Freedom," in *The University in the American Experience* (New York: Fordham University Press, 1966), and a discussion he edited: *Religious Liberty: an end and a beginning, the declaration on religious freedom, an ecumenical discussion* (New York: Macmillan, 1966).

American Proposition is...eviscerated at one stroke....The American Proposition rests on the...traditional conviction that there are truths; that they can be known; that they must be held; for, if they are not held, assented to, consented to, worked into the fabric of institutions, there can be no hope of founding a true City, in which men may dwell in dignity, peace, unity, justice, well-being, freedom" (ix). As the last words indicate, the truths he has in mind chiefly concern the human good: that it consists in justice and dignity, in freedom and peace. These goods are grounded in human nature and discernible to reason. And this is what the natural law tradition asserts.

Murray's claim is that the American Proposition implicitly rests on that tradition; he will allow that the foundation might not have been *explicit*, and that the Founders could have built "better than they knew" (30).[4] He does not want to claim that the details of that tradition were explicit and clearly part of its foundation. America had, after all, fought a Civil War precisely because its commitment to freedom (e.g. states' rights) had clashed with its commitment to justice and equality for all. Just how conflicting claims should be adjudicated is often not clear. The tradition only provided the argument's general principles, and the commitment to reasoning from them to what they entail.

Such a "gentlemanly" approach to civil discourse, however, is only a hope and not a present reality. It is blocked first by the fact that even the most basic terms of the discussion are understood differently: "we have no common universe of discourse. In particular, diverse mental equivalents attach to all the words in which the constitutional consensus must finally be discussed—truth, freedom, justice, prudence, order, law, authority, power, knowledge, certainty, unity, peace, virtue, morality, religion, God, and perhaps even man. Our intellectual experience is one of sheer confusion, in which soliloquy succeeds to argument" (16). If this were not bad enough, the problem is compounded by the intractable weight of history and prejudice: "man is not only a creature of thought but also a vibrant subject of sympathies; and in the realm of philosophy and religion today the communal experiences are so divergent that they create not

[4] He is here quoting from the American Catholic Church's Third Plenary Council of Baltimore (1884).

sympathies but alienations as between groups" (17). He cites the common Protestant suspicion of the natural law tradition itself as but one instance, among many possible.

Murray locates four main groups in the American conversation: Protestant, Catholic, Jew, and Secular (18-22). Of these, the furthest from the Catholic point of view is clearly the secular; for the other two share the conviction that there is a level of religious truth transcendent to the secular, whereas the latter opposes this. He has little good to say of the "pseudo-morality of secular liberalism,"[5] regarding its innate relativism as already discredited (293). He also has little to say of the Jewish tradition, and focuses instead on the Protestant, as being, historically, the American "majority view." Until recently, this view could be characterized by four traits (276-77): it was *voluntarist*—the good was based on God's commands or will (and not on His wisdom, or what was intrinsically the case); it was *scriptural*—what the Bible enjoined was sufficient, and should be accepted in its literal sense; it was *subjective*—what one did was less important than why one did it (one's intentions or motives); and it was *individualistic*—social ills could be solved by each individual loving his neighbor as himself. Yet he finds that Protestants have seriously called this ethic into question in his time, as being unduly simplistic. Social ills required social solutions, not just well-intentioned individuals; and politics and the public sphere were different from the private, and far more ambiguous, thus requiring an emphasis upon differing contexts and pragmatic solutions, which could not be reduced to Biblical injunctions (277-78). The former morality was "still around" (278), but it was now on the defensive, and with good reason (277).

As he looks at the American scene, Murray finds a most uncertain landscape. His work is filled with sober remarks: "The work of the barbarian [is] to undermine rational standards of judgment, to corrupt

---

[5] Murray's work seems rather dated in his easy dismissal of a tradition that has proven stronger than he seems to have supposed it would. In particular, he does not distinguish an ideological secularism—in principle opposed to an Absolute and inevitably committed to relativism—from a political secularism that seeks to construct a polity in separation from any religious faith or moral tradition. This latter view seems to be more in continuity with the Deism of many Founders and remains a force to be reckoned with.

the inherited intuitive wisdom by which people have always lived, and to do this...by spreading a climate of doubt and bewilderment in which clarity about the larger aims of life is dimmed and the self-confidence of people is destroyed ...[as is] now presently appearing on university campuses" (12). Or "we are not really a group of men singly engaged in the search for truth...[but] the variant ideas and allegiances among us are entrenched as social powers; they occupy ground; they have developed interests; and they have persons to fight for them" (19). Again, "there is no public philosophy in America. By one cause or another it has been eroded" (86). And, "the vacuum in public life...is a vacuum in philosophy, a public philosophy with affirmative tenets that determine positive goals" (94). Thus, "the general uneasiness among the public—here at home and abroad—derives from an instinctive sense that America does not know what it is trying to do" (246). Finally, in sum, "the ethic which launched Western constitutionalism and endured long enough as a popular heritage to give essential form to the American system of government has now ceased to sustain the structure and direct the action of this constitutional commonwealth" (293).

When Douglas Auchincloss wrote his excellent summary of Murray and his work for his *Time* cover story of December 12, 1960,[6] he began as follows: "John Courtney Murray sees his native America entering a new era of 'post-modern man' in a sorry state of ideological impoverishment that, unless repaired, must doom the best political skill and dedication."[7] And he "summed up" Murray's view of America in the following terms: "The modern rationalistic and pragmatist experiment he feels has failed. That experiment tried to carry on Western liberalism, whose roots are Christian, without Christianity. The individual conscience, lacking religion to inform and support it, is collapsing under the burden—'poor little conscience,' says Murray. Only the monistic state threatens to remain. If this goes on, a spiritual vacuum will grow at the heart of life and into it will rush violence, 'the mark of the Architect of Chaos, the Evil One.'"[8] This is a sobering

---

[6] Douglas Auchincloss, "City of God & Man" (*Time*, December 12, 1960): 64-70.

[7] Ibid., p. 64.

[8] Ibid., p. 70.

conclusion indeed, and all the more evidently so next to Maritain's more optimistic assessment.[9]

Given this intellectual situation, the aim of Murray's work is modest: to lessen the "warfare" that lies hidden under the surface of civil discourse and to help us dedicate ourselves to the project of finding common ground and attempting an argument (23). In his judgment, the Catholic community was uniquely placed to attempt such a project. For, as he saw it, "the American university [had] long since bade quiet goodbye to the whole notion of an American consensus, as implying that there are truths that we hold in common, and a natural law that makes known to all of us the structure of the moral universe in such ways that all of us are bound by it in common obedience" (40). The Catholic community, on the other hand, still adhered to this tradition (41). Thus, by an irony of history, it could now reinvigorate and defend a polity founded first mainly by Protestants. In words that echo Maritain's call for an integral humanism—but without ever once referring to him—Murray argues for a Christian humanism of the temporal order:[10] "The Christian heart must cultivate a contempt for the world, but diligently cherish its reverence for the work of the Creator, who is Creator not only of heaven but of earth, of the visible as well as the invisible" (189-90). Yet—even more than Maritain—he remains dubious of the success of this project, for a broad American commitment to such a theistic humanism has been much eroded. Throughout, he finds the American Proposition deeply menaced from within.

He nevertheless takes up and argues cases, thereby displaying what such an argument might look like. For example, on the basis of distributive justice, he argues that the state ought to aid *parochial*

---

[9] Thus, the concluding chapter of *Reflections on America* (New York: Scribner, 1958) reads "America is Promise," a title that accurately conveys the abiding hope for America that runs throughout this work. (Of course, it could be argued that Maritain saw America as "promise" relative to Europe. Given the latter's recent inability to acknowledge, much less defend, its Christian heritage, that seems more prescient.)

[10] For his forthright advancement of this project, see his early (1940) "The Construction of a Christian Culture," in Harpers, *Bridging the Sacred and the Secular*, pp. 101-23.

schools (148). In relation to *censorship*, he argues the need to distinguish the moral from the legal and the private from the public: thus, contraception may be a sin, but that need not make it a crime (158). Repression of *pornography* is reasonable, but the standard should be the maintenance of "that minimum of actualized morality that is necessary for the healthy function of the social order" (166), and he defends the American presumption in favor of freedom, the burden of proof rightly resting on the advocate of restraint (164). He argues that thinking on the American *economy* lacks a clear set of political principles to guide its policies (180-01). And he long ponders communism and America's opposition to it, and finds the country's thought on *war and peace*—and on its international commitments and responsibilities—to be confused, and its course adrift. He argues for a sensible theory of just war (272), while lamenting its virtual absence from discourse on public policy (265).

I raise these cases only to remind us of what can be found within Murray's pages. And with these I am done: I have only desired to remind us of his fundamental argument.

3. Protestant and Jewish assessment of Murray's position

Before giving my own assessment of what Murray proposes, I would like to examine its reception by Protestant intellectuals. Their critiques will lead to my own.

I turn first to George Lindbeck, of Yale University, who offers a sympathetic and highly intelligent review.[11] He points out that Murray was hardly the first Catholic to argue in favor of religious freedom.[12] He claims that it has recently been argued even more ably by various European theologians (*inter alia*, he cites Rahner, von Balthasar, and de

---

[11] George A. Lindbeck, "John Courtney Murray, S.J.: An Evaluation," *Christianity and Crisis* 21 (1961): 213-16.

[12] Ibid., p. 213. Indeed, this tradition seems to go back at least to that great American Catholic of the 19th century, Orestes Brownson: see his "Civil and Religious Freedom," in *Brownson's Quarterly* (July, 1864), reprinted in *The Brownson Reader*, edited by Alvan S. Ryan (New York: P. Kennedy & Sons, 1955), pp. 350-56, and his "magnum opus": *The American Republic* (New York: O'Shea, 1866).

Lubac),[13] and affirms "the theological issue is no longer in doubt." [14] Harvey Cox, writing from Harvard,[15] goes even further, noting that a European such as the Belgian Catholic Augustin Leonard, O.P., had argued that religious freedom was a "religious concern" and a "sacred duty,"[16] thereby seconding the Protestant commitment that it was "one of the rights conferred by God on man."[17] Cox worries that Murray's commitment to it may be more shallow (although Vatican II was to demonstrate that his worry was unnecessary).

In general, the reviews of his stance on religious freedom are (not surprisingly) favorable, with Martin Marty from Chicago adding his own praise to that of Cox and Lindbeck.[18] The latter, however, goes further, even supporting the nature of Murray's reasoning, and comparing his talents to "those of a first-rate constitutional lawyer."[19] He recognizes Murray's right to read magisterial directives narrowly, without being bound by the personal opinions of popes (e.g. their views about democracy, in the 19th century). Indeed, not only has that been the standard way of reading such directives, but he argues that "no other procedure is possible"[20] for one who thinks within a particular

---

[13] Ibid., p. 215.

[14] Ibid., p. 214.

[15] Harvey Cox, "Notes and Reviews: We Hold These Truths," *Cross Currents* 11 (1961): 79-83.

[16] Ibid., p. 81.

[17] Ibid., p. 79.

[18] Martin E. Marty, *The Christian Century* 77 (November 9, 1960): 1315-17, especially its first page.

[19] Lindbeck, op. cit., p. 215.

[20] Ibid., p. 214. For a counter-argument--that Murray distorted, rather than developed, papal teaching (e.g. Leo XIII's)--see Michael J. Schuck's "John Courtney Murray's Problematic Interpretations of Leo XIII And The American Founders," *Thomist* 55 (1991): 592-612. However, any theory of development requires that the essential be separated from the accidental and the implicit discovered beneath the explicit, even though such distinctions would have not been made by an earlier figure within the tradition. Thus, it is indisputable that Murray and Vatican II both advance a more limited role for the State than that advocated by Aquinas or by Leo XIII.

tradition. Thus, he accepts that it is not special pleading to argue that the Church can be consistent in its support of American democracy, even though it was not of its Jacobin form.[21]

When it comes to Murray's argument in favor of natural law, however, his admiration (again not surprisingly) is only lukewarm. Interestingly, what concerns him is less the idea of natural law itself as it is Murray's apparent "unreconstructed and rationalist" version of it.[22] He again notes that some European Catholic theologians, while remaining within a Thomistic framework, recognize that, "without the support of revelation, our rational knowledge of the normative structure of human nature is likely to be dangerously inadequate and confused."[23] He does not find Murray as cautious; on the contrary, he seems to assume "that all major precepts and conclusions of the natural law as traditionally set forth can be demonstrated in such a way as to be objectively convincing to any man of sufficient intelligence."[24] If so, he must disagree. The same complaint can be found in Marty, who says that "the Catholic 'natural law' argument on birth control ...looks to non-Catholics for all the world like particular, positive, 'revealed' law."[25]

The problem these three theologians raise is less with general principles than with cases. While Lindbeck finds him thoughtful on the issue of censorship, he finds him again too rationalistic in his distributive justice argument for public aid to private schools: this is to forget the importance of political prudence, for such aid could lead to

---

That does not mean that the past role assigned a Christian Emperor, King, or State was essential to Catholic doctrine, nor does it exclude the doctrine that these should have a more limited role from being implicit in the principles of an earlier Doctor or nascent in the ideas of an earlier Pope.

[21] This argument had likewise been made earlier by Brownson: see, especially, the final chapter of *The American Republic.*

[22] Lindbeck, op. cit., p. 215.

[23] Ibid.

[24] Ibid.

[25] Marty, op. cit., p. 1316.

"a chaos of competing sectarian educational systems."[26] Likewise, he thinks his analysis of communism, and American responses to it, may be inadequately informed by political experience and prudence.[27] Marty seems to object not only to contraception, but to his views on public aid to private schools and censorship (although he gives no reasons for his objections).[28] Cox argues that Murray's description of public policy decisions as "merely complicated, and not ambiguous" may be unduly "sentimental about the efficacy of reason."[29] "Would that it were so!" he exclaims, but this would be to forget that "moral problems are more than intellectual," and that our fallen will and self-deception will surely skew our deliberations.[30] Lindbeck is also puzzled over Murray's objection to moral ambiguity, since human fallibility and sinfulness are consonant with natural law, and he regrets what he sees as an unfair attack on Reinhold Niebuhr[31] (although George Weigel plausibly suggests that the probable target of Murray's attack on "ambiguists" is not Niebuhr—his personal friend—but "political realists" such as Hans Morgenthau).[32]

In any event, one can fairly summarize these Protestant reviewers as exhibiting a common tendency of the Reformers: they argue that our fallen condition should make us ready to suspect that unaided reason cannot get us as far as Murray seemingly implies.

---

[26] Lindbeck, op. cit., p. 215.

[27] Ibid., p. 216.

[28] Marty, op. cit., p. 1316. Marty seems the least sympathetic to Murray, finding him rather "removed" from common Protestant convictions. For example, he notes Murray's facile dismissal of the nominalism that is common to much modern Protestant thinking (p. 1316). Murray's work does seem somewhat "dated" in the ease with which he dispenses with this position: a sign, perhaps, of an overly confident Thomistic realism.

[29] Cox, op. cit., p. 82.

[30] Ibid.

[31] Lindbeck, op. cit., p. 216.

[32] George Weigel, *Tranquillitas Ordinis: The Present Failure and Future Promise of American Thought on War and Peace* (Oxford: Oxford University Press, 1987), chapter 4—"The John Courtney Murray Project"—p. 124.

Before offering my own assessment, I'd like to bring in a Jewish voice, that of Rabbi David Novak, who is quite familiar to Maritainians.[33] He is himself a defender of natural law[34] and thus a natural ally of Murray. Indeed, his 1992 essay on Murray is basically quite sympathetic.[35] Nevertheless, he argues that the Aristotelian metaphysic that undergirds Murray's account of natural law will not be regarded as plausible by our contemporaries. Murray's idea "that there is a definable human nature to which everyone can refer without prior allegiance to any religious tradition, and from which natural law precepts can be derived," is simply not convincing.[36] Instead of requiring such an impractical standard, one should appeal to the *ius gentium*, to what the community "constitutes as generally normative in and for the world....one will have to appeal to historically evident data, rather than to the type of metaphysics Murray suggested."[37] Thus, a religiously-based political ethic ought to begin by acknowledging its own faith commitments and its own embrace of natural law within that commitment. It can then offer its tradition to the larger and broader community, as a means of illumining and supporting what that larger community's historic commitments have been. There will be no need for any member of that community to accept the philosophical truths

---

[33] He gave a fine speech to the 1991 American Maritain Association conference, which unfortunately could not be included in the volume devoted to that year's papers: see *Jacques Maritain and the Jews*, edited by Robert Royal (Notre Dame: University of Notre Dame Press, 1994), p. 1, footnote #1.

[34] See his *Natural Law in Judaism* (Cambridge: Cambridge University Press, 1998).

[35] David Novak, "John Courtney Murray, S.J.: A Jewish Appraisal," in *Jewish Social Ethics* (New York: Oxford University Press, 1992), pp. 67-83.

[36] Ibid, p. 76.

[37] Ibid, p. 77. Orestes Brownson had much earlier made use of the *ius gentium*, but precisely because it grounded law not in mere convention—which was potentially subject to abuse and tyranny—but in God Himself. (For one example, see *The American Republic*, p. 135.) Indeed, absent an ultimate appeal to the Lawgiver implicit in the concept of *ius gentium*, it is hard to see how this can supply the basis for the agreed-upon laws that Novak desires to establish or how it will not be vulnerable to the charge of being merely conventional. International agreements, like natural law, finally rest on the authority of a Lawgiver.

that undergird the natural law tradition. It will be sufficient for the community that this tradition renders its own commitments more coherent. In this way, natural law can be defended without an appeal to Aristotle, or even without a commitment to certain fundamental ideas, such as human nature itself.[38]

Novak's critique indicates that the Jewish tradition (at least as he understands and defends it) is quite close to the Catholic one (just as Maimonides is close to Aquinas).[39] Indeed, his assessment of Murray is more positive even than Lindbeck's. Yet, as with the Protestant critics, so here the criticism is that Murray is too "rationalistic," too inclined to argue for an abstract natural law theory accessible to all, rather than seeing that such an argument is bound to be a non-starter for many contemporaries, and that it will make them suspicious that a religious tradition is surreptitiously being smuggled in under the guise of a "neutral philosophy," based upon the "common light of reason."

4. Conclusion

I come, then, to my own assessment of Murray. How should we see the judgment of his critics? How viable or how flawed is his own defense of natural law reasoning, as the indispensable "*lingua franca*" that America needs to recover, to be true to its traditions?

We should probably begin by acknowledging that America has changed considerably in 50 years. To hear Murray chastising Protestants for criminalizing contraception (157) is to measure some of the distance we have come![40] He wrote before the media and feminist revolutions, the race riots, the quagmire of Vietnam and Watergate, before Vatican II and its aftermath, Roe vs. Wade, and the gay revolution. The public conversation has shifted, and its tone is quite different. For example, save in the South, or perhaps in the Midwest, the Protestant ethic he regarded as previously dominant, if challenged,

---

[38] Ibid., p. 76 ff.

[39] Novak himself notes the similarity, precisely in relation to American Jews and Catholics: Ibid., pp. 68-70.

[40] For his fine and most careful analysis of the issue of contraception, see his "Memo to Cardinal Cushing on Contraception Legislation," in Harpers, *Bridging the Sacred and the Secular*, pp. 81-86.

seems much less in evidence. And it would no doubt surprise—and perhaps even shock—him to find a Catholic candidate for the White House publicly disputing and actively attacking the Catholic Church's clear and constant defense of the unborn and its equally evident rejection of contraception and "homosexual marriage." Again, since 1989, America seems even less clear of its vision for the world, or how it should lead in it. Certainly, the landscape of our public discourse has altered, and seemingly not for the better.

Yet one could, I think, also point to certain gains. For example, the just war tradition seems to inform our public discourse about war and peace more than it did in his day. No doubt one of the reasons is that our present thinking—ever since Vietnam—has been more about conventional than nuclear war. It is easier to employ just war arguments when you are not contemplating a 'nuclear exchange'! Still, the difference is notable. Also, it seems that Murray might be surprised—but this time surely pleased—that the American bishops have taken stands on war and peace, and the economy, and that their voice is a more accepted part of our "national debate." Finally, the plight of the unborn since Roe vs. Wade has kept the American Proposition's commitment to equality for all as alive for our time as the plight of slaves did after Dred Scott.

Granting that the nation's discourse is in another, and perhaps more dire, "key" than 50 years ago, the question earlier posed still remains: what should we make of Murray and his project today? I have two evaluations to offer: one positive, the other more critical.

In the first place, then, it seems to me that Murray is entirely correct in asserting both that America has historically stood for certain discernible truths, and that this is implicitly to embrace the natural law tradition. It is to do so, that is, in relation to its most general principles. Rightly, Americans regard human beings as naturally engaged in "the pursuit of happiness." Rightly, they see them as fundamentally social and committed to the enterprise of living together co-operatively for the common good. Rightly, they remain committed to the search for and support of human dignity, to an "ever more perfect" union based on justice and equality for all. A commitment to the highest level of natural law precepts is one that remains common, and for which a convincing case can be made.

Of course the "clerks," the university professors (85), are bound to raise the usual objections. Nominalists may question the existence of a common human nature. Skeptics may attack our ability to discern even its broadest outlines. And radicals of all stripes may find the limits imposed by nature an affront to their independence. There is nothing new about these arguments and the natural law tradition has weapons in its armament sufficient to take on such challenges. It is here, in the discourse of academe, that I believe we should understand Murray's claim that the natural law tradition is rooted in a larger philosophy. Contrary to what Novak says, that tradition need not depend on Aristotle's outmoded "astrophysics," although it will require much of his anthropology.[41] The intellectual in-fighting will continue, but the natural law tradition appears as vigorous today as ever, as ready to enter the fray. In fact, the University since his day has seen the renewal of "virtue ethics," and the natural law tradition itself is less marginalized in current ethical debates. Yet Murray was right to distinguish *this* contest from the task of convincing ordinary citizens of the basic terms of public discourse and policy. This remains no easy task, yet it is still possible, for University arguments—some sophistic, some more reasonable—hardly touch the common sense of the intelligent public.

Indeed, it seems possible not merely to defend our innate grasp of the basic precepts to preserve our life, to educate our children, to seek the truth, and to live sociably, but the next level of precepts, the *ius gentium*. The bases of our law and polity remain the truths given in the Ten Commandments, which are accessible to human reason unaided by such revelation: injunctions against murder, adultery, theft, and perjury remain basic and defensible, as do the positive injunctions to

---

[41] Novak rather curiously asserts that "physical teleology...is normative in the Aristotelian system because it is primarily seen in astrophysics" ("John Courtney Murray," op. cit., p. 71). I say "curious," because Aristotle's reflection on the heavenly objects (e.g. in *De Caelo*) is expressly taken up *consequent* upon his analyses in the *Physics* that establish the necessity of the teleology at issue. Teleology is normative by virtue of a philosophical analysis of all natural activity (including man's), not primarily because instanced in some "astrophysics."

honor God and parents.[42] At the level of the *professor*, it will be necessary to avert to a sound anthropology; but, at the level of *public policy* and political discourse, this is hardly necessary. Here what we need instead, as Novak rightly claims, is to argue from the nation's historic commitments. Let the professors argue about ultimate foundations or their absence! For the argument to advance at the level of common discourse, it is enough to draw attention to past and present commitments in law and the national ethos and to argue that not to support the truths enshrined in these is to undermine what most citizens hold most dear. It seems to me that a defender of Murray can be entirely sympathetic to Novak's public strategy.

As any natural law theorist knows, however, the greater the particularity of the precept, the greater its uncertainty. Indeed, as any Thomist knows, Aquinas famously allowed that a society could even be mistaken at the very high level of the *ius gentium*: the Germans of old, he supposed, did not even recognize that theft was wrong![43] It seems to me, then, that some of the criticism of Murray is misplaced. He can hardly have supposed that all precepts of the natural law could be set forth in a way that would convince "any man of sufficient intelligence[!]"[44] To take but one instance, if the Theological

---

[42] The fact that the Third Commandment specifies the Sabbath rest, as a means of honoring God, poses a thorny political problem for a pluralist society: how to honor God without unduly favoring one religion. The present policy (of differing nations and religious traditions) is to favor holy days of the main religion within that society, while seeking to make some allowance for the observance of other traditions. However this political problem is solved, it is separable from the almost universally felt need to honor the sacred. (Furthermore, contrary to what many today seem to assert, affirming the existence of one God is neither the prerogative of religion nor does it enjoin any religious behavior, as Deists among America's Founders well knew. That Theism is a philosophical position is historically obvious. To assert that God's existence has no relevance for the law of a pluralist society, because this would mean affirming the basis of a religion, would be as misguided as not to criminalize murder because one of the Ten Commandments condemns it.)

[43] Thomas Aquinas, *ST* I-II.94.4.

[44] Not only is this *prima facie* improbable, requiring as it does an unreasonably virtuous and educated populace, but it can hardly be squared with his many

Commission on contraception could disagree about whether each contraceptive act was intrinsically wrong, we are obviously dealing with a level of precept that is bound to be dubious and contested. After all, if the truth was not clear to a majority of Roman Catholic natural law theologians, it is hardly likely to be so for a non-Catholic population of ordinary citizens! And if one society could miss the truth that theft is wrong, another obviously could miss this truth. In a similar vein, when Lindbeck says that political prudence may argue against Murray's views on parochial education and his tactics to oppose communism, it is hard to imagine him not welcoming such criticism. This, after all, is precisely to "engage in the quarrel," as we should, and Lindbeck's arguments do have some merit.

In addition, Protestant insistence on man's sinfulness, fallibility, and "moral ambiguity" seems to misunderstand Murray's concern. Surely (as Lindbeck himself suggests), Murray could concur with this assertion (even if Jesuits as a group have tended to be more optimistic about fallen human nature). His target is not such a view of nature, but a political "realism" that reaches back to thinkers such as Thucydides or Machiavelli, and that is predictably trotted out to justify a willingness to sacrifice moral principle in the face of hard political choices. However tempting, this will not do. He is right to argue this, and I suspect that his Protestant critics might concur. On the whole, it seems to me that they do in fact engage Murray in "gentlemanly converse." I believe he could welcome their very critique, as implying a natural law conversation.

We come, then, to my criticism of his argument, which demonstrates some sympathy for the concern that he is overly "rationalistic." Having argued persuasively for the salutary impact of the Catholic natural law tradition upon America, he seems all too blind to the deleterious impact of "American confusion" upon the Catholic community. He is too ready to assume that the Catholic community will happily embrace its own tradition, and will be impervious to the

---

sober—not to say dire!—critiques of America. For confirmation of what he expected of the general populace, see his "Memo" cited above (note #40).

corruptive influences of the culture.[45] He makes this assumption even while Catholics migrated from "Catholic ghettos" to mixed suburbs and made ready to assume their rightful place in the American firmament, with the first Catholic president. I realize that it would be unfair to require Murray to foresee, in the 1950s, the ferment and chaos that was to beset the Church after Vatican II. Nevertheless, from his own diagnosis of the "American malaise," some of this was predictable; yet he almost entirely misses it.

For, consider this. In the first place, it is a natural human reaction to find common ground with our neighbor and friends, and to minimize what divides us. It is a hard command that we should hate sin while loving the sinner, and living closely with our neighbors will make it hard to find their differing views wrong. In the second place, the Catholic commitment to certain acts being unexceptionably bad will be met by hard cases that call this into question. Thus, when Lambeth broke with the previous "Christian consensus" on *contraception*, it did so because of the legitimate concern that a family might not be able to afford more children. *Abortion* is pushed for the cases of rape or incest. *Euthanasia* is urged for the few terminal cases where pain killers cannot be employed. *Harvesting embryos* is to be permitted, because stem cells are believed to be able to save lives. *Homosexual marriage* is demanded for those who love each other (and who may desire to raise children). It will be impossible for Catholics not to have some sympathy for such

---

[45] He is not without some recognition of this influence, as this passage from his "Memo" indicates: "Catholics themselves must be made to understand that, although contraception is not an issue of public morality to be dealt with by civil law, it remains for them a moral issue in their family lives, to be decided according to the teaching of the Church. Because contraception is made legal it is not therefore made moral, any more than it should be made illegal simply because it is immoral" (p. 84). Yet, in arguing against its being a matter of public morality, it never occurs to him that it might develop from being a matter of a doctor's prescription to being advertised and dispensed by vending machines or that one of the effects of a likely increase in extra-marital sexual activity and likely increase in unwanted pregnancies would be an increase in public pressure for abortion on demand: in short, that its legalization could have public consequences that indirectly did plausibly argue for its being an issue of public morality. He misses, or underestimates, the potentially revolutionary impact of contraception on society.

hard cases, yet they all undermine the Church's stand on such matters.[46] Thirdly, this will be especially hard to maintain in a culture that has traditionally looked to motive more than act to determine personal morality. Finally, as Murray himself both noted and endorsed, the American "default position" is to favor freedom over restraint, and thus to place the initial burden of proof on the Catholic limitation of one's freedom in such cases. This historical commitment is bound to put Catholic teaching on the defensive and will likely undermine the Catholic community's confidence in some of it traditional moral teaching.

The fact that so many of the issues just mentioned were non-issues for Murray's time marks the distance our society has traveled in the last 50 years. If he did not see how the Catholic community was likely to be challenged, perhaps we should not blame him. For America was not then ready to compromise on these matters, as it is today. Nevertheless, the fact of living closely with others, in a society with an ethic based on motive, and prejudiced in favor of personal choice, was bound to create difficulties for Catholics.[47] Furthermore, he held that many moral precepts are clear only to the few, who are wise: "society is rescued from chaos only by a few men, not by the many. It is only the few who understand the disciplines of civility and are able to sustain them in being and thus hold in check the forces of barbarism that are always threatening to force the gates of the City"(13). He noted that

---

[46] The Catholic position in relation to such hard cases acknowledges both the good motives and the hard circumstances involved, and the perplexity and pain these create, while maintaining we should still avoid the act in question. This is a complex position and one that requires strength of mind and will to maintain. (Indeed, it may even require the grace of God and a willingness to share in the suffering of the Redeemer.)

[47] Most of the controversial public issues of the day concern life and, centrally, our sexuality (which is not surprising, since it is intimately ordered to life). Murray certainly could have recognized that this was an area of likely controversy. From the beginning, the Reformers had taken a different view from Catholics on this subject: e.g. in rejecting the perpetual virginity of Mary, a celibate clergy, and the sacramentality of marriage, in permitting divorce, and in their more recent support of contraception. Given the historical strength of Protestant culture in America, it should not have been impossible to discern "trouble ahead."

Aquinas held the same: the laws "of more particular import reached the people through the lawgiver, Moses" (116).[48] Now, today's debated issues are just at this level of precept. Thus, just as the prohibition of all lying is such a truth, so is the precept against all contraception, rightly held to be a kind of "bodily lie."[49] He could have seen, then, that the times posed a significant problem for Catholic educators, above all for the bishops.

Several years ago, I heard an intelligent bishop claim that the Church had "lost the natural law argument" on contraception when it came to the laity, who found it unconvincing. His assertion was both remarkable and seriously erroneous for three reasons. First, contrary to what he may think, the Catholic community is likely to be more convinced by natural law argumentation than by any other. Not only is it true, and in touch with its common sense, but Catholics are predisposed to honor it as their own tradition, rather than to be skeptical of it. Second, the reason the bishops have failed to convince

---

[48] It is worth noting what precepts Aquinas claims (in *ST* I-II 100.11) are *not* evident to all, but only to the wise: amongst others, commandments against witchcraft, blasphemy, violence against one's neighbor, prostitution, homosexual acts, fraud, robbery, and lying! It is precisely these "corollaries" to natural law precepts that we should expect to be contested in a democracy governed less by the wisdom of the few than of the many. And this is, in fact, just what we do find. Thomas's list underlines what the Founders often argued: that a democracy absent the salutary impact of religious education—which in effect impresses the wisdom of the few upon the many—will end in license.

[49] Thus, in contraception, the body is made to "say" what is not the case: sexual union is an intimate act of self-donation...except that one's greatest bodily power, to procreate (which, insofar as it can create a body prepared to receive a human soul, is a "co-creator" of something immortal and "divine") is not given, but reserved; or, rather, this power of life is given, but then immediately taken back, the bodily equivalent of "double-speak." Now, it is not hard to see that periodic abstinence respects the truth that sex is essentially ordered to life—sexual union being avoided when a new life is not wanted—whereas contraception does not respect this, but sterilizes the sexual union. However, it is much harder to see just why this difference is so important. In a similar way, it can be hard to see why lying is never justified, even in difficult circumstances.

the laity is that they have hardly tried. Not once in the last twenty years, for example, have I ever heard a sermon from the pulpit against contraception. They thus now find themselves belatedly arguing against homosexual marriage because it is an intrinsically sterile union, even though they have remained virtually silent about the sterilization of the sexual union systematically practiced by heterosexuals. But, leaving aside these two arguments, what most appalled me was that a bishop should think he needed to *persuade* the laity by such *argument*. The foundational reason why the Catholic laity should reject contraception is because this is what their Church teaches. They should hold Catholic doctrine out of their prior faith commitment and what it enjoins on them, not because they agree with a rational argument.

Natural law arguments function in two very different ways, depending upon who is being addressed. If we are seeking common ground with those of a different or no faith tradition, then these must stand on their own, without further appeal. Rightly, Murray urges this approach, as the legitimate basis of a public policy rooted in historic American commitments. But natural law arguments function quite differently for those within a faith community. For the *reason* why a person of that community holds a view (and this will be as true for one community as for another, as true for Jews as for Catholics, say) is because this view is part of their sacred community and its sacred commitments. For this person, the natural law argument is merely *supportive*, not *probative*. He or she should already hold the position, before encountering any argument: not because of the truth of the latter, but because of his or her adherence to the community's teaching.[50] A Catholic holds on faith that the Holy Spirit protects the

[50] Natural law argumentation, when philosophical, is based on the wisdom of God, who orders or provides for creatures according to what they are; thus, for example, it argues that we can see that we should act with justice towards our neighbor, because this accords with our social nature, our basic need to co-operate with others (an argument as old as Socrates' reply to Thrasymachus and the Ring of Gyges in the *Republic*). But natural law argumentation, when theological, is based on the holy will of God, who has commanded that certain acts be done. This is held on faith, and the natural law reasoning supplies an *ex post facto* justification of this; that is, it seeks to show that God's holy commands are truly wise, in accord with what is good for us. But it holds open the possibility that we may not be able to see fully

Church and leads it into the truth, even into truths that may be theoretically open to reason, but that may be quite difficult to see given both our fallen condition and our historical context. Thus, a Catholic should hold that contraception is wrong before ever attempting an account of why this is so, and he or she should continue to hold this position, even if finding all proposed arguments weak.

Today, we find ourselves confronted with the noxious—and truly scandalous—spectacle of Catholic politicians asserting that they "respect" the view of their Church that abortion is an intolerable crime, but that they will actively work against this view. This is a scandal not only because they dishonestly characterize a sin against the Fifth Commandment as one against the Sixth, and an anti-abortion stance as a private affair of faith. It is just as scandalous because of their apparent conviction that they can merely "respect" Catholic doctrine, while refusing it their assent, even regarding one of the few sins that incurs the Church's automatic excommunication. Whatever comfort they may seek to draw from "minimalist"' theologians, this is intolerable nonsense.[51] The Catholic teaching is and ever has been that the Catholic laity owes Catholic doctrine a religious *assent* of their will and not merely intellectual "respect." By rights, they ought to "respect" and take seriously the views of other traditions! The Church does not say and never has said that this is all they owe *Her* teaching! It may be hard, but so is holiness.[52]

---

what really is good for us, just as a child may not fully appreciate the wise commands of his parents. One wonders whether making this distinction and point clear would not go a good ways towards relieving the uneasiness felt by Murray's Protestant critics (and by Novak) concerning what is felt to be his undue "rationalism."

[51] Some Catholic theologians today claim that Catholics are free in conscience not to follow their Church's moral teaching on matters with which they cannot agree. These theologians apparently think the Church does not mean what She says in authoritative documents, of Council or Catechism. This is sheer sophistry.

[52] Indeed, one should go further: it is not merely hard to follow the Lord's commands; without His aid, it is impossible (as He Himself declared in Matthew 19:26). The fundamental reason a non-Catholic society will likely reject certain of the Church's harder moral precepts is that many in it reject

Now I do not say that Murray is responsible for the state of affairs presently besetting the Catholic community. However, I do say that there was and is one way of clearing up the confusions that confront us. And that is to begin by acknowledging two evident facts. First, a Catholic discovers the natural law tradition as part of his or her faith community. Second, as this tradition descends to details and to hard cases, it becomes more and more doubtful and will likely less and less persuade those outside that tradition. A Catholic should forthrightly acknowledge that what is theoretically open to the light of reason may fail to persuade, and that his own commitment to some particular conclusions of his tradition owes as much or more to his faith commitment than to his argument. Novak is right. Religious people need to be forthright about the fact that they are offering to the larger community a tradition of their own: one that they indeed believe illumines common commitments, but that comes from their context, not some "neutral ground."

Would Murray endorse such a position? It seems to me that he would. Yet this is evidently not the way he proceeded to make his argument. Otherwise, why are all his critics so worried about his rationalism, his confidence in deducing the details of the tradition as Catholics see them, and his apparent requirement that we hold a common philosophy in depth, in its metaphysical commitments? Had he argued his case as I believe it needs to be argued, and made more of the differing levels and certitude of natural law precepts, these kinds of misunderstandings and criticisms could hardly have been made. And, had he done what I have suggested he needed to do, he would have been more ready to warn his Catholic readers that their commitments to truths supported by natural law arguments did not derive first from them, but from their commitment to the Holy Spirit watching over their Church. The Catholic community in America has become seriously confused about its historic and present commitment to Catholic doctrine.[53] I do not say that John Courtney Murray helped cause this.

---

or do not have the divine faith that helps one fulfill them. Her standard is higher than that of paganism, and the best among the pagans recognized that only the wise few could meet even their standard of moral virtue.

[53] Since a Catholic believer's supposed right not to practice what the Church teaches undermines the ability to entrust oneself unreservedly to the

That indeed would not be true. But neither did his way of presenting his argument help waylay this confusion.

My conclusions, then, are twofold. First, his project remains as a task to be fully attempted and carried forward. It is sensible and right. But we must recognize that natural law argument—by its own admission—diminishes in its clarity and application as it descends to particulars. Catholics should therefore be prepared to find their own tradition far from convincing on some particulars to non-Catholics, and should be forthright about this. Second, the Catholic community needs to be quite clear that its faithful hold the views that they do not because of a natural law argument (however supportive and thus comforting some may truly find this as being), but because of their faith commitment to their sacred community and its traditions. They must hold themselves to their own standard, even when this seems too "high" or too unreasonable to others. Indeed, others are more likely to be persuaded by the holiness of their witness than by the strength of their arguments. I believe Murray himself would endorse both of these conclusions.

---

guidance of the Holy Spirit in the Church, as well as compromises the virtue of obedience to the Lord's teaching that is essential to Catholic life, this crisis is particularly grave.

THE REAL ALTERNATIVES TO JUST WAR[1]

James V. Schall, S. J.

If there is a great European war in the near future, it will not be a capitalist war for markets, but a war of creeds for the possession of men's minds. And each side will be firmly convinced of the justice of its cause.... The war-makers will not be capitalists and armament manufacturers but the idealists and propagandists, and principles will be as important as poison gas.... But any peace propaganda which shuts the eyes to realities is worthless and may even increase the danger which it sets out to combat. It has been the fault of both pacifism and liberalism in the past that they have ignored the immense burden of inherited evil under which society and civilization labour and have planned an imaginary world for an impossible humanity. We must recognize that we are living in an imperfect world in which human and superhuman forces of evil are at work and so long as those forces affect the political behaviour of mankind there can be no hope of abiding peace.... For war is not only the work of man. It is also willed by God as the punishment of sin and as its instrument by which the Divine Justice performs its inscrutable judgment.

- Christopher Dawson[2]

While the effects of sin abound - greed, dishonesty and corruption, broken relationships and exploitation of persons, pornography and violence - the recognition of individual sinfulness has waned. In its place a disturbing culture of blame and litigiousness has arisen with speaks more of revenge than justice and fails to acknowledge that in every man and woman there is a wound which, in the light of faith, we call original sin.

- John Paul II[3]

---

[1] This article originally appeared in *Policy Review* 128 (December, 2004): 59-70.

[2] Christopher Dawson, "The Catholic Attitude to War," *Tablet* 169 (March 13, 1937).

[3] John Paul II, "Address to American Bishops," #4, *L'Osservatore Romano*, May 19, 2004, p. 3.

1. The case for war

A calm and reasonable case can and should be made for the possession and effective use of force in today's world. It is irresponsible not to plan for the necessary use of force in the face of real turmoil and enemies actually present in the world. No talk of peace, justice, truth, or virtue is complete without a clear understanding that certain individuals, groups, and nations must be dealt with by the use of measured force, however much we would like to deal with them in a more peaceful or pleasant manner. Without the threat of force, many will not talk seriously at all, and some not even then. Moral and economic problems are greater today because of the lack of adequate military force or, more often, because of the failure to use it when necessary. This view goes against the rhetorical grain, but it is a fact that needs attention and comprehension. We do not live in a new "world-historic" age that can "by-pass" these "outmoded" instruments of power, however rhetorically attractive it is to talk that way. Human nature has not changed, either for better or worse. Human institutions, both at the national and international level, have not so improved that they cannot be threats to the human good. Who watches the watchdogs remains a fundamental, if not *the* fundamental, question of the human condition. It is an issue with philosophical, theological, and political dimensions.

This is a counter-cultural position. It goes against much articulate liberal and religious sentiment. These sentiments about abolishing war, which are often ungrounded, are themselves one of the dangers of war. For example, on the wall above General Douglas MacArthur's tomb in the old city of Norfolk Virginia there is a plaque with the memorable and eloquent words that this military commander spoke on the occasion of the Japanese Surrender in 1945. They now appear to the author to be part of the problem, not the solution, as once appeared to be the case:

> It is my earnest hope and indeed the hope of all mankind that from this solemn occasion a better world shall emerge out of the blood and carnage of the past – a world founded upon faith and understanding – a world dedicated to the dignity of man and the fulfillment of his most cherished wish, for freedom, tolerance, and justice.... We have had our last chance. If we do not now devise some greater and more equitable system, Armageddon

> will be at our door. The problem is basically theological, and involves a spiritual recrudescence and improvement of human character that will synchronize with our almost matchless advances in science, art, and literature, and all material and cultural developments in the past two thousand years. It must be of the spirit if we are to save the flesh.

Since MacArthur spoke these words over sixty years ago, we have had thousands of wars of varying types and degrees. We thought that we had founded a system to prevent wars, especially small ones. MacArthur assumed that such a perfect system could be established. But his view was utopian, not realistic. As a result, the means whereby many small wars could actually have been stopped were lacking and the work of converting the whole world to a better "system," resulted in little being done that was truly effective.

The inspiration for this argument is taken from Maritain's phrase that "justice, brains, and strength" can and should belong together.[4] We need not collapse before tyranny or terrorism, and those who sponsor either. But we must do something effective about them. "Peace and dialogue" rhetoric does not work in the absence of a force component. The more the reality of measured force is present, the more dialogue and peaceful, including religious, means of conflict resolution are possible. Intense concern about "weapons of mass destruction," including how to make them, how to use them, and also how to insure they do not fall into the hands of radical groups, is not fanciful. Every holiday since 9/11, some e-mail arrives warning of the possible use of "dirty bombs" in some American or world city. That they have not been used, however, is more likely because those who would use them have actually been prevented by force. Units who would blow up major installations, if they could, do exist. All they lack are delivery capabilities.

In light of these considerations, this analysis argues that our main problems are not concerning the use of too much force, but too little. A peaceful world is not a world without ready forces, but one with

---

[4] See James V. Schall, "Justice, Brains, and Strength: Machiavelli and Modernity in Political Philosophy," in *Jacques Maritain: The Philosopher in Society* (Lanham, Maryland: Rowman & Littlefield, 1998), Chapter I, pp. 1-20.

adequate, responsible, and superior force that is used when necessary. The failure to have or to use such forces causes terror and war to grow exponentially. Unused force, when needed at a particular time and place, ceases to be force. But force is meaningless if one does not know that he has an enemy or how this enemy works and thinks. That latter problem is spiritual and philosophical, not technical. Many an adequately armed country has been destroyed because it did not recognize its real enemy. Neither is this an argument for force "for force's sake." It is an argument for force for justice's sake. This argument does not endorse the pursuit of an "eternal peace," which is a this-worldly myth, but real peace of actual men in an actual and fallen world. Peace is not a goal, but a consequence of doing what is right and preventing what is wrong and, yes, knowing the difference between the two.

Justice and force require one another in the actual world. Too often they are placed in opposition in a way that renders both unbalanced and ineffective. It is not a virtue to praise justice as if it need not be actually enforced and worthy things defended. The greatest crimes often are grounded in a utopian vision that is blind to living persons, and that does not see how to limit and control the disruptive forces that arise continually in human life. These forces are not substitutes for the virtue of justice. Indeed, this difficult virtue relies also on the existence and proper use of force for it effectively to exist. Contrary to much rhetoric, we do not live in a world in which diplomacy, dialogue, diversity, and law, however valuable, have replaced force. We can hopefully reach an adequate public order. But failure to understand that law and dialogue at some level also need the presence of reasoned force ends up not in creating more peace but less.

2. War is not the answer?

In late spring, in Baltimore, I walked to the end of Chestnut Street where it meets Joppa Road. On one corner was a large official-looking residence called "Mission Helpers Center." On both sides of its entrance gate were large blue and white signs that read, "War Is Not the Answer." These placards recall the many too simple slogans about war one often sees, including, like this one apparently, from religious sources. Here are some other examples that I recall seeing in recent years: "War is obsolete." "War is never justified." "The answer to violence is not more violence." "War does no good." "No one wins a war." "Love, not war." "Diplomacy, not war." "Dialogue, not war." "Stop violence." "Only the U.N. can declare war." "Justice, not war." "No war is legitimate." "Everyone loses in war." "War, Never Again."

When I saw the "war-is-not-the-answer" sign, I said to myself, "but to what question is war *not* an answer?" On the other hand, is there no question to which war *is* the only sensible answer? Must we be pacifists and draw no lines in the sand? Does nothing ever need defending? Can we choose not to defend what needs defending and still be honorable? If war is not the "answer," what is? Without being naïve, how do we rid ourselves of tyrants or protect ourselves from ideologues or fanatics who attack us with their own principles and weapons, not ours?

Machiavelli advised that a prince should spend most of his time preparing for war. The prince was not pious except when useful to his own end of staying in power. If we are this prince's neighbors, do we take no notice of his preparations? Do we give him the answer he most wants to hear from us, namely, "war is not the answer?" Those who practice this doctrine of no war make easy targets. The prince thinks war *is* an answer. It can help him in his goal of acquiring and keeping power. We may have to suffer a defeat. We should not choose to bring one on ourselves.

Even though much carnage and chaos happen in war, on every side, still we cannot blithely conclude from this fact alone that "war is not the answer." It may not be the *only* answer. But, a mere ungrounded velleity consisting in the frivolous hope that nothing bad will happen no matter what we do or fail to do is not a viable alternative. Any presumed alternative to war, employing other putatively more effective methods, has to stop what war seeks to prevent by its own reasoned use of measured force. The general opinion of most sensible men throughout history has been that war certainly is one answer, even a reasonable answer, in the light of consequences that would likely ensue without it. More than a few "un-fought" wars have made things considerably worse. Many wars that have been fought have made things better. The honor classically associated with war heroes is explained by the following proclamations: "Our cause is just." "Give me liberty or give me death." "Eternal vigilance is the price of liberty." "Walk softly but carry a big stick."

We often rightly ponder the horrors of war. It is a growth industry, particularly for those who do not choose to fight. Soldiers usually know more about the horrors of war than journalists. They also know more about what it is like to live under a tyrannical system. The gulags and concentration camps ought to cause us to reflect deeply on what happens when unjust regimes acquire and remain in power. 9/11 could have been prevented with but a small use of force, had we known that our enemy would utterly surprise us by using passenger planes as weapons.

Nietzsche, since he thought Platonism and Christianity had failed because both lauded weakness, was open to the idea of a certain nobility to war and the pursuit of power for its own dramatic sake. Like many moderns, he did not think there is any order in the universe except that imposed by his own will. Most sensible people, however, can see that the primary way to prevent or remove the threat of takeover by forms of unlimited power is the legitimate use of adequate force against them. Thus, we must not reflect about war's atrocities in isolation from real situations and without balance. Peace is not simply the absence of war. "No war" can, and often does, mean the victory of tyranny and the subsequent disarming of any opposition. "No moral use of war" can, by the same logic, result in no freedom and no dignity.

We need more serious reflection on the consequences for others and ourselves when we lose wars or fail to act and, as a result, something worse happens. Those who cry "peace, peace," often have unacknowledged blood on their hands because they failed to use adequate force when needed "To the victors go the spoils" is an ancient matter of fact, not a principle of justice. Cowardice has never been considered a virtue. Similarly, "turning the other cheek" should not serve as an excuse for allowing some evil to conquer, especially one that we could prevent, except because our theories prevented us from trying. Not a few worthy things have been eradicated forever because a war was lost. Eternal vigilance remains the price of liberty, and much else that is worthy.

For this very reason we should read ancient history. We can meditate with profit on the enormous cultural consequences of the final success of Xerxes in Greece, had Sparta and Athens not successfully defended themselves. Nevertheless, good causes do not always win wars; neither do bad causes always lose them. The "God of Battles" is often ironic. Fortune is difficult to conquer, and its consequences do not guarantee justice. St. Paul, as Dawson reminds us, even suggests that wars and the sword punish our wrongdoings. Pope John Paul II observed that we live in a world in which we want to deny that we commit any wrongdoing, and hence we fail to see the need for correcting our faults.

Still, we must think about the fact that failure to act can make things worse. Nor can we deny that there is a comparative difference between "bad" things and "terrible" things. We can be just as immoral and as inhuman by failing to act as by acting. The history of lost wars is as important as the history of victorious ones, perhaps more so. The idea of an absolutely war-less world, a world "already made safe for democracy," is more likely, in practice, to be either a sign of utopia or a madhouse. A world in which war is "outlawed" is more likely to mean either that we are no longer in the real world or that the devils and the tyrants have finally won. They allow us only to agree with them and do as they say. We are naive if we think that formal democratic procedures, lacking any reference to the content of laws, cannot have deleterious effects. A democratic tyranny is quite conceivable, many think likely, and on a global scale. "Globalization is not neutral." Not a few of the worst tyrants of history have been very popular and have died peacefully in bed in their old age, amidst family and friends.

3. National frontiers

The frontiers of most countries are where they are because of wars, won or lost. This is true even of the relatively peaceful Canadian-American border, whose drawing, even whose existence, is related to the American Revolution, the War of 1812, and to "54.40 or Fight!" The northern Mexican border does not include California, Texas, Arizona, and New Mexico, as it once did, because a war was lost. I have seen Mexican maps that still include these states within Mexican frontiers. This means that many Mexicans think the present borders are unjust; thus we are not wholly at peace. Lord Acton believed that had the South won the American Civil War, it probably would have taken over Mexico.

The so-called "evil empire" covered a quarter or more of the globe because of war and revolution. Ironically, it got its start when Lenin precipitously pulled out of bloody World War I to eradicate his domestic enemies on the right and the enemies of his Bolshevism on the left. The demise of the Soviet Union surprised most social scientists because it was not destroyed by war or by any force subject to their analytical methods. However, as we were reminded by the Reagan funeral, a major cause of the collapse of communism, besides the spiritual one for which the Polish Pope stood, was the massive American preparations for war, including nuclear war. They were sufficient to convince the Soviets finally to recognize communism's own internal bankruptcy. Many, at the time, thought this build-up was itself "immoral." Had it not occurred, the Soviet Union might well still be in existence and its demise might not have been so peaceful, if indeed it was not victorious.

In the case of World War II, we can surely "thank" the lack of early French and English preparedness for and initial unwillingness to engage in war to be a major cause of the more lethal war that, by almost any standard, had to be fought and fortunately won, but only with the aid of others. "Peace in our time," the slogan of the British prime minister, led to World War II. "War was not an answer?" What is the "answer" to terrorism if not war at some level? Terrorists, as they often testify, think that terrorism is a legitimate, even divinely commanded duty. Is capitulation the answer? Roman history, in fact, is filled with such wars and capitulations.

In the abstract, the view that non-combatant alternatives to war are always available may well be true. But there are things worse than war. Not to know what they are is tantamount to losing any real contact with or understanding of human experience and history. Machiavelli did not study the "history of war" for merely idle reasons. Many "peaceful" alternatives to war are not happy ones. One of them consists in being conquered by a hostile power and experiencing complete civilizational destruction. We read of Muslim and Mongolian armies before whose swords we would not like to fall, knowing that if we do, our culture, religion, and way of life, not to mention many of our lives, would disappear. No one in the decade before the sudden appearance of Mohammedan armies in the seventh century could have imagined the configuration of the world map today, a configuration in many areas due precisely to the permanent conquests of these earlier and later armies. The modern integrity of Europe is unimaginable without two victories over Muslim forces, one at Tours in France, and one at Vienna.

4. Wars of civilization

These reflections do not propose further to define the over-analyzed question concerning the conditions of just war in the modern age of weapons of mass destruction. The most "lethal" weapons are today turning out to be car bombs and ordinary passenger planes. The problem with nuclear weapons was never really the weapons themselves, but the will and purpose for which they might be used. Reading the American bishops' documents on nuclear war in the retrospective light of the bombing of the World Trade Centers makes them seem almost irrelevant. The fact is, deterrence did work, however reluctant we may be, usually for ideological reasons, to admit it. The earlier considerations about "absolute weapons" also seem wholly out of touch with what has become the primary defense concern in the 21st century.

We do have a concern that "terrorists," as we are wont to call them in lieu of calling them what they call themselves, will gain possession of nuclear weapons. We could reasonably suppose that communists did not want to be destroyed. We are not so sure about radical Muslim war planners. The "suicide bomber" may prove to be more lethal, and more intellectually perplexing, than any nuclear weapon ever was.

Nuclear and conventional weapons, in fact, have become so accurate, so down-sized, and so controlled that all the elements of the just war theory devised by the most scrupulous moralist are in place and in operation. One might even argue that current American weaponry is constructed the way it is precisely because it is living up to just war concerns. Again, the problem is not the weapons themselves, but who uses them. The knowledge of how to make such weapons is widely available, along with the technology to make them. We cannot think these plans out of existence without thinking much of modern science out of existence. And we have no reason to think that present day terrorists, who have a different religious philosophy, will not use nuclear weapons if they can, even if they destroy themselves in the process.

What is not in place today is how to deal with or even understand the "suicide bomber." Just war theory is relatively useless in this area. As I read somewhere, what after all does a fully armed GI do in confrontation with a pregnant Muslim woman who has bombs strapped inside her dress and intends to blow him, herself, her baby, and dozens of others up? All the literature and normal understanding about "innocent women and children" have become, if not irrelevant, at least maddeningly difficult to apply in such increasingly common cases. The reason for this problem is not military, but ideological or theological.

The answer to the question of why a radical Muslim man or woman will blow him or herself up is not simply political or military. Aristotle had said that if someone is willing to die in the process, no one can really prevent him from trying to kill us. Augustine had a similar problem with the Donatists. A Muslim extremist who blows himself up, along with fifteen others, can pretty much rest assured that this same utterly irresponsible type of weapon will not be used against his own people. This is a civilizational divide, not just a matter of taste, nor even of the end justifying the means. It is the consequence of a faulty theology and it must be addressed at that level.

The central issue raised by the foregoing analysis is Christopher Dawson's question from the 1930's, namely: Is the current situation we are facing a new war of civilization? Much vested interest is devoted to the proposition that it is not. Insisting that there is no such conflict is itself an ideological commitment. Our civil and religious leaders have been loathe to designate the current situation as a civilizational war. Islam is a religion of peace. To suspect that it is a threat on a much broader scale is one of those things that must be classified as "secret writing." It goes against the dominant religious mood, namely, ecumenism, and against the liberal mode, namely, tolerance, according to which all issues can be resolved without war. But neither of these viewpoints are proper to certain Muslim ways of looking at the world which, in their missionary view ought to be Muslim, even if by war, and even if by suicide bombings. War can be precisely "holy." Until we understand that, we simply will not be able to grasp the essence of the problem.

There is considerable talk, both in the West and in some sectors of the Muslim world, that Islam can be accommodated to certain politically acceptable forms without having to change any of its basic beliefs. This radical reconstruction of Islam is said to be the main "neo-conservative" project. The proposed project of rewriting or re-founding Islam is a concomitant of identifying the current attacks as coming from a minority "terrorist" movement and not from Islam in any genuine form.

One can defend this program on prudential grounds. No one, on the other hand, including churches and religious groups, is willing to examine in a serious way the truth claims of Islam, not only its self-understanding of Allah and its view of Judaism and Christianity, but also its practiced way of life and the direct relation of its religion and its politics. Until this latter effort is undertaken in a much more serious way, the prudential approach can be justified as a holding operation. But even in the effort to provide models and forms of "democratic" and "free" political systems, what is ultimately behind this thinking is the effort to undermine those teachings and customs of Islam that cause the problem, the first of which is the claim of the truth of Islamic revelation and its understanding of the absolute will of God as arbitrary. In this sense, MacArthur was right. Political problems often have theological import as their basis.

The Italian paper *Il Giornale* recently published an interview with Caesare Mazzolari, bishop of Rumbek in the Sudan, a place in which Christian-Muslim relations are those of war, war against the Christians. His remarks perhaps serve to contextualize this issue, particularly in the light of the Dawson thesis:

> Q. "Is there a clash of civilizations...?"
>
> A. "The Church has defeated communism but is just starting to understand its next challenge – Islamism, which is much worse. The Holy Father has not been able to take up this challenge due to his old age. But the next pope will find himself having to face it...."
>
> Q. "Some bishops in Italy have allowed chapels to be used as mosques."
>
> A. "It will be the Muslims who convert us, not the other way around. Wherever they settle down, sooner or later they end up becoming a leading political force..."

> Q. "Does it make sense to export our democracy to agricultural and sheep-herding societies that make no distinction between religion and politics?"
>
> A. "No. This is idiotic. Islamic people base their decisions only and exclusively on the umma. They don't even know what individual rights are."[5]

This is, no doubt, a blunt analysis from someone located in a country where over two million people have been killed in Muslim attacks on Christians and their own dissidents. Whether we look on it as the wave of the future or as an exceptional, isolated case will pretty much decide the kind of attitude we have to war and the necessity of the retention and use of military power.

5. Use of force

The topic of this analysis, however, is not Islam but war. An essential ingredient of this discussion is a current understanding of what Islam is and intends. But our relationship with Islam is not the only civilizational challenge we face, and Islam itself is not necessarily a monolithic worldview. Furthermore, Western secularist ideology is as absolutist in its own way as Islam. The thesis that the "terrorists" are merely a side-show, a tiny minority, which will naturally pass away, provides an easy but inadequate way out of considering the more fundamental challenges of the religion as a civilizational movement. According to the judgment of some of its more radical leaders, there is suddenly the possibility that the religion can continue its historic mission of expansion, in some cases spreading the religion by force or other means.

The question of how to "disarm" or to "dissuade" this expansion, which now has a demographic component through immigration into Western nations with low birth rates, is bound up with the question of a continued capacity and willingness of a nation to defend itself. It is still necessary to defeat those who hold violence to be a legitimate form of political activity, no matter how small or large we think their forces

---

[5] Interview of Stefano Lorenzetto with Msgr. Caesare Mazzolari, May 26, 2004, http://www.chiesawysiwyg://213.92.16.98/ESW_articolo/0,2393,42160,00.html.

might be. They remind us of Augustine's dealings with the Donatists in which, after exhausting all possible peaceful and accommodating means to deter them, he concluded that they must change their minds even by the use of force, at least to pacify them. Augustine has often been criticized for this conclusion. But, even if we assume that it does work, which is dubious, it is clear that those with whom we are dealing today are not going to be "converted." They look upon suicide bombing in service of their cause as martyrdom and as guaranteeing entrance to heaven. The fact that this position seems preposterous to many of us is one of the main reasons we cannot effectively deal with it.

A common theory about war today is that we have evolved or progressed beyond it. The claim that war may still be needed is looked upon as "anti-progressive," or a sin against "history." No "reasonable" person can hold the view that war may be necessary. The "we-have-outgrown-war" position, with its Hegelian overtones, is part of a broader evolutionary hypothesis that holds, generally speaking, the world is getting morally better. According to this view, we have learned how to "overcome" violence with dialogue or psychological counseling. The older realist hypothesis, by contrast, which is more attuned to the Fall and the natural difficulties of the practice of virtue, maintains that as the world improves in technological or political means, the potential for greater evil also increased. According to this latter view, we will never be in a situation where some use of force is completely unnecessary for the achievement of what limited goods we can and should attain.

The hypothesis that war is no longer necessary has little justification. Behind this view, we find operative an ancient controversy concerning the idea of a world state as the primary inner-worldly purpose of mankind. Indeed, after denying any other transcendent purpose, it becomes the only purpose of mankind. The framework of "world" or "global" government is now said to be already in place. Though the United Nations was not legally erected to be a "world government" or "world state," no political controversy involving war, it is now claimed, erroneously, can be "unilaterally," and hence morally, decided outside of its jurisdiction. This view is designed to take away any consideration of national self-interest or of independently coming to the aid of those under attack. This newly discovered veto on war evidently comes from custom, not law, though even there it is difficult to know how such a momentous structural change could be legitimated in this unarticulated way.

This assumption of a benign United Nations already legally established depends upon a misguided view of the institution and the ideological currents within it. Many positions on moral and economic questions within the United Nations are extremely troubling. There are "missionary" efforts to impose these ideas on the world. Furthermore, this position implies that there are never circumstances in which either truth or good will have to be protected *against* the United Nations, and that it should logically absorb all the world's military capacity within itself. United Nations citizenship and courts should replace national citizenship and courts. The ultimate appeal, in this view, ought not to be to national courts but to international courts. International criminal and civil courts will be the primary arbitrators who decide justice within the nations. International courts will claim immediate jurisdiction over all rights cases wherever they occur. Any appeal to national "self-interest" against their decisions will be looked upon as a crime against humanity.

In his discussion of "restitution," the primary act of justice in all its forms, Josef Pieper made the following observation:

> The dynamic character of man's communal life finds its image within the very structure of every act of justice. If the basic act of commutative justice is called "re-stitution," the very word implies that it is never possible for men to realize an ideal and definitive condition. What it means is, rather, that the fundamental condition of man and his world is provisory, temporary, non-definitive, tentative, as is proved by the patchwork character of all historical activity, and that, consequently, any claim to erect a definitive and unalterable order in this world must of necessity lead to something inhuman.[6]

This "something inhuman" is what we are concerned about when we address the question of whether war is obsolete. The grounds of this

---

[6] Josef Pieper, *Josef Pieper: An Anthology* (San Francisco: Ignatius Press, 1989), p. 63.

latter assumption are that we actually do have in place the means to prevent war. The historic realism that argued that war would always be with us is now said to be effectively bypassed.

In response to this assertion, we may cite the following summation of Augustine's view of war by Herbert Deane: "Wars are inevitable as long as men and their societies are moved by avarice, greed, and lust for power, the permanent drives of sinful men. It is, therefore, self-delusion and folly to expect that a time will ever come in this world when wars will cease and 'men will beat their swords into ploughshares.'"[7] Yet, we are asked to believe the implausible supposition that the institutions designed to replace the national state will not themselves be threats against freedom and justice. On the contrary, a vital question remains as to whether the world would be better off with national states that can maintain their own judgments and forces. This analysis argues that, whatever the logic of the international state, its practice is too dangerous both on the large scale and on the small scale ever to trust it with anything more than minimal powers that are for the most part merely advisory. When it comes to modern tyrannies, international organizations have not been successful and they are often part of the problem.

Jean Elshtain has written, "I would argue that true international justice is defined as the equal claim of all persons, whatever their political location or condition, to having coercive force deployed in their behalf if they are victims of one or the many horrors attendant upon radical political instability."[8] What Elshtain implies is that there is and must be room for the existence and use of force that understands and works for right order. I would maintain, therefore, that much of the thinking about how war is obsolete is itself a major contributor to war, particularly to the new kinds of war that we see in the 21st century. Such a view prevents quick and effective action. Without denying that this alternative can also be abused, we can never arrive at a clear

---

[7] Herbert Deane, *Political and Social Ideas of St. Augustine* (New York: Columbia University Press, 1956), p. 155.

[8] Jean Bethke Elshtain, *Just War against Terror* (New York: Basic Books, 2003), p. 168.

concept of the problem if the mechanisms designed to address it include it.

6. In conclusion

In conclusion, we are left with the need to see force and power, when used rightly, as actual servants of justice. C. S. Lewis wrote in his essay, "Why I Am Not a Pacifist:"

> It is arguable that a criminal can always be satisfactorily dealt with without the death penalty. It is certain that a whole nation cannot be prevented from taking what it wants except by war. It is almost equally certain that the absorption of certain societies by certain other societies is a great evil. The doctrine that war is always a greater evil seems to imply a materialist ethic, a belief that death and pain are the greatest evils. But I do not think they are. I think the suppression of a higher religion by a lower, of even a higher secular culture by a lower, a much greater evil.... The question is whether war is the greatest evil in the world, so that any state of affairs, which might result from submission, is certainly preferable. And I do not see any really cogent argument for this view.[9]

Lewis, as usual, on the grounds of principle, had it about right. War is not the greatest evil, but at times the only means to prevent it. This is true on both a large and small scale. What we are left with is that the effective use of force is still best and most properly left in the national state. This is not the war of all against all, but the war of those who can limit terrorism and tyranny when and where it occurs. The worst modern tyranny in the 21st century will not come from armies but from their lack, or better from the lack of the capacity and courage to use them wherever needed to protect justice, freedom, and truth when it is at stake.

The real alternatives to just war cannot be viable without including the necessity and ability to deal with those who do not know or listen to reason. As a *Wall Street Journal* editorial put it, do we "treat terrorism

---

[9] C. S. Lewis, "Why I Am Not a Pacifist," in *The Weight of Glory and Other Addresses* (New York: Macmillan, 1965), p. 43.

as a problem of law enforcement or an act of war?"[10] Law enforcement does not work unless there is a more fundamental possibility of dealing with those who are bound by no concept of legal order as we understand it. There is no alternative to just war that does not depend on and include the possibility and the exercise, when reasonable, of just war.

[10] The Wall Street Journal, July 21, 2004.

Toward a Recovery of the Moral Sense

Alice Ramos

In 2008, Pope John Paul II's *Veritatis Splendor* marked its fifteenth anniversary. A critical task for philosophers and theologians alike in the light of *Veritatis Splendor* is the recovery of the moral sense, given its decline and obscuring in a culture that has also lost its religious sense.[1] The position a person takes toward the greatest of mysteries, that is, the mystery of God, is at the heart of every culture. Different cultures also involve different ways of pondering the mystery of the world, of the human person, and of giving expression to the transcendent dimension of human life. Present-day culture all too often has a very narrow sense of human life, because it emphasizes the physical and the psychic, not the divine. But in the midst of such a culture, at times characterized by a closed skepticism, there are also human beings marked by a restless incredulity and with these it is necessary to dialogue. Among them certainly there are those driven by the natural desire to know the truth, the kind of persons who, not having found God yet, possibly spend their time seeking Him because they do seek truth. An example of this restless incredulity can be found in the celebrated semiotician Umberto Eco. A recent translation of Eco's correspondence with Carlo Maria Cardinal Martini entitled *Belief or Unbelief?* recounts a discussion on various questions, including the ethical question. Eco frames his answer to Martini in terms of an ethics "born in the presence of the other."[2] Eco believes in a natural ethics that can match the principles of an ethics grounded on faith in transcendence. The purpose of this chapter is to show how an agnostic's understanding of ethics can be better understood as the intellect's desire for the truth and as "the work of the Law written in the hearts" of men. This will lead to a discussion of the moral sense as a capacity which all human beings have for recognizing the true good, a

---

[1] Pope John Paul II, *Veritatis Splendor* (Boston: St. Paul Editions, 1993), no. 98, p. 120.

[2] Umberto Eco and Cardinal Martini, *Belief or Unbelief?*, translated by Minna Proctor (New York: Arcade Publishing, 2000), p. 89.

sense rooted in the religious sense, in man's relatedness to the other who is God. This capacity for recognition is in particular need of help in our culture, and as Christian academics I think that we can provide much needed help, through both word and deed.

Let me begin with a number of claims made by Eco; a universal semantics, that is, elementary notions common to everyone in the human race, provide for Eco the basis for an ethical system. The acceptance of this semantics enables us, for example, to respect others, including their needs and rights as physical and also thinking beings. He maintains that we can only understand and interpret ourselves through others; in fact, he speaks of "the other that is in us."[3] Consciousness of the other's importance provides for Eco a strong foundation for ethical behavior, much as the existence of the totally other, that is God, would provide for the believer an unshakeable foundation for morality. What Eco terms a "secular ethics" is, according to him, a natural ethics, one that not even a believer would deny, and which does have sufficient impetus for virtue. The nonbeliever, like the believer, will know that he has done wrong and that he stands in need of correction and more importantly, of forgiveness. As Eco graphically puts it:

> ...a nonbeliever might think the evil he is doing in secret goes unseen. But keep in mind, if the nonbeliever thinks that no one is watching him from on high, he thereby knows--for this very reason--that no one will forgive him. Knowing he's done evil, his solitude will be infinite, his death desperate. This person is more likely than the believer to attempt to purify himself through public confession; he will ask forgiveness from others. He knows his predicament from the core of his being, and so he also knows in advance that he must forgive others. Otherwise how does one explain that nonbelievers are also capable of feeling remorse?[4]

It is interesting to find a prominent agnostic intellectual such as Eco speaking in this way; he considers his ethics to be animated by a deep religiosity, albeit a secular religiosity, which is based on "a sense of the

---

[3] Ibid., p. 94. See also pp. 91-94.

[4] Ibid., pp. 98-99.

sacred, of the finite, of investigation and expectation, of a communion with something greater--even in the absence of faith in a personal and provident divinity."[5] The principles of this natural ethics cannot be in disharmony with the principles of a supernatural ethics, which according to Eco, recognizes that "natural principles were carved into our hearts in anticipation of salvation."[6] Granted that men who hold to a natural ethics will not always act justly, Eco considers that even an ethics grounded on an absolute foundation does not keep believers from sinning, because the temptation to evil is found even in those who have a revealed notion of the good.

That a natural ethics can be the basis for a supernatural ethics should not be disputed, for grace builds on nature. Thomas Aquinas tells us that because the proper form of man is his rational soul, there is in every man a natural inclination to act according to reason, and this is to act according to virtue. Thus, our reason naturally directs us to act virtuously.[7] But nature wounded by sin does not do all the good that it would have done in the state of original justice. Sin not only disorders our faculties, it also diminishes the natural tendency to virtue.[8] The good of nature, however, is threefold, according to Aquinas, and the first good of nature, which consists in the principles out of which nature is constituted, was neither destroyed nor diminished by sin.[9] Consequently, Aquinas says "virtue is natural to man according to a kind of beginning."[10] In human reason "are to be found instilled by nature certain naturally known principles of both knowledge and action, which are the nurseries of intellectual and moral virtues," and in the will there is "a natural aptitude for good in accordance with reason."[11] Because of these natural principles, which are the "seeds of the virtues" and are found in every man's reason, we can understand

---

[5] Ibid., p. 90.

[6] Ibid., p. 102.

[7] *ST* I-II 94.3c.

[8] *ST* I-II 85.2c-3c.

[9] *ST* I-II 85.1c.

[10] *ST* I-II 63.1c.

[11] Ibid.

how someone like Oscar Wilde in his depraved period might see Martin of Tours cutting his cloak in half for a beggar as a noble or beautiful gesture, but a foolish one nonetheless.[12] The intelligibility and attractiveness of virtue is recognized and appreciated not only by the good man. As Aquinas says, ". . . although not all men have virtues in the complete habit, yet they have them according to certain seminal principles in the reason, in force of which principles the man who is not virtuous loves the virtuous man, as being in conformity with his own natural reason."[13]

Aquinas's argument enables us to understand Eco's description of what happens in the person who commits evil, feels remorse and seeks to purify himself through the forgiveness of others. Just as a human being can project himself into the future and recognize the inappropriateness of a possible action through the use of his intellect, so he can also look back on the act and recognize its dishonorable character, consequently experiencing remorse, guilt, or shame. The experience of shame is found in the reasoning faculty. Shame shrinks from what is dishonorable itself, that is, from the morally bad act, which is not in consonance with human dignity, and not simply from its consequences.[14] The remorse or shame experienced is evidence that the evil performed is not in harmony with reason. There is thus a rupture or disharmony that is produced within the human person as a result of a bad choice, and also a rupture in his ties to others. For this reason, Eco says that the man who does evil "knows his predicament from the core of his being." It is in the nature of human spirit to see and know itself and its acts, to look toward the other and back upon itself—matter is incapable of this.[15] The person is relational or dialogical in his very being. And so, when Eco says that ethics is "born in the presence of the other," and that the experience of evil is known "from the core of his being," the other cannot simply be other human persons such as himself, even if Eco says that "the ethical dimension

[12] I am indebted to my colleague Marie George for this example.

[13] *ST* I-II 27.3 ad 4.

[14] Aristotle, *Rhetoric* 1384a24, 1384a14-16.

[15] Joseph Ratzinger, "Concerning the Notion of Person in Theology," *Communio* 17 (Fall, 1990): 451.

comes into play when the other arrives on the scene."[16] Rather, "in the core of his being" man is inherently moral and made for communion with that totally other, the ultimate true good who is God. While recognizing that the inner man needs purification and forgiveness from others for the evil committed, that he needs, as it were, to be known with approval, Eco's reasoning does not go far enough.

In order better to understand the desperate and solitary situation of Eco's nonbeliever, which may be characteristic of many people in our culture, we will refer to Aquinas's distinction between synderesis and conscience found in his treatment of man's intellectual powers in the *Summa Theologiae.* While our rational powers admit of opposite things, synderesis inclines us to the good only, and therefore Aquinas calls it a habit rather than a power, although he notes that some consider it to be a power higher than reason, while others say that it is reason itself, not as reason, but as nature.[17] Just as speculative reason proceeds from speculative principles that are bestowed on us by nature, so practical reason proceeds from certain practical principles. Aquinas speaks of the first practical principles as belonging to synderesis, a special natural habit, which inclines us to the good and draws us away from evil. Synderesis provides us with a universal and unerring principle, in reference to which all human works are examined.[18] Because of the permanent and unchangeable character of this practical principle, human knowledge participates to some extent in the same knowledge that exists in higher substances. The intellectual simplicity from which our reason moves due to the habit of first principles is similar to angelic knowing, which is said to be godlike since angels receive knowledge of truth without any movement or reasoning.[19] Aquinas puts it more emphatically when he says: "... that something is known with certainty is due to the light of reason divinely implanted with us, by which God speaks within us."[20]

---

[16] Eco and Martini, *Belief or Unbelief?*, pp. 93-94.

[17] *ST* I 79.12c.

[18] See *DV* 16.2c.

[19] See *DV* 15.1c.

[20] *DV* 11.1 ad 13.

The important question is: How should this be understood in relation to synderesis? Aquinas says that synderesis is a habitual light which cannot be extinguished from the human soul, just as it is impossible to deprive the soul of the light of the agent intellect, through which the first principles in both speculative and practical matters are made known to us. This light belongs to the nature of the soul and by it the soul is intellectual. It is precisely the intellectual soul, the mind, or the understanding[21] which is said to be formed by the first truth itself, as a copy is formed to the likeness of the exemplar;[22] the intellectual soul or mind is thus said to be made in the image of God. Aquinas quotes Augustine in this regard who says, "The image of God exists in the mind, not because it has remembrance of itself, loves itself, and understands itself; but because it can also remember, love, and understand God by Whom it was made."[23] The remembrance of God, of which man's mind as image of God is capable, can help us better to understand the notion of synderesis, for it is possible to interpret the latter by means of the Platonic concept of *anamnesis* (that is, remembrance or recollection).[24]

This concept is also in accordance with a certain Biblical anthropology; in his Epistle to the Romans, St. Paul says, "In truth, when the Gentiles, guided by natural reason, who have no law do what the Law prescribes, these having no law are a law unto themselves. They show the work of the Law written in their hearts. Their conscience bears witness to them."[25] A similar idea can be read in the monastic rules of St. Basil who says, "The love of God is not based on some discipline imposed on us from without, but rather is constitutively infused in our reason as a capacity and a necessity."[26] St. Basil even says that a "spark of divine love is lodged within us."[27] And

---

[21] *DV* 15.1sc 5.

[22] *DV* 18.1 ad 7.

[23] *ST* I 93.8sc.

[24] See Joseph Cardinal Ratzinger, *Verdad, Valores, Poder*, translated and introduced by José Luis del Barco (Madrid: Rialp, 2000), pp. 64-74.

[25] Rom. 2:14-15.

[26] *Regulae fusius tractatae* Res 2, 1: *PG* 31, 908, quoted in Ratzinger, p. 66.

[27] Ibid.

since love of God is manifested in doing His will, in fulfilling His law, then the "spark of divine love" means that we have received in our mind—and not as something imposed from without—the capacity and disposition to do what the law prescribes. We can say with certainty that one thing is better than another because there is engraved in us, as it were, a fundamental understanding of the good.[28] There is thus inserted in us a primordial remembrance of the true and the good, of the true good, and in this remembrance there is a natural tendency of beings created in the image of God to do what is fitting to God. Man's very being from its origin is in harmony with certain things and in contradiction with others.[29]

This *anamnesis* of the origin, resulting from the very constitution of our being, which is made for God, is not a conceptually articulated knowledge but rather a certain inner sense, a capacity for recognizing the true good, which beckons the human person who is not interiorly divided to recognize its echo deep within himself. Such a person sees that this good befits his nature (because it is that for which his nature is made) and he thus wants to direct himself to that befitting good.[30] We might also say that the true good which is recognized by this capacity or inner sense is a participation in the ultimate true good, that is, God, and thus this inner sense, or moral sense, is rooted in the religious sense, in man's relatedness to God.[31] We can now understand what the Apostle Paul means when he says that the Gentiles are a law unto themselves: this is not to be taken in the sense of the autonomous subject who creates, as it were, his own law, but rather that one's own self, one's interiority, is the site of self-transcendence, since it is there where we are touched by the One from whom we originate and to whom we are destined.[32]

So when the sense of the good is not heeded, it is not surprising that the mind should pronounce itself against this evil, against what is

---

[28] St. Augustine, *De Trinitate* VIII, 3, 4; *PL* 42, 949, quoted in Ratzinger, p. 67.

[29] Ratzinger, *Verdad, Valores, Poder*, p. 67.

[30] Ibid.

[31] See Pope John Paul II, *Veritatis Splendor*, nos. 98 and 106, pp. 120 and 128.

[32] Ratzinger, *Verdad, Valores, Poder*, p. 68.

unfitting and disproportionate to it. Aquinas calls conscience "a certain pronouncement of the mind," which bears us witness.[33] Insofar as something has already been done which is evil, conscience is said to accuse or to cause remorse, because what has been done "is found to be out of harmony with the knowledge according to which it is examined."[34] In such a case, Aquinas tells us, we have a defiled conscience because we are conscious within ourselves of the act's wrongness or inappropriateness, and thus conscious of some disorder within our very selves.[35] We may say that the remorse experienced by conscience is the mind's recognition that what was done was not in keeping with its nature. The object of the act was not a truly human good, and thus not in consonance with what Aquinas calls "the law of understanding," which is the habit of synderesis or natural reason.[36] We can now better reinterpret Eco's concept of the feeling of remorse, which is not simply a feeling, but rather the mind's pronouncement against evil, and the need for purification and forgiveness, given the defilement of conscience and of self mentioned by Aquinas. The case of Eco's non-believer clearly shows the working of synderesis, the law of understanding present in the mind of the Gentiles, according to Aquinas. And so the non-believer's conscience experiences remorse for evil-doing, since conscience examines the act against this law or principle.

Knowledge of the first principles contained in synderesis is the same for all human beings and cannot be blotted out from their hearts. But, as Aquinas tells us, it can be neglected in the case of particular actions, in so far as reason is hindered from applying the general principle to a particular act on account of some passion.[37] Something that is not good can appear as good to reason in a particular instance because of a passion, or disorder in the will itself. Provided the judgment of reason retains its freedom, it is in the power of the will not to will, or not to

---

[33] *ST* I 79.13 ad 1.

[34] *DV* 17.1c.

[35] *DV* 17.1 ad 2 (1st series).

[36] *DV* 17.2 ad 3.

[37] *ST* I-II 94.6c.

consent to the passion.[38] Human beings thus retain dominion over the passions. If a man's will is rectified, that is if he has a good will, which is not interiorly divided, then he will be rightly disposed in regard to the principles of practical reason. He will then love the true good rather than what simply appears good. So, knowledge of the good must also be accompanied by love of the true good. In the case of Eco's non-believer, in whom knowledge of the first principles is at work given the remorse of conscience, it would seem that rectitude of the will is lacking. This might also account for his lack of belief, since as Augustine puts it: "no man believes, unless he will."[39] Our will, our loves, need to be ordered by virtue and in the final analysis, by grace.

To return then to the *anamnesis* of man's origin—the remembrance of God, of the true good—to which we have related synderesis, we can also interpret this as the foundation for what Pope John Paul II in *Veritatis Splendor* calls the "new evangelization."[40] This *anamnesis* lodged within the core of man's being needs help from the outside in order to be actualized. After having had the truth of the Gospel proclaimed to them, the Gentiles recognized this truth as that for which they had been interiorly longing, since it was the development of that seed of truth already present in and constitutive of their being. The light of faith thus perfects and elevates the natural light of synderesis. Robert Hugh Benson, in perhaps his most celebrated book, recounts an anecdote which is illustrative of how the truth already lives in the human heart and how it can be fully recognized: "An old Hindu, it is related, after hearing one sermon on the life of Christ, begged for baptism. 'But how can you ask for it so soon?' inquired the preacher. 'Have you ever heard the name of Jesus before today?' 'No,' said the old man, 'but I have known him and have been seeking him all my life.'"[41]

The truths of faith need not only to be proclaimed, they also need to be lived. *Veritatis Splendor* reminds us that faith becomes a witness before God and before men precisely through the moral life. Eco

---

[38] *ST* I-II 10.3c.

[39] *ST* I-II 56.3c.

[40] See Pope John Paul II, *Veritatis Splendor*, no. 107, p. 128.

[41] Robert H. Benson, *The Friendship of Christ* (New York: Scepter, 1991), pp. 51-52.

himself recognizes this to be the case, and so after lamenting the sins of colleagues at a Catholic university, he says, "The power of an ethical system is judged by the behavior of the saints."[42] Certainly, it is the saints whose lives reflect the splendor of truth. Just as the beauty of nature has led in the past to the knowledge of God, now the beauty of a life consistent with the faith can lead people to wonder at the cause of such a life and can thus become for many a new access to God. While contemporary culture is to a great extent very secularized, de-Christianized as the Pope puts it, it is nevertheless also sensitive to the presence of signs in its midst. The believer committed to moral truth can therefore become a sign and a compelling force that will lead persons to faith. In speaking of the consistent ethical life commitment to which faith calls us, Pope John Paul II puts before us the example of numerous saints: "By their eloquent and attractive example of a life completely transfigured by the splendor of moral truth, the martyrs and, in general, all the Church's Saints, light up every period of history by *reawakening its moral sense*. By witnessing fully to the good, they are a living reproof to those who transgress the law. . . ."[43] There is no doubt that many in our world have forgotten about God and also the distinction between good and evil. They have converted human life into something without meaning, drowned in nihilism.[44] The moral sense needs to be reawakened in these persons, and we as Christians are challenged by Pope John Paul II to give witness to the absoluteness of moral truth, and to the Truth itself who is Christ. As the Pope puts it: "This is a daunting task if we consider our human weakness, which so often renders us opaque and full of shadows. But it is a task which we can accomplish if we turn to the light of Christ and open ourselves to the grace which makes us a new creation."[45]

We cannot expect to renew and transform our culture unless there is an interior renewal of persons. We should therefore remember the

---

[42] Eco and Martini, *Belief or Unbelief?*, p. 97.

[43] Pope John Paul II, *Veritatis Splendor*, no. 93, p. 115; author's emphasis.

[44] Leszek Kolakowski, "La Filosofía de la Modernidad," *Nuestro Tiempo* (October, 1985): 112.

[45] Pope John Paul II, *Novo Millennio Ineunte* (Boston: St. Paul Editions, 2001), no. 54, pp. 70-71.

words of Léon Bloy, which made such an impression on the young Raïssa and Jacques Maritain: *Il n'y a qu'une tristesse, c'est de n'être pas des saints* ("There is only one sadness, not to be a saint").[46] Through their quest for and love of the truth which interiorly transformed them, the Maritains were able to bring about a spiritual renewal in their midst. Only through a life so lived, aided by the grace that makes all things new, can we hope not only to reawaken the moral sense in so many around us, but also to dialogue with those who recognize a natural ethics but have not yet come to the full discovery of truth.

---

[46] Raïssa Maritain, *We Have Been Friends Together*, translated by Julie Kernan (New York: Doubleday, 1961), p. 88.

Aquinas on Trust and Our Social Nature

Marie I. George

One evening, two friends of mine were discussing whether one could really trust one's spouse. It seemed to me unduly cynical to conclude that one could not, and so I decided to see whether Aquinas could shed some light on the matter. In researching the matter, I was struck by how Aquinas both affirms a moral obligation on our part to trust others and ties it to our social nature.

First, a brief account of what Aquinas takes trust to be is in order. It is hard to define trust because it seems to be something we directly experience--there does not seem to be something better known than it. Moreover, Aquinas never offers a definition of trust. He does, however, often speak about it when discussing the supernatural virtues of faith and hope. He sees our belief in certain truths about God, and our hope to get to heaven, to be founded upon our trust in God. Aquinas thus characterizes trust as an assured reliance on someone for either knowledge or for help.

The obvious reason why someone would think one can not trust anyone is the simple fact that all human beings are fallible and are thus liable to let one down, friends included. As Aquinas points out: "An infallible opinion of the goodness of any mere man could not be sustained, however, for even the most holy men are found to fail as to certain things."[1]

If even the mostly holy men fail, the average person is even more likely to do so. Whence, as Aquinas notes, while the one who relies on God is never disappointed, for God's goodness is unchanging, the one who hopes in man is sometimes disappointed, for human goodness is subject to failure.[2]

---

[1] *SCG*, IV 55.

[2] See *In Ps.* 30, p. 250b: "Secondly he posits the stability [of hope in God]--'Let me never be put to shame,'--because this hope relies on God who is unchanging; but the one who hopes in man who fails is sometimes confounded."

A second reason not to trust others can be seen by considering the fact that we cannot even entirely trust ourselves. We have an inside view on our intentions, values, and virtues, but not on those of others. Despite this, we cannot be entirely sure of our intentions, nor that we would resist sin under trying circumstances. As Aquinas observes: "Peter was saying this [i.e., that he would lay down his life for Christ] to the extent it seemed so to him, and not with a lying heart (*animo*). But nevertheless man does not know the strength of his heart (*affectus*), and above all not when danger is at hand."[3]

Our ignorance about ourselves is perhaps best exemplified by the fact that we cannot be sure that we are in the state of grace[4]--which we could be, if we had certitude about our intentions, and especially about our repentance of serious sins. Thus, Job says: "Though I think myself right, his mouth may condemn me; though I count myself innocent, it may declare me a hypocrite. But am I innocent after all? Not even I know that...." (Jb. 9:20, 21)

In addition, Aquinas in his commentary on Job affirms more generally that no one by himself can know the state of his soul with certitude.[5]

Aquinas also speaks about self-doubt when commenting on the Apostles' reaction to Christ's words that one of them would betray him by each asking "is it I?" As Aquinas notes, they are sure that Christ is speaking the truth, and this causes each of them to doubt himself.[6] The betrayal of Christ was plainly an exceedingly grave offense, and yet the Apostles, who were not wicked men, realized that they were capable of it.

If we then sometimes have reason to doubt ourselves, despite a privileged vantage point when it comes to knowledge of our morals and motives, how can we be expected to trust others whose morals and

---

[3] *In Io*, edited by P. Raphaelis Cai, O.P. (Rome: Marietti, 1952), #1843.

[4] See *ST* I-II 112.5: "Another manner in which a human being could know something is on his own with certitude. And in this manner no one can know that he possesses grace."

[5] *In Iob*, p. 64a "[H]omo se ipsum non cognoscit statum suum..."

[6] See *In Io* #1801.

motives are not apparent to us? Even if others were more reliable than ourselves in the past, it is apparent that we cannot be entirely sure of how reliable they are. As Aquinas observes: "For a human being, even if he knows others, nevertheless is not able to have certain knowledge about them, because he only sees those things which are apparent; and therefore for him work[s] provide the means of proof in regard to others."[7]

A third reason for not trusting any human being is that Scripture admonishes us not to do so.[8] However, I do not intend to take up this theological objection here.[9]

Given that Aquinas notes that all human beings are fallible, even the good, and that he observes that we do not entirely know how reliable we are, and we know others less well, one might gather that he would advocate a mistrustful attitude towards our fellow man. However, this proves far from being the case. And this is where man's social nature enters in. As Aquinas notes:

> because in the life we share in common it is necessary for one man to make use of another as if this other were himself as to those things where he himself does not suffice, therefore it is necessary that he rely on those things which another knows and are unknown to himself as on those things which he himself knows: and thence it is that in human affairs (*hominum conversatione*) faith is necessary, by which one man believes the things said by another; and this is the foundation of justice... and thence it is that no lie is without sin, since this faith is detracted from by every lie as from something which is necessary. [10]

---

[7] *In Io* #422.

[8] "A curse on the man who put his trust in man, who relies on things of flesh, whose heart turns from Yahweh. ... A blessing on the man who puts his trust in Yahweh, with Yahweh for his hope" (Jr. 17:5).

[9] Aquinas, in a number of places, explicitly addresses the scripture passages that state that we should trust no one but God. See, *inter alia*, *CT*, q. 253, *ST* II-II 17.4, and *ST* II-II 25.1 ad 3.

[10] *In Boeth. De Trin.* 3, art. 1. See *ST* II-II 129.6 ad 1: "[I]t belong to the magnanimous person 'to be in need of nothing,' because being so belongs to

We all need others. People need to rely on us, and we need to rely on them. The former is the basis for the moral responsibility to act in a trustworthy manner. However, the presence of trustworthy individuals does not by itself suffice for collaboration; they have in fact to be trusted. From this fact arises a corresponding moral obligation to trust others: "Nevertheless people do not owe their parents every honor.... A person, however, owes to his friends and brothers trust (*fiduciam*) and the sharing of things, and similarly to blood relatives and to those who belong to one tribe, and to fellow citizens, and so forth."[11]

Aquinas is fully aware that (as Scripture says): "Even a man at peace with me, in whom I hoped, and who ate bread at my table, exalts at my fall." But, he does not take this line, which he understands as a prophecy concerning Christ, to undermine the notion that there is a moral obligation to trust others:

> Judas was counted as one of the friends [of Christ]. This prophecy came about in fact because he betrayed Christ with a kiss which is a sign of friendship and peace. Whence the Lord said (Lk., c. 22): "Judas, do you betray the son of man with a kiss?" ... Further he [Judas] was one of his intimates; whence "someone in whom I hoped." But was Christ then deceived in his hope? No. And therefore he says "in whom I hoped," i.e., in whom I seemed to hope, i.e., to trust (*confidere*), because he entrusted to him the administration of his goods. Alternately, "in whom I hoped," i.e., on account of his condition: I so stood to him as I *ought* to hope in him. But sometimes a person hopes in someone whom he believes to be a friend, and whom he *ought* to trust, and nevertheless he is disappointed: "Do not trust any of

---

one who is deficient; this nevertheless ought to be understood according to the human condition; whence he [Aristotle] adds 'or almost nothing'. For it is above man to be in need of absolutely nothing. [E]very human being...needs human assistance, because man is naturally a social animal so that he is not sufficient unto himself as to his life. Therefore, insofar as the magnanimous person is in need of others, thus it belongs to him that he have trust in others...."

[11] *In Eth.* #1783.

> your brothers" (Jr., c. 9); "Do not trust your friend, and have no confidence in your leader" (Mi., c. 7).[12]

We see that Aquinas does not understand the Old Testament passages here to contradict the notion that we owe people trust despite the fact they may let us down--"I so stood to him as I ought to hope in him." This is consistent with his position on caution, which will be discussed further on. He is insistent that we should give people in general the benefit of the doubt--mistrust should not be our default attitude: "a man ought to presume of any person what is good being ignorant [of the contrary]." [13] Aquinas praises those who are trusting: "But this certainly was commendable in Peter, namely, his trust because he was suspecting no evil of his comrades [for he affirmed without exception that all of the Apostles believed in Christ]; but to be admired in the Lord is his wisdom, which perceived hidden things."[14]

For Aquinas, a person's lack of suspicion often bespeaks of his own moral goodness: "[I]t is the wont of a good and innocent soul that he believes others as well to be far from any evil-doing which he knows himself to be free of. And therefore because John was the most innocent disciple, and the evil-doing of betrayal was far from his mind, he never suspected that a disciple could go ahead with such an evil act."[15]

Aquinas's praise here of John's innocence should not, however, be taken as an endorsement of naiveté. Innocence and naiveté are similar in meaning, as both involve a lack of knowledge and dispose one to credulity.[16] The innocent person, however, is one who is unfamiliar with evil, as is the case of a young person lacking experience of life who is himself good. The naive person, on the other hand, has sufficient

---

[12] *In Ps.* 40, p. 307a, b; emphasis added.

[13] *In Io* #421.

[14] *In Io* #1006.

[15] *In Io* #1818.

[16] See *Webster's New Collegiate Dictionary* (Springfield, Massachusetts: G. & C. Merriam Company, 1980): "Naive: deficient in worldly wisdom or informed judgment; esp. credulous. Innocent: free from guilt or sin esp. through lack of knowledge of evil: blameless."

experience of fallen human nature to know better than to trust people indiscriminately—the question: "How could you be so naive?" expresses blame. Naiveté is a form of imprudence opposed to caution.[17] Thus, the trust Aquinas advises is not without restrictions: "One is to presume what is good about any and every person unless the contrary is apparent, so long as this does not tend towards the endangerment of another. For then caution is to be exhibited, such that one does not believe just anybody..."[18]

Aquinas adds here two qualifications to the trust we in general owe people. First, one need not give the benefit of the doubt to someone who is manifestly bad. Secondly, one is obligated to exercise caution in those cases where being taking in can result in harm to someone, instead of proceeding on the assumption that the person is trustworthy until proven otherwise. Aquinas applies both of these criteria in the specific case of whether one can legitimately reject someone's testimony:

> [T]estimony... does not have infallible certitude, but probable certitude. And therefore anything which carries probability with it in the opposite direction renders testimony ineffectual. Sometimes that someone lacks solidity in testifying to the truth is rendered probable due to some fault of the person (such as infidelity and ill-repute; further those who are guilty of public crimes and who cannot accuse) and sometimes in the absence of fault. And the latter is either due to a defect of reason, as it plain in the case of children, the insane and women [sic]; or due to emotion, as is plain in the case of enemies, relatives, and household members; or even from some external condition, as is the case of paupers, servants and those who can be commanded, concerning whom it is probable that they can be easily induced

[17] See *ST* II-II 49.8 ("Whether caution is part of prudence"): "The things that prudence is concerned with are contingent things that can be done, in which just as truth is able to be mixed with falsehood, so too evil with good on account of the multi-form character of things to be done where it is common for the good to be impeded by the bad, and for the bad to have the appearance of goodness. And therefore caution is necessary for prudence, as it is taken to be a good thing that a bad thing is avoided."

[18] *ST* II-II 70.3 ad 2.

> to bearing witness contrary to the truth. And thus it is manifest that the testimony of someone can be rejected, both with and without fault on his part.[19]

Obviously, if a judge or jury believes a false witness, this can result in great harm, namely, the condemnation of an innocent person. Thus, caution and mistrust have a rightful place in trials, and sometimes even distrust (understanding here mistrust as doubting someone's reliability and distrust as taking the person to be unreliable—the two are sometimes taken as synonyms[20]). In addition to setting aside the testimony of those whose untrustworthiness is apparent, such as that given by convicted criminals, one can also set aside the testimony of those who can be easily coerced or persuaded to give false testimony. One need not give the benefit of the doubt to a witness who was an enemy or a relative of the accused.

Aquinas also finds mistrust and suspicion warranted when one discovers that one's fiancé has been unfaithful: "Although those who have become engaged have not given each other power over their respective bodies, nevertheless if either (or both) engage in fornication, it then becomes suspect whether he or she will be faithful in the future. And therefore one can protect oneself from the other by breaking off the engagement."[21] The unfaithful party is of proven unreliability, and lack of trust in him or her is thus warranted.[22]

Aquinas's explanation of why the formation of a true friendship takes time and much mutual frequentation suggests another point about trust, namely, that there are different degrees of trust or caution

---

[19] *ST* II-II 70.3.

[20] It is one thing to have no reason either way to trust a person or not; it is another to have reason not to trust a person. For this reason "mistrust" in these two cases does not mean the same thing.

[21] *ST* Suppl. 43.3 ad 6 ("Whether an engagement can be broken off...on account of fornication by the other party").

[22] Aquinas never directly addresses the difficult question of whether one should ever go back to trusting a spouse who was guilty of marital infidelity.

one should display towards others.[23] Trust is not all or nothing, but develops over time, during which we can observe the other person's reliability. Plainly, one need not have spent extensive time with someone in order to trust him to water one's plants, whereas one does if one is to trust him with intimate details of one's life. Prudence dictates that one display greater caution when the potential for harm is greater.

Thus far we have seen that Aquinas does not tell us that we should give others the benefit of the doubt without qualification. If he is not against keeping one's eyes open, and indeed blames those who believe others too readily,[24] why does he counsel trust rather that mistrust as the normative attitude? Again, it is because he regards the continued existence of society as dependent upon its members trusting one another and not offending each other.[25] Mistrust imperils the survival of society by its negative impact both on group efforts and on the dissemination of knowledge crucial for survival; in similar ways, mistrust affects society's well-being as well. In addition, mistrust often constitutes an insult, which also contributes to the breakdown of society. And on top of this, mistrust engenders more mistrust, thus

---

[23] See *In Eth.* #1582: "[A second reason why true friendship is rare is] because friendship of this sort requires a long period of time and getting used to each other in order that they know each other to be virtuous and friends; for as the proverb goes, it does not happen that people know each other until they have eaten together a measure of salt. For it is not appropriate that one accept another person as one's friend before one appears to the other [as someone] to be loved, and is trusted to be such...."

[24] In the gospel account of the woman at the well, the townspeople told the woman: "Now we no longer believe because of what you told us; we have heard him ourselves and we know that he really is the savior of the world" (Jn. 4:42). Aquinas, commenting on this passage, says: "granted that to believe men quickly pertains to superficiality (*levitas*)..., nevertheless, to believe God quickly is, to the contrary, praiseworthy" (*In Io* #662).

[25] *ST* I-II 94.2: "In a third manner there is an inclination in man to the good according to the nature of reason...as man has a natural inclination... to live in society. And according to this, those things which regard an inclination of this sort pertain to natural law, such as that... he not offend others whom he must frequent."

multiplying both of its ill effects. Let us see how Aquinas develops these points.

The central role Aquinas attributes to trust for the well-being of society comes out in numerous places, including his discussions of lying,[26] keeping secrets,[27] oath-taking,[28] as well as in his treatment of the virtue "*veritas*" or genuineness (the opposite of which is phoniness or fakeness). Perhaps one of the clearest passages expressing Aquinas's view on trust in society is his response to an objection that claims that genuineness is not part of justice:

> Since man is a social animal, one man naturally owes another that without which human society cannot be preserved. Men would not be able to live with one another unless they were able to trust one another (*nisi sibi invicem crederent*), as when manifesting the truth to one another. And therefore the virtue of genuineness (*veritas*) in some manner answers to the notion of debt.[29]

Here, Aquinas speaks explicitly of the obligation to show oneself to be a trustworthy person. Trust, however, is a two-way street—the other person then has a corresponding obligation to trust people who appear to be sincere.[30] The failure to do so would imperil human society:

---

[26] See *In Boeth. De. Trin.*, q. 3, art. 1 quoted earlier in the main text: "no lie is without sin."

[27] *ST* II-II 70.1 ad 2: "There are sometimes things of the sort that one is not held to denounce. Whence one can be bound [not to reveal them] by the fact they are confided to one as a secret. And then one cannot in any manner be held to make them known, not even on the command of a superior, for to preserve trust (*servare fidem*) belongs to the natural law; the command of a man has no power against what belongs to natural law."

[28] See *In Duo praecepta caritatis* in *Opuscula Theologica*, vol. 2, edited by Raymundi M. Spiazzi, O.P. (Turin: Marietti, 1954), #1206: "Further [false oaths made in God's name] injure other men. For no society can endure among people unless they trust (*credant*) one another. However, things that are doubtful are confirmed by oaths."

[29] *ST* II-II 109.3 ad 1.

[30] Aquinas maintains that the failure to rely on the human assistance that is available is sinful: "And therefore if people rely on God alone, they do not on

> That without which human society cannot be preserved is above all necessary for man, and to humanity as a whole (*toti generi humano*), since man is a political animal (as is said in 8 *Ethic.*). But without trust (*fide*) human society cannot be preserved, because it is necessary that one man believe another as to promises and testimony and other things of this sort which are necessary for men to remain together. Therefore, trust (*fides*) is in the highest degree necessary to humankind.[31]

If people dismissed the testimony of every witness, it would be impossible to maintain justice in society, justice, of course, being essential for a genuine political community. And if people set no store on the promises of others, it would be difficult for any cooperative enterprise to get off the ground. As Aquinas notes, human society is useful for survival,[32] for survival generally requires the coordinated efforts of many individuals, as is the case of hunting large animals, constructing sizeable shelters, and defending one's property against attackers. Where distrust is present, people often attempt to compensate for those whom they perceive to be likely slackers ("I cannot count on him to do his job"), and in doing so often jeopardize the project at hand, as they are liable to interfere with each other and not do their own job as well as they might.[33] There are also many truths useful for survival that need to be passed on from one individual to another, e.g., that such-and-such a plant is poisonous or safe to eat. Here, too, when distrust is present, people tend to refrain from acting ("I do not believe him when he says this is safe to eat"), and thus miss out on things that would help them stay alive.

---

account of this tempt God. But if without any utility or necessity they would abandon human aid, they would be tempting God" (*ST* II-II 97.1 ad 3).

[31] *In Boeth. De Trin.*, q. 3, a.1, 3rd sed contra.

[32] See *In Pol.* #387: "life in common is also useful for the sake of staying alive, as long as each of those present in a community ordered to life helps the other to sustain life and to ward off the dangers of death."

[33] I used to clean houses when I was in college. I remember one client who on my first visit followed me around the house as I vacuumed, dusted, etc. For all practical purposes she might as well have done the work herself.

Aquinas also appears to agree with Aristotle's view that a society held together only by bonds of justice and not also by bonds of friendship is at risk for disintegrating.[34] Trust is essential for friendly relationships.[35] Even though trust is needed simply for society to survive, it is also plainly needed for society to thrive: to have a system of education, to offer care for those in need, to foster cultural activities such as concerts, etc., all require the joint efforts of many individuals.

In addition to seriously hampering cooperation, mistrust is also harmful to social life insofar as a person who is mistrusted is liable to perceive this as an insult or injustice to the extent it entails an erroneous and temerarious judgment of his character. Aquinas says as much in his discussion of whether one ought to interpret questionable behavior, appearance, etc. in a more rather than a less favorable manner:

> When someone has a bad opinion about another without sufficient cause, he injures the other and treats him with contempt. No one ought to contemn another or harm him in any way in the absence of a compelling reason. And therefore where there do not appear any manifest indications of a person's badness, we ought to hold him to be good, and anything doubtful ought to be given the more positive interpretation.[36]

Plainly, harming others in this manner is destructive of harmonious social relationships.

Aquinas does not deny that those who put a positive spin on a person's doubtful behavior, demeanor, etc. may be mistaken more often than not. However, he maintains that: "It is better that someone frequently err in having a good opinion of some bad man, than that he more infrequently err in having a bad opinion about someone good, for

---

[34] See *In Eth.* #1542: "And he [Aristotle] says that states seem to be conserved through friendship. Whence legislators are more eager to preserve friendship among citizens than even justice, for they sometimes set justice aside, e.g., in cases where punishment is to be inflicted, lest dissent arise."

[35] See *In Eth.* #1592-93.

[36] *ST* II-II 60.4. The question is entitled: "Utrum dubia sint in meliorem partem interpretanda."

the reason that the latter causes injury to someone, whereas the former does not."[37] In addition to being insulting, misjudgment of a good person is further injurious because it is liable to affect his reputation: "a person is held as honorable by the fact he is judged good, and contemptible by the fact that he is judged bad."[38]

Aquinas does not deny that in some cases holding a good opinion about someone bad may have harmful consequences; for this could plainly happen if one went on to rely on such a person because of one's mistaken opinion. Aquinas is simply saying that as *a general rule* one should shy away from thinking ill of anyone. Accordingly, one should be disposed to display trust as a general rule. Again, this does not mean that one's trust should be blind. Where the possibility of trusting someone who is not trustworthy carries the risk of harm, one has an obligation to display caution rather than trust.

To prevent serious harm to its citizens, society puts in place various institutions and agencies in order to ascertain the reliability of individuals exercising various tasks. Some of them ascertain reliability from the point of view of competence, e.g., the Department of Motor Vehicles grants licenses for driving big trucks to those who pass tests. Some of them ascertain reliability from the point of view of whether the professional did the work for which he was contracted, e.g., the Better Business Bureau. Background checks are run for those who work with children, and so forth. Arguably, making use of these resources to determine whether one will rely on a given person is not to mistrust that person in the first place, but is rather simply to assess whether it is apparent that the person is unreliable (e.g., the chimney man who advertises having a permit, but in fact no longer holds a current one). In such cases, one's assessment is not apt to be taken as an insult, as it is impersonal, being based on the prior assessment of a societal agency or group (which one trusts rightly or wrongly to have made a suitable evaluation).[39] In any case, the possibility of serious harm would legitimate a certain mistrust.

---

[37] *ST* II-II 60.4 ad 1.

[38] *ST* II-II 60.4 ad 2.

[39] Aquinas never makes this distinction, but I think there is reason to distinguish "impersonal mistrust" from "personal mistrust." Doing a

One might object that Aquinas does not think that trust should be our default attitude on the grounds that he apparently regarded oaths to be legitimate due to many different causes.[40] One requests an oath from someone whom one does not entirely trust.[41] However, Aquinas maintains that the situations in which one can legitimately require another to take an oath are limited to "*causa necessaria*," such as in judicial proceedings.[42] There are times we really need to know that what the person is saying is true in order to avoid serious harm. As Aquinas puts it in the *Summa Theologiae,* oaths are like medicines, to be used only when really needed.[43] And while, according to the *reportatio* of Petrus de Scala, Aquinas held that "it is licit to swear for many reasons," when one looks at the nine reasons that are given, all of them involve serious matters such as "restoring peace" and "putting

---

background check on a person applying for a job working with children would be an example of the former, whereas not trusting a fiancé that has never cheated on one would be an example of the latter. Impersonal mistrust is not of the sort that is damaging to society, as people ordinarily understand that it is necessary; those who take it as a personal insult are at fault for doing so.

[40] According to the *reportatio* of Petrus de Scala in *Super Evangelium S. Matthaei*, edited by P. Raphaelis Cai, O.P. (Rome: Marietti, 1951), ch. 5, lec. 8.

[41] *ST* II-II 89.5: "An oath is sought to alleviate some defect, namely, that by which one man mistrusts another." *Per accidens*, it might happen that the person in court who swears in witnesses is a close friend of a person sworn in. See also *ST* II-II 98.4 ad 1: "[the private individual] does not always know [whether] the person swears truly or falsely, but he sometimes may be in doubt about what actually happened and believe that the other person will swear truly, and then he demands an oath in order to have greater certitude."

[42] See III *Sent.* d. 39, art. 5, q'la 2, solutio 2 and ad 2.

[43] See *ST* II-II 89.5c and ad 3. *ST* II-II 89.5: "It ought to be said that that which is not sought except in order to remedy some defect is not numbered among those things which are to be desired per se, but among things which are necessary, as is manifest in the case of medicine, which is sought to remedy infirmity. An oath, however, is sought to remedy some defect, namely that by which one man instructs another."

calumny to rest in legal proceedings."[44] This, of course, fits with what was said above about the need to show caution, and thus some degree of mistrust towards people when there is a risk of serious harm. It does not support the notion that our initial attitude towards others should generally be that of mistrust.

There are many situations in life where one risks little by trusting others without doing a background check or having extensive familiarity with them.[45] Maybe one's coworkers will eat the lunch one puts in the common fridge; maybe one's neighbors will fail to return tools one lent them; maybe the person one carpools with will not show up on time. But these are small prices to pay considering the reaction one's coworkers and neighbors would have if one treated them as if

---

[44] See the *reportatio* of Petrus de Scala in *Super Evangelium S. Matthaei,* , ch. 5, lec. 8, #536: "Whence, note that it is licit to swear for many causes. First, for confirming the truth to the incredulous; II Cor. 1, 18: 'By the faithful God, I swear that there was not in what we said to you yes and no' [context: people may have had doubts whether Paul had acted in their best interest]; secondly for restoring peace, as Jacob swore to Laban (Gen. 31:53); thirdly, for contracting friendly ties (Gen. 26:28: 'The men of Gerar said to Isaac: "Let there be an oath between us"' [context: Isaac thinks that they hate him]); fourthly, for manifesting the truth: 'Testimony in the mouths of two or three witnesses sustains any charge' (Deut. 19:15); fifthly, for the preservation of fidelity: 'The elders of Israel came to the king, and he struck a treaty with them' (II Reg. 5:3); sixthly, for the recognition of obedience and subjection, as the men of Galaad to Jephtha [Judges 11:10]; seventhly, to respect the custom of the Church, as canons do [e.g., the sons of Israel swore to serve the Lord]. And these seven reasons are put forth for the sake of some good. There are two other reasons for the sake of removing evil, namely, for putting calumny to rest in legal proceedings: 'The end of all controversy is an oath for confirmation' (Heb. 6:16). The other reason is to purge infamy: 'When the cadaver of a killed man was found, and it was unknown who was guilty, the elders and the judges went out...and said: "Our hands did not shed the blood here, nor did our eyes see it. Be favorable, Lord, to your people Israel whom you have redeemed" (Dt. 21:1).'"

[45] It is plain that the degree of trust we owe people varies with the situation. Some situations call for more caution than others. It is one thing to hire a gardener and another to hire a kindergarten teacher; one need not, and indeed ought not, trust a butcher like one trusts a bosom friend.

they were unworthy of trust. They would be insulted and consequently would be liable to mistrust one in return.

We have seen that mistrust is detrimental to society, hampering collaboration and generating indignation on the part of those unfairly mistrusted. As just mentioned, to make matters worse, mistrust breeds mistrust. This is a further reason to be reticent to mistrust others. Aquinas speaks about how mistrust engenders mistrust when commenting on an incident recounted in John's gospel: "[S]ince he [Christ] knew that they trusted him imperfectly, he himself did not trust them."[46] Aquinas does not elaborate on exactly why the mistrust of the people in question engendered mistrust on the part of Christ. However, Aquinas notes elsewhere that we often judge others according as we are ourselves.[47] A person who is mistrusted for no reason is led to wonder whether the other's mistrust is not due to the other's lack of trustworthiness.[48] Also, we generally do not trust those who harm us, and so others' unjustified mistrust of us leads us not to trust them.

In conclusion, Aquinas does not think that most people are virtuous, and he is fully aware that everyone is fallible, even the virtuous, and

---

[46] *In Io* #421.

[47] See *In Io* #1818. See also *In Io* #2399: "[I]t often happens that people think the same things [to be true] about others which they themselves suffer from."

[48] Although I could not find any place where Aquinas affirms it, I think that it is evident that trust breeds trust. We perceive people who trust us to be trustworthy themselves, and we also perceive them as paying us the compliment of regarding us as trustworthy. Lack of trust, on the other hand, tends to incline the mistrusted party toward becoming untrustworthy. It is a commonplace that people live up to the expectation one has of them. A child or young person who is mistrusted to do the right thing, despite possessing sufficient judgment and character to do so, is tempted to adopt the attitude, "my parents already think badly of me, so I might as well do the bad things they think I'm liable to do if it were not for their watchful eye." This fits with Aquinas's observation that "a person will abstain from sins many times for the sake of preserving his reputation. And therefore when someone sees that he has already lost his reputation he gravitates towards sinning for no good reason..." (*De Correctione Fraterna*, in *Quaestiones Disputatae*, vol. 2, edited by P. Bazzi [Turin: Marietti, 1965], q. unicus, a. 2).

that our judgments of others' intentions and character are not infallible either (people can be fake and deceive us). For this reason, he does not advocate an attitude of blind trust. Indeed, in the fickle realm of human action, where the bad often has the appearance of good, Aquinas holds that a person would be lacking in the virtue of prudence not to be cautious and mistrustful when harm to others may ensue. Nonetheless, he holds that trust rather than mistrust should be the normal attitude we adopt towards others due to the essential role it plays in society. Lack of trust seriously compromises the collaboration necessary for life and for living well. We cannot profit from the knowledge and help other members of society have to offer us, if we mistrust them. In addition, if we presume that people are likely to fail us at any moment, they are rightly insulted, and our mistrust thus weakens the harmony within a society. Moreover, mistrust generally engenders more mistrust, which is another reason that it should not be our default attitude, but one we adopt only when there is reasonable evidence of the other's untrustworthiness or when serious harm can ensue. For all these reasons, it is of the utmost importance to trust people, giving them the benefit of the doubt, while exercising caution as the circumstances demand.

PART II:

Civilization and the Arts

VISUAL INTELLIGENCE IN PAINTING[1]

Robert Sokolowski

1. Introduction

Philosophers have long agreed that thinking is expressed in the use of language, that we "think in the medium of words."[2] It is also true, however, that we think in the medium of pictures, and it is likely that these two ways of thinking are interrelated; certainly, we could not think in pictures if we did not have words, and perhaps we could not use words, in principle, unless we were also engaged in some sort of picturing, at least in our imagination. An ideographic language like Chinese would give greater support to the latter possibility than would our phonetically based form of writing.

Philosophically, words and pictures can be used to illuminate one another and to shed light on what it is to think. In both words and pictures, we deal with compositions, and in both cases the compositions are, to use a phrase of Michael Oakeshott, "exhibitions of intelligence."[3] There is a difference between the two that we notice immediately: spoken words are fleeting and pictures are durable; words and pictures differ in their temporality. They also differ in other ways that are philosophically important. Let us explore these differences.

---

[1] This essay has also appeared in the *Review of Metaphysics*. Reprinted with permission.

[2] The phrase is from David Braine, *The Human Person: Animal and Spirit* (Notre Dame, Indiana: University of Notre Dame Press, 1992), p. xxii.

[3] See Michael Oakeshott, *On Human Conduct* (Oxford: Clarendon Press, 1975), p. 15: "Thus the movement of a human eyelid is a categorially ambiguous identity; it may be a wink or a blink, a wink which is an exhibition of intelligence, a subscription to a 'practice' and has a reason, and a blink which is a component of a 'process' to be understood in terms of a 'law' or a 'cause'." See also p. 32.

2. Words and their structure

We begin with spoken words and we ask what it means to think in the medium of speech.[4] When we speak, we present things as articulated into wholes and parts, and we do so for ourselves and for others. The paradigmatic form of speech is found in conversation, whether between two people or among many, whether in private or in public. The focus of speech is not the speech itself but the things that are spoken about. Thoughtful speech is like a magic wand that we wave over things. As we wave the wand, the parts and wholes of things become disclosed: their identity, their features, their relationships, their essentials and their accidentals, in a word, their intelligibility, all come to light, for ourselves and for our interlocutors.

However, we do not articulate just the *things* that we present. While we explicate things, we also conjugate the words we speak. The speech that we declare is itself segmented into its own kinds of parts and wholes. That is, we continually assemble and reassemble the wand itself as well as the things we wave it over. We display things by structuring our speech. Our listeners are intent on the things we talk about, but they must also be aware, marginally, of the words we speak. The eye is caught by the thing and the ear is caught by the sound, but the mind is shaped by both: we attend to what is seen as we listen to what is said.

Speech is articulated on two levels. First, on the higher level, each sentence and each argument is made up of lexicon and grammar, of content and syntax. Second, on the lower level, each word is internally made up of phonemes, of vowels and consonants. The phonemic structure inside a word establishes each word as a word, and these words are conjoined in grammatical and lexical sequences. When all this happens on the side of speech, parts of the world come to light. The artful combinatorics in words and sentences lets the articulation of things take place, and such exhibition occurs whether we speak of things in their presence or their absence. Human reason can articulate on all these levels; it keeps all of these dimensions in mind, and all of

---

[4] In the next six paragraphs, I use, with additions and revisions, some material that I have published in "Language, the Human Person, and Christian Faith," *Proceedings of the American Catholic Philosophical Association* 76 (2003): 29-30.

them are significant: human intelligence composes words out of phonemes and statements out of words, and simultaneously it displays things in their parts and wholes. We charge our words with so much intelligence that things themselves begin to appear in the light that the words give off. The person who accomplishes this, furthermore, does so for himself and for others. All discourse is in principle a matter of conversational reciprocity. Thinking in the medium of words is inherently intersubjective and so is human reason.

The most conspicuous and most tangible feature of our verbal articulation is the way in which phrases are embedded into one another. This is the work of syntax; it makes it possible for us to segment our speech, and also to segment our displays, into parts that are not just concatenated sequentially one after the other, but parts that are stacked within one another, in the fashion of Chinese boxes or Russian dolls.[5] Because of this syntactic embedding, speeches of unlimited complexity and exquisite intricacy become possible: think of the multilayered "boxing" that takes place in a novel or a scholarly book. It is specifically the syntactic element in speech that raises our verbalization into rational discourse. Syntax provides the rational form for the more material contents of what we say, and the syntax works not only in individual statements but also in long arguments, not only in particular judgments but also in extended reasoning. Speech is governed not only by predicate but also by propositional logic. We should not focus so much on the simple judgment that we forget the larger conversation in which each judgment is embedded.

Syntax, furthermore, should not be taken just by itself. Syntax has to be related to the phonemic structure within each word, and within each word it is specifically the consonants that function in a manner

---

[5] I have found the work of the American linguist Derek Bickerton to be very helpful in regard to syntax as constitutive of human speech. See his *Language and Species* (Chicago: University of Chicago Press, 1990), and *Language and Human Behavior* (Seattle: University of Washington Press, 1995). His work belongs to the tradition initiated by Noam Chomsky with *Syntactic Structures* (The Hague: Mouton, 1957) and *Aspects of the Theory of Syntax* (Cambridge, Massachusetts: The MIT Press, 1965). The relation of these notions of syntax to Husserl's doctrine on categorial intentions and categorial intuitions calls for investigation.

analogous to syntax. Consonants are like the syntax within words. Consonants clip and trim the words we speak, and we have to be socialized into them, just as we have to be socialized into syntax and judgment. Consonants order the more elementary vowel sounds of speech. The vowels require far less instruction. We come into the world crying and no one has to teach us how, nor do we need to be taught the wails and whimpers and giggles that make up the basis for other vowel sounds. Vowels by themselves would be unlettered; it is the consonants that make the sounds rational. This phonemic structuring of words, moreover, does not come to pass apart from the higher, syntactic structuring; rather, the consonantal shaping of sound occurs under the teleology of syntactic patterning. Consonants are introduced under the downward pressure of syntax. We shape sounds into words *because* we want to combine words into phrases and discourse (and we combine words into phrases *because* we want to display things).

The dimension of vowels in words is more associated with emotion, and the structure of consonants is more associated with reason. Vowels are especially involved with feeling, with our biological and sensory appreciation of what is going on and what is happening to us. The emotive dimension of vowels comes to the fore in singing, but human singing requires the clipping and cutting of consonants if it is to become thoughtful melody and not just humming and cooing, if it is to become a song that exhibits intelligence.[6] Consonants introduce the rigor and determination of reason into the melody of vowels.

Vowels are the work of the lungs and vocal chords, consonants the work of teeth, tongue, and lips, with some help from the throat. Forming consonants is more under human control. It is also the more visible performance and it makes speech seem like eating in reverse. Maritain has said that the human body is the most beautiful thing in the world and that the human face is naturally sacred.[7] The face

---

[6] I once attended a master class given, in public, by Elly Ameling at the University of Maryland, and one of the things that impressed me most was the accuracy and force with which this wonderful soprano registered the consonants in her singing. She emphasized the importance of such precision in what she told the students.

[7] Jacques Maritain, *Creative Intuition in Art and Poetry* (New York: Meridian Books, 1954), p. 152.

certainly has a cadence of its own, and this is due partly to the consonant-work of the lower face and partly to the expressiveness of the eyes. Its natural design is "finished" by the life the person has lived; a baby's face does not yet show what one has done or what one can be expected to say.[8]

Human rationality is also expressed in laughter, which also requires the demarcation of consonants to be what it is. Laughter is made up of vowel sounds segmented into short bursts by simple consonants, as in ho-ho-ho, or ha-ha, or, in a more discreet manner, tee-hee. A plain, drawn-out vowel sound is not constituted as laughter and it does not express an intelligent appreciation, because it contains no consonants. It expresses anxiety or pain rather than rational amusement.

There is a still deeper level of linguistic structure, one that underlies both the grammatical patterns in sentences and the sound patterns in words. It is the level of prosody, the rhythms and beats that are proper to a language. In fact, the unborn child in the mother's womb is already sensitive to this aspect of the mother's voice, which reaches the child by being filtered through the amniotic fluid. Two writers on children's language, Kyra Karmiloff and Annette Kamiloff-Smith, observe that this form of speaking and listening, between the mother and the child in the womb, "blurs phonetic information but leaves intact the rhythmic properties of speech." They say that the baby "is learning to recognize the melody and rhythms of language," that is, the intonation contours and the stress patterns that constitute the particularities of both its mother's voice and the sounds that will become its native tongue.[9] Thus the unborn child already has some experience of language and, therefore, "the newborn comes into the world prepared to pay special

---

[8] I am grateful to Kevin White for much of the material in this paragraph, as well as for many other remarks and suggestions that I have used in this paper. On the distinguished status of the human face: it is now often said that the human brain is the most complicated thing in the universe. It would be interesting to ask whether the brain or the face should enjoy the greater prestige.

[9] Kyra Karmiloff and Annette Karmiloff-Smith, *Pathways to Language. From Fetus to Adolescent* (Cambridge, Massachusetts: Harvard University Press, 2001), p. 43.

attention to human speech and specifically to his mother's voice."[10] The child becomes familiar with his mother's tongue and his mother tongue even before he is born.

The rhythmic dimension of speech, the cadence of language, cushions the grammar and morphology that will take shape within it. For example, the child, as he grows, begins to express the rhythm and prosody of sentences and questions before actually stating and asking things: "By the end of the first year, the baby's babbling rises and falls in intonation to mimic questions and statements."[11] The prosodic level of speech also comes into play, with great sophistication, in poetry, singing, and music. Think of how music enhances the emotional meaning of words, how it expresses the human response to what is being presented in the song, and how it does so by engaging the dimensions of both vowels and rhythms.

We have distinguished three levels of human speech: the sentential and argumentative level, made up of vocabulary and grammar, or lexicon and syntax; the phonemic level, made up of vowels and consonants; and the deep prosodic level, made up of rhythms and beats.[12] Let us now explore parallels to these three levels in painting.

---

[10] Ibid., p. 2.

[11] Ibid., p. 151.

[12] The syntax in language makes it possible for us to go beyond stating things in speech; it permits us also to appropriate what we are saying. We do so when we use the first-person pronoun in what I would want to call a "declarative" manner, as opposed to a merely "informational" usage. We can say not only, "It is raining," but also, "I know it is raining." When Nietzsche says that "only the spirit of music allows us to understand why we feel joy at the destruction of the individual," he wishes to reduce speech to the rhythms that underlie both syntax and phonemes, a reduction that also removes any declarative expression of myself as speaker. See *The Birth of Tragedy and Other Writings*, translated by Ronald Speirs, edited by Raymond Geuss and Ronald Speirs (New York: Cambridge University Press, 1999), p. 80.

3. Pictures and their structure

In speech, the highest and most tangible level we have described is that of words and grammar, that of syntactic structure in sentences and arguments. We begin with this more visible level.

In pictures, the analogy to vocabulary and grammar, the analogy to syntactic structure, is the arrangement of images into a larger whole. A painting is one image, just as an argument or a sentence is one statement, but the painting also contains parts, which in turn also are pictures, and the parts are placed by the artist into an ordered whole. These parts are not randomly distributed, no more than are the words in a statement. The painting enjoys a pictorial grammar. Consider two paintings of the Blessed Virgin by Murillo, *The Immaculate Conception* and *The Assumption*. The placement of the cherubs in each of the paintings is obviously significant, expressing the Virgin's innocence, her affinity with the angels, and her superiority over them. Consider the painting of *Napoleon at the Battle of Wagram*, by Horace Vernet. The emperor and his horse are both looking in the same direction, both are tensed and alert, Napoleon is looking through a spyglass and receiving dispatches and is clearly in control. The smoky darkness of the battle in the distance, the wounded officer to the right, the mounted grenadiers and officers in their tall hats—all these elements combine to make a single statement or narrative about the general and the battle. For another image of the same personage, consider the triumphal *Consecration of the Emperor Napoleon and Coronation of the Empress Josephine* by Jacques-Louis David, with the arrangement, expression, and attire of the crowd of people in the image.[13] All these partial pictures are like so many subordinate clauses in a sentence or so many steps in an argument: they are linked by pictorial grammar into one thought, one complex thing being stated. The location of the subordinate images within the overriding image, the overriding statement, is analogous to the syntactic placement of phrases within phrases in speech. The location of images within images is the syntax of the painting, and it is a structure that the viewer himself has to "pronounce" if he is to take in the image.

---

[13] The full title of David's painting is *Consecration of the Emperor Napoleon and Coronation of the Empress Josephine at the Cathedral of Notre-Dame in Paris on 2 December 1804.*

In speech, we move downward from syntactic composition to phonemes, to the composition of vowels and consonants within words. Phonemes are deeper than nouns and verbs and other grammatical forms. I would suggest that in picturing, the analogue to vowels is color and the analogue to consonants is line. Here also, color and line are deeper, they are more elementary, than are images and their position. Furthermore, color is related to line much as vowels are related to consonants. Vowels are the fundamental, spontaneous, and emotive component in words, while consonants are more rational and need to be learned. Analogously, color is chthonic and affective, while line, *disegno*, is more rational and determinative. Lines clip, cut, and trim colors just as consonants define vowels. Indeed, it is often possible to convey the meaning of a sentence by writing down the consonants without the vowels, by giving only the instructions for pronunciation. The correlative to this in pictures is the drawing or the sketch, lines encompassing space without color. Shading, I might add, is an interesting intermediate case: it reflects the play of light into the bright and the dark, but it does not differentiate light into the color spectrum. Movies in black and white employ line and shading but no color, and they exhibit no less intelligence for that.

The British art historian Norbert Lynton recognizes the subrational character of color. In a review of an exhibition at the Royal Academy, he writes, "Color is notoriously difficult to engage with intellectually."[14] He quotes John Gage as saying, "[I]n the nineteenth century color was still regarded with suspicion by many critics."[15] The academic tradition considered color an ornament added to *disegno*, subversive if unconstrained by correct draughtsmanship and truth, revealing base animal instincts. To draw out my analogy, sheer color would be like sheer vowels, a wail rather than a word, or, as the poet Allen Ginsburg

---

[14] Norbert Lynton, "Masters of Color: Derain to Kandinsky. Eighty masterpieces from the Merzbacher Collection," *Times Literary Supplement* (13 September 2002). See also John Gage, *Color and Culture. Practice and Meaning from Antiquity to Abstraction* (Berkeley, California: University of California Press, 1999), Chapter 7, "Disegno versus Colore."

[15] Ibid.

would have it, a "Howl" without the definition of reason.[16] Ginsburg's poem, incidentally, despite its title, had to make use of consonants and syntax if it was to be a poem at all, and even the title is more than a howl; the word *howl* frames, and so humanizes, the wolf's "ow" with two consonants. Something similar happens with *bark*. The affinity of color with vowels is confirmed by Arthur Rimbaud's *Sonnet des Voyelles*, in which he attributes a particular color to each of the five vowels; the first line of the poem reads, "A noir, E blanc, I rouge, U vert, O bleu: voyelles."[17]

We have claimed that in pictures the syntax of images is analogous to the syntax of phrases in speech, and that color and line are analogous to vowels and consonants. Let us move on to the third and deepest level of language, the prosody or rhythm that underlies both words and sounds. There is something analogous to this in a picture, although it is not obvious what we should name it. We could use the terms applied to language and simply call it the rhythm or the cadence of the painting. The word *cadence* is not inappropriate. The *Oxford English Dictionary* lists one of its meanings as, "Harmonious combination of colors," and it quotes Swinburne, "The cadence of colors is just and noble: witness the red-leaved book . . . on the white cloth, the clear green jug on the table, the dim green bronze of the pitcher." Adrian Stokes speaks about this rhythm and calls it "movement." He describes having an experience in which colors entered into unexpected harmony with one another: "[T]he young leaf-greens of intense luminosity and of the right area and disposition...had entered into

---

[16] Mark Rothko and Jackson Pollock both give up on *disegno* as well as representation, but they cannot do away with color. Their work is the opposite of a line drawing. It is interesting to note, however, that Rothko claimed that his work was governed by a metric and not just by color. In a response to a claim that it is the color that dominates in Rothko's work, John Gage writes, "For the painter himself this was far from being a matter of course, and he told Phillips [Duncan Phillips of the Phillips collection in Washington, D.C.] that 'not color, but measures were of greatest importance to him.'" "Rothko: Color as Subject," in *Mark Rothko*, edited by Jeffrey Weiss (New Haven, Connecticut: Yale University Press, 1998), p. 248.

[17] My thanks to Kevin White for the reference to Rimbaud, as well as for some of the finer points about consonants in the words howl and bark.

companionship with the red, and with each other...In my opinion every picture that really 'works' possesses in infinite reduplication this kind of relationship, this kind of *movement*."[18] Still another name for this phenomenon can be found in a remark by Jeryldene M. Wood, who writes about a painting by Piero della Francesca and mentions "the *fluency* of Piero's picture as a whole."[19] The remark is especially pertinent, because the rhythm of an image can be presented only when the picture is taken as a whole.

The rhythm of a picture lies not only in the balance of colors, in which, for example, this red patch on the one side picks up something red on the other; it is also the cadence of the images as they make up the whole; it is the visual rhapsody of meanings, colors, and lines. Even the monochromatic, shaded background of a painting, such as the brown backdrop in a Rembrandt portrait or the charcoal grey or burnt and raw umber background in a work by Chardin, enters into this pictorial rhythm. This prosody is harder to distinguish than the more clearly defined images, lines, and colors, but we do sense this rhythm and we know when it is violated, when the colors do not rhyme, or when the lines and images look clumsy or when they unintentionally jar the viewer. A good positive example of such rhythm, one that is almost tangible, can be found in Piet Mondrian's aptly named *Broadway Boogie-Woogie*, which captures not only the beat of the music but the tempo of New York City, as would be obvious to anyone who has spent some time there. A sense for such cadence is probably the most unteachable thing in picturing. It underlies and encases both the sensibility and the intelligence in painting.[20]

---

[18] Adrian Stokes, *Colour and Form* (London: Faber and Faber Ltd., 1950 [1937]), p. 109; italics original.

[19] Jeryldene M. Wood, "Introduction," in *The Cambridge Companion to Piero della Francesca*, edited by Jeryldene M. Wood (New York: Cambridge University Press, 2002), p. 7; my italics.

[20] Piero della Francesca wrote a treatise on painting entitled *De Prospectiva Pingendi* (Ravenna: Danilo Montanari, 2000). At the beginning of the work (p. 7) he says, "Painting contains in itself three principal parts, which we say are design (disegno), composition (commensuratio), and color (colorare)." His list encompasses only two of the three dimensions that we have distinguished (composition of images, and color and line). He does not

In speech, rhythm comes into clear prominence in singing, where it underlies both the vowels and the thoughts, and it is more perceptible and measurable because of the temporal nature of speech and song, but cadence is also present in the arrangement of colors, lines, and images. After all, it takes time to be able to "read" a painting. We appreciate a painting properly only when we have lingered over it, when we have seen it many times and have looked at it at different times of day and during different moods of our own. It is especially the rhythm of the painting that needs this kind of repeated, protracted study, and only if the cadences of the picture have been caught (and the noun is plural because there will be many of them) will the significance of the image come to light. Indeed, the rhythm is a kind of repository in which further meanings, further articulations in the painting are kept in store, and it introduces a temporal aspect into the activity of viewing a painting.[21]

I wish to conclude this comparison of pictures and words by using some sentences from Edith Wharton. In her short novel, *False Dawn*, she tells about a man, Lewis Raycie, who in the 1840s bought some old Italian paintings and tried to exhibit them at his home in New York. They were in fact painted by important artists, but no one recognized or appreciated them. Wharton describes the situation by mingling terms that pertain to pictures with terms that pertain to speech. She describes the man's hopes: "Once let the pictures be seen by educated and intelligent people, and they would speak for themselves especially if he were at hand to interpret them." But the exhibition was a catastrophic failure: "Even with Lewis as interpreter, the pictures failed to make themselves heard."[22] What does it mean for a picture to "make itself heard"? It means that the image will provoke the viewer into the

---

mention anything equivalent to cadence, but the reason for this omission may be the fact that the book gives instruction on how to use perspective. Rhythm is too deep in the structure of painting to be teachable.

[21] An important contrast between speech and painting lies in the fact that speech moves us away from the words to the thing, while pictures bring the thing into themselves. There is, therefore, an interesting "spatial" difference between the two modes of presentation.

[22] Edith Wharton, "False Dawn," in *Old New York* (New York: Charles Scribner's Sons, 1952 [1924]), pp. 60-61.

syntactic action that lets the composition of images, the patterning of colors and lines, and the cadences of the whole come to light. The viewer will also be able to speak intelligently about the picture, but only as an indication that he has taken in what the picture is, that is, that he has grasped what is identifiable within it.

4. Pictorial intelligence and human happiness

So far my remarks have been rather formal. We have discussed the three linguistic levels of syntax, phonemes, and prosody, and the three pictorial levels of configuration, line and color, and cadence. So far we have not spoken about the content, about what is said or what is depicted, nor have we discussed the kind of intelligence that is needed for such presentation. Let us speak primarily about the intelligence that occurs in depiction. What does it reveal and how does it reveal it?

I wish to claim that picturing deals with human happiness, the *eudaimonia* described in the *Nicomachean Ethics*. We as human beings, by our simple existence, introduce the most dramatic activity in the universe, the activity of choosing the things that either achieve or lose our beatitude. We are the kind of thing that can be, or can fail to be, happy, the kind of thing for whom happiness becomes an issue. We are caught up in this pursuit, and hence we become an issue for ourselves. We never just want to get something done; we always know that *we* are doing it and that what we do will modify how we will be. We are ineluctably so involved; we can't help it; we do not have a choice in the matter. We can make choices that either achieve or prevent our happiness (it can be achieved in no other way except through our choosing), but we do not have any choice about being the kind of thing that wants and needs to be happy. When philosophy describes the human being as wanting and needing to be happy, it describes an essential necessity, something neither cultural nor optional. We are that kind of part of the universe, that kind of entity, and we install that kind of activity into the world. In an unpublished lecture on Henry James, Francis Slade, echoing and modifying Aristotle, says, "This is what poetry imitates: the action that actualizes or destroys our beatitude."[23] The term *poetry* does not mean just the sonnet, epic, or

---

[23] The lecture was given at St. Francis College on April 22, 2003. I am grateful to Francis Slade for notes of his lecture and permission to quote from them. I

tragedy; it can mean the novel, and it can also mean a depiction. Specifically, it can mean a portrait.

We must distinguish between a likeness and a portrait. A likeness is a mere copy of a person; it shows what he looks like. It gives you enough to be able to identify the person. A portrait is more than this; it is a depiction of an essay at beatitude. It presents, poetically, someone's shot at happiness and self-identity. It presents what Aristotle would call a "first substance," an individual entity, an instance of the species man, but it does not present that substance as a mere compound; it presents that entity as an essence, with a necessity and a definition. This definition is individualized (it is a *first* substance), but it is also able to be universal, that is, it can flow back on life, and more specifically it can become identifiable with the persons who view it, the other individuals who are also an issue for themselves, who are also engaged in beatitude.[24] The portrait contains a lot of images, a lot of subordinate clauses. It presents the person's face, but also his configuration, his posture, his clothing, and some of his things, those relevant to his way of being. If the portrait is serious and successful, if it is poetic and not a mere likeness, the person depicted in it will look out at us and declare, "This is what I have done and what, consequently, I am. This is what I have done with the chance I was given." The face and the things express a life, a choice and choices for or against beatitude. It is up to the painter to capture this, and to do so by his combinatorics of image within image, lines enclosing colors, and the cadences underlying it all. A mere likeness is a lot less than this; it succeeds if the viewer can

---

am also grateful to him for telling me about Edmund Waller's poem, which I use at the end of this essay.

[24] One might ask whether the association of portraits with an individual's happiness is found especially in art that has been influenced by Christian belief. See Alain Besançon, *The Forbidden Image. An Intellectual History of Iconoclasm*, translated by Jane Marie Todd (Chicago: University of Chicago Press, 2000), p. 265: "The unrepeatable and continuing individuality of the human subject, the presence of a personal soul within, animates the portrait as it has been practiced in Europe since the Middle Ages." As a further point, we might say that the memory we each have of ourselves is something like a portrait, presenting, in a dramatic way, to ourselves as the exclusive audience, the self-identity we carry with us so long as we live.

simply recognize who the subject is, if he can just *identify* him; a portrait of someone succeeds if it enables the viewer to *understand* him. It does not just show; it portrays. As Sir Joshua Reynolds put it, "It is not the eye, it is the mind which the painter of genius desires to address..."[25]

Like all works of art, a portrait exercises what Thomas Prufer has called "reflux" on life.[26] The image does not just present itself to us; it "flows back" on life and enables us to experience things as articulated wholes. In Hans-Georg Gadamer's phrase, we see the world "with sight schooled by art."[27] John Gage expresses this in an elegantly compressed way; he describes harmonious combinations of colors and says, "It is in pictures, *or when we see in terms of pictures*, that these color-relationships take on a coherence."[28] We not only see pictures; we also become able to "see in terms of pictures," that is, we learn to experience the world in the terms the image conferred on us, and, when we do so, patterns show up that would not have been visible otherwise. What Gage says about colors is true about human action; life and action become framed into wholes and parts that they would not enjoy without the imprint of drama and picturing. As Slade puts it, "The imitated action flows back over...actual action, and it is by virtue of the reflux of imitated action, which is 'tragic,' that the actual action is seeable as tragic, is displayed as tragic."[29] We become able to experience life in the terms the depiction affords us: "This is how art makes us see life. Without the art of tragedy, life could not be experienced as tragic." We come to see

---

[25] Sir Joshua Reynolds, *Discourses on Art*, edited by Robert R. Wark (San Marino, California: Huntington Library, 1959), p. 50. See also p. 57, where Reynolds mentions "this exertion of mind, which is the only circumstance that truly ennobles our art."

[26] Thomas Prufer, "Providence and Imitation: Sophocles' Oedipus Rex and Aristotle's Poetics," in *Recapitulations* (Washington, D.C.: Catholic University of America Press, 1993), pp. 18-19.

[27] Hans-Georg Gadamer, *The Relevance of the Beautiful, and Other Essays*, edited by Robert Bernasconi (New York: Cambridge University Press, 1986), p. 31. The German reads, "mit durch die Kunst erzogenen Augen."

[28] Gage, *Color and Culture*, p. 9; italics added.

[29] Slade makes this point in the lecture mentioned above in note #23.

objects and other people in terms of pictures, but more importantly, we also come to "see" ourselves in a more understandable way, as also engaged in the attempt at happiness that is depicted in the portrait. An image conveys not just knowledge about the world but self-knowledge as well; as Slade says, "Art is entangled with life with the aim of untangling life by making it clear to itself." Everyone, the greatest and the least, needs such imaging to help define himself.

A portrait is the clearest instance of a visual imitation of "the action that actualizes or destroys our beatitude," but other forms of painting, such as landscapes and street scenes, can also be related to human conduct. I would like to quote Francis Slade again, this time from a conversation. He and I once went to an exhibition of the paintings of John Singer Sargent. Some of the pictures in the show represented people in various settings: on the bank of a river, in a restaurant, on a street, in an interior. Slade observed that in Sargent's paintings the settings were always such that people could be at home in them. I replied that Sargent was very different from Edward Hopper in that respect; in Hopper's paintings, nobody is at home. And Slade responded: "It's more than that. They aren't at home "*and they know it.*" Not without reason has Hopper been called "the visual laureate of heartbreak hotel."[30]

The point I wish to make is that landscapes, seascapes, and street scenes are presented as backgrounds for the possibility of human choices. They present worlds in which something like us can be. Even in landscapes and seascapes, poetry imitates and intimates action or at least a setting for action, and a setting with a certain quality: as enabling the action, or as hindering, threatening, inviting, absorbing, scorning, or annihilating it. Even Jackson Pollock and Mark Rothko express a context for human being. They present a particular setting, or even, by implication, the universe as such, as a place that is or is not habitable, a place where beatitude can or cannot be sought. In extreme instances, they may present a place where it would be laughable to seek happiness, but even then they cannot extinguish our search for it.

---

[30] Peter Campbell, "At Tate Modern," *London Review of Books* (24 June 2004): p. 33. Slade added the observation that Hopper's *Nighthawks* was a favorite of Jean-Paul Sartre, and it is obvious why.

Eliminating any context in which beatitude can be sought, while still keeping the search for it alive, is precisely what nihilism is. Among contemporary artists Francis Bacon may be the most vivid example of this combination.

5. Pictorial categoriality

What kind of intelligence is at work when we thoughtfully read a portrait as expressing an attempt at happiness? What sort of categoriality is at work, what kind of categorial intuition takes place? Consider as an analogue the way in which a diagram functions to illustrate and condense a complicated set of events and relationships in the world. Just drawing the right lines in a diagram will present a situation in a simple and easily perceptible way; it will provide a solution to a problem and put a confused, troubled mind to rest. A diagram conjugates a complex situation. Likewise, suppose that we know a certain person, perhaps a famous individual or just a friend who has lived a largely private life, and suppose we see a thoughtful portrait of him. What we see there is something like a few strategic, diagrammatic lines drawn through the shape of that person. The portrait is like a diagram in which not just a mathematical but a moral unity is constituted, and in which more than lines are put into composition. It is a presentation of a whole life in its significant, articulated parts. It provides just the right phantasm for an insight into *this* substance. The artist knew which lines to draw, what colors to choose, what things and features to highlight as the properties of that person. He thereby reveals the substance of that person and the substance of that life, which is, after all, simply the person unfolded. The portrait enfolds what the life unfolds. If the artist succeeds in capturing his subject, if he does depict this particular attempt at beatitude, he achieves a solution and a resolution of the presentational problem he undertook when he began the painting. He has exercised his artistic intelligence, not just in resolving the formal structures of composition, line and color, and rhythm, but in depicting an attempt at happiness, a human being.

The portrait calls for intelligence (*intellectus* or *nous*) and not reasoning (*ratiocinatio* or *syllogismos*). You do not draw inferences when you view the painting. You might carry out inferences when you are studying the painting, when you are decoding the symbols, being informed about the iconography, and examining the patterns of line and color; but when you see the painting as a whole, you engage not in inference but in articulated identification, in categorial synthesis, in an act of intelligence, an act of understanding. Furthermore, this insight makes an impact on you as the viewer, because of the way art flows back into life, the way in which the form expressed in the depiction shapes our own being and the life we live. We are therefore moved, we rejoice or we are stunned, not because we have solved a puzzle but because we have understood something about the kind of actuality we call happiness. We do not *infer* that the fact depicted in the portrait also applies to us; we grasp the form and its application in a single insight, a kind of "pairing," to use Husserl's term.[31] The intelligence in question encompasses the images and their relationships, the colors and lines, and also the cadences of the portrait, which envelop the picture in a way different from the way the frame encloses it and makes it one. The underlying rhythm is the reservoir for the painting while the frame is the fence that surrounds it.

The frame of a painting isolates the image. The image so detached then flows back on life; it rejoins the word through its reflux, not through its spatial contiguity. Henry James gives a striking illustration of these two themes, the frame of a picture and the merging of a painting with life. In *The Ambassadors*, the protagonist, Lambert Strether, makes an excursion from Paris into the French countryside.[32] His outing is described as taking place within "a certain small Lambinet," a landscape painting that he saw years earlier at a Boston dealer's, which he could not afford but had never forgotten. The frame is mentioned: "The oblong gilt frame disposed its enclosing lines," and an identification between image and life takes place: "It was what he wanted: it was Tremont Street, it was France, it was Lambinet. Moreover, he was freely walking about in it." Later, as he lay on the grass and took a nap, he "lost himself anew in Lambinet," and "He really continued in the picture . . . all the rest of this rambling day." No matter where he walked, he had "not once overstepped the oblong gilt frame. The frame had drawn itself out for him, as much as you please."

---

[31] On the concept of pairing see Husserl, *Cartesian Meditations*, translated by Dorion Cairns (The Hague: Martinus Nijhoff, 1977), p. 51.

[32] Henry James, *The Ambassadors*, book 11, chapter 3.

Strether's excursion sets the stage for the novel's central discovery and reversal. Something analogous happens, with a similar play of identities and differences, in *The Wings of the Dove*, when Milly Theall views a portrait of a woman by Agnolo Bronzino and finds herself identified with the personage.[33] This event also involves something of a discovery and reversal, because it immediately precedes the first intimation of Milly's fatal illness.

I have a final point to make about the cadence of a work of art. My understanding of this dimension must be distinguished from the theory that lay behind nonrepresentational painting in the 20th century. The original members of this movement, Kandinsky, Malevich, and to a lesser degree Mondrian, were theosophists.[34] They thought that art could express ultimate, quasi-divine powers of the universe. To reach these forces the artists bypassed individual things. The rhythms they were after were cosmic, analogous to the laws of nature that Francis Bacon said were behind the more particular forms of things, the laws of nature into which individual things and species could be resolved. These artists wanted to express not the truth of particular objects or even particular kinds of objects, not things they might imitate, not a nature that they might repeat, but the truth that lay hidden *behind* such particularities and not in them, a truth that only artists could reach and one that they could reveal to others. They wanted something analogous to a song without words. In what was called "supremacist" art, the artist was taken to be a prophet and not just a craftsman. He would share in the creative process of the universe and would be in touch with rhythms that were universal. The artist posits and does not copy; he does not subordinate himself to the way things seem to be. As Alain Besançon says about Malevich, "Ecstasy and mystical knowledge give access to the infinite, to the unreality of the phenomenon..."[35] and, "The task of man is to wrest himself from the phenomenon, the

---

[33] Henry James, *The Wings of the Dove*, chapter 11.

[34] See the treatment of these artists by Besançon, *The Forbidden Image*, pp. 321-77. He considers their ideas a modern version of iconoclasm. At the end of his career, however, Kandinsky returned to representation and depicted fanciful biomorphic images.

[35] Ibid., p. 366.

figurative, and to sink into the mystery of the universe...But the universe—in other words, God—does not think. Only man thinks, and it is through thought that he will identify with the universe, that is, with God."[36]

My treatment of the rhythmic level in speech and in painting would keep us from overshooting the individual object. I would claim that the cadence in question is proper to this individual speech and this individual painting; it is not cosmic or universal. The rhythm underlies these particular lines, colors, and images, and it could not exist without them. The formal causes define the more material elements and make them be what they are. Furthermore, I would observe that not only speech and depiction but individual entities each have their own built-in tempo, their own temporality, as part of their substance.[37] All living things have their biological rhythms, their daily and seasonal cycles, as well as their deeper genetic cadences that let them unfold as entities. The expression of genes in a cell needs an internal clock, as the regulatory genes turn the others on and off, and even atoms and molecules have their vibrations and harmonies. Things do not dissolve into cosmic laws; there are forms and finalities; things are differentiated from one another; in a word, there *are* entities and light

---

[36] Ibid., pp. 369-70. I would have to differ with Gadamer's analysis of nonrepresentational art in "Art and Imitation," in *The Relevance of the Beautiful*, pp. 92-104. He sees it as mimetic, but not in either a Kantian or Aristotelian way; he says that it calls to mind Pythagorean doctrines about mathematical order in the cosmos. Modern art, he says, reflects and imitates this deep-seated pattern, not the forms of things. He claims that such a reduction is necessary because our modern industrial world has marginalized ritual and myth and has "also succeeded in destroying things," so that nothing familiar remains to be imitated or expressed in art (p. 102). What modern art does offer is "a pledge of order" when everything familiar is dissolving (p. 104). I would reply that Gadamer concedes too much to the technological age, and seems, in this passage, to capitulate to it. There still are things that provide a measure and a telos: not only organic entities, but also relationships, situations, and actions that need to be artistically registered for us.

[37] See Russell Foster and Leon Kreitzman, *Rhythms of Life. The Biological Clocks that Control the Daily Lives of Every Living Thing* (New Haven, Connecticut: Yale University Press, 2004).

plays on them. Things are real and they can be imitated. The rhythms of particular things are differentiated from one another. In the case of human beings, the biological time provides a context for a temporality that involves memories, anticipations, and choices, which make up a human life. The end of speech and depiction is to show what things and persons are and how they present themselves, not to dissolve them in view of a deeper truth. Phenomena are not unreal; the cadences in speech and pictures bear witness to the way things are.

6. Christian intelligence in pictures

Christian art, the depiction of Christian things, is also an imitation of the action directed toward beatitude, but the action in question and the beatitude it is involved with take on a different tone. The modification is not just cultural but theological. Christian belief understands itself to transcend cultures even while it finds its place in them. The decisive action for Christian faith is what God has done in the world, the action of Incarnation and Redemption. God's work of Creation provides a background for this redemptive performance, and so the world itself is also depicted differently. The landscape of the world is not just a habitation for men but a place in which the Son of God can dwell and has dwelt. Christian art, therefore, presents and celebrates God's own beatitude, the happiness that is God's own life, which he has presented to us through the Death and Resurrection of Christ. Every Christian painting presents God's glory, his *doxa*, a Greek term that must be taken in its multiple senses of glory, appearance, doctrine, and truth, all of which are present in the compound term *orthodoxy*. Every Christian painting serves to convey the central message of the gospels that is summarized in the line of the *Benedictus*: "to give knowledge of salvation to his people, *ad dandam scientiam salutis plebi eius*."

What would the Christian faith be without its images? The Creed calls for the complementarity of depiction. How would the manifestation of the Incarnation be sustained without its reflection in pictures? Without images would it not become only a matter of words, and hence a gnostic illumination, a matter of thinking and not action? The iconoclastic heresy takes on deeper meaning when we ask this question, and the inevitability of its condemnation becomes more apparent. In Christian liturgy, the mystery of the sacrament must be played off against the glorious and brilliant iconostasis, as well as the statues and stained-glass windows. Christian images are not just pedagogical devices; they are witnesses to the truth of the Incarnation and the embodiment of grace. They help distinguish Christian faith from the Jewish and the Muslim by presenting the Incarnation to us in a way that words alone could not do. One might also think of the complex visual beauty of a fine cathedral at Solemn Mass. Catholicism seems to know how to compose very simple images into very complex ones. Not only Jews and Muslims but also some Protestants seem to be in principle people of the word alone, and hence iconoclastic. Picturing seems to be a pagan remnant that Catholicism can incorporate and transform but that the other religions cannot.[38]

The primary location for Christian images is not the art gallery but the church, monastery, convent, or home. Such pictures are meant to be lived with. In religious imagery, the "lingering examination of the original"[39] that every painting demands is carried out, not as a merely intellectual inquiry, but as a prayer, which achieves its focus and intensity because the image makes present, pictorially, God's glory or its presence in one of the saints. Christian images can present a human being, an essay at happiness, but in this case the beatitude is accomplished not just by deeds but by grace. The image presents God's grace and glory shining through, but in a way specific to this particular saint, to the Blessed Virgin or St. Peter, to St. Francis Xavier or St. Teresa of Avila. Jan van Eyck and Fra Angelico depict more than people who have no regrets for what they have done with their lives. They depict people who have entered into a kind of happiness different from the kind determined simply by what we do ourselves, and it is also different, in ways that deserve exploration, from the beatitude depicted in images of the Buddha and his attendant Boddhisatvas.

---

[38] This affinity with imaging has been less true of the Catholic liturgy of the past thirty-five years, which is much more verbal and less ritualistic, less visually compositional, than the centuries-old liturgy that preceded it.

[39] The phrase is from John Walsh, "Pictures, Tears, Lights, and Seats," in *Whose Muse? Museums and the Public Trust*, edited by James Cuno (Princeton: Princeton University Press, 2004), p. 79.

Landscapes are also modified in Christian art. Here I would like to quote Besançon again. He writes about French Impressionist painting and says: "One is struck by the well-being (*le bien-être*) that radiates from it, its joyful harmony, its pleasure in contemplating creatures and landscapes, all of which is more in keeping with the Christian spirit than are the troubled and suspicious works of symbolism..."[40] He admits that people like Cézanne and Monet might have been anticlerical, "*parfaits mangeurs de curés*," but he insists that they were children of a civilization that the Catholic Church had marked by her education,[41] and he also claims that "the great epochs of *Christianisme* are always marked by the flowering of a happy lay culture (*une culture laïque heureuse*)."[42] Christian art, even as an unconscious inheritance, rejoices in the world as created by God, as a place where beatitude can be attained, where, one believes, the incoherence of life has been resolved by the redemptive Death and Resurrection of the Incarnate Son of God.[43]

Christian truth is present not only in the iconography of a work of Christian art. It extends to the other levels, from the placement of images to the combination of line and color to the cadences of the picture. All of these bodily elements become ingredient in the truth that is disclosed. They become ingredient not only as elements in the picture, but also as representing elements of the material world, which was created by God in the beginning, was incorporated into his act of Redemption, and will be transformed at the end of time, when it will become obvious what the body and flesh really are. Robert E. Wood has

---

[40] Alain Besançon, *La confusion des langues. La crise idéologique de l'Église* (Paris: Calmann-Levy, 1978), p. 43. See also, *Trois tentations dans l'Église* (Paris: Calmann-Levy, 1996), p. 28.

[41] Besançon, *La confusion des langues*, p. 44.

[42] Ibid., p. 43.

[43] Besançon makes similar points in other passages. See *The Forbidden Image*, p. 33: "Plato posits the fundamental theological principle on which all art rests: that the world is good." On page 265: "These points, it seems, can be reduced to one: creation is good." On page 238, he speaks about 17th and 18th century French painting and says, "The reflection of that image [of God] . . . illuminated profane art, provided a sense of well-being, a happiness about being in the world which was also praise of its Creator."

examined Christian art in relation to "the fundamentally incarnate character of Christian religion, rooted in the belief in God's own incarnation and culminating in the resurrection of the body."[44] Christian truth could not have been disclosed without the body, and so Christian intelligence does not escape from the material substrate but incorporates it into its faith. It is not gnostic and therefore eschews iconoclasm of any form, whether Byzantine, Reformed, or Modern. Christian art is essentially representational, and it depicts each thing and person, each *tode ti*, with its own internal necessity, as existing in its own form of being, both created and graced.[45]

---

[44] Robert E. Wood, *Placing Aesthetics. Reflections on the Philosophic Tradition* (Athens, Ohio: Ohio University Press, 1999), p. 327.

[45] As an epilogue to my essay, I comment on Edmund Waller's poem, *To Vandyck.* It speaks eloquently about the presentational possibilities in a picture and about the effect a portrait has on the viewer. The artist's skill does not just entertain the viewer but makes him love the thing depicted:

Rare Artisan, whose pencil moves
Not our delights alone, but loves!
From thy shop of beauty we
Slaves return, that enter'd free.

People respond not simply to the image but to the thing imaged. In the one case, it is a response to someone unknown:

The heedless lover does not know
Whose eyes they are that wound him so;
But, confounded with thy art,
Inquires her name that has his heart.

In the other case, a response to someone once known:

Another, who did long refrain,
Feels his old wound bleed fresh again
With dear remembrance of that face,
Where now he reads new hope of grace

The painter's work is not just an inert likeness or an aesthetic object, but presents the thing itself, in this case the face, with its own causal efficiency:

Strange! that thy hand should not inspire
The beauty only, but the fire;
Not the form alone, and grace,
But act and power of a face.

When Art Fails Humanity:

Jacques Maritain on Jean Cocteau, Modernism and the Crisis of European Civilization

Cornelia A. Tsakiridou

1. Introduction

Jacques Maritain's relationship with French artist, playwright and cinematographer Jean Cocteau is a good example of his attempt to rescue modernism from some of its most dangerous fallacies, an effort that he took to a personal level. He and Raïssa tried to save Cocteau from addiction and despair and convince him to return to Catholicism. Maritain felt great compassion for Cocteau as he did for other artists in whose conversion and work he took a loving interest. But he was also deeply troubled by Cocteau's aestheticism, his superficial approach to morality and self-indulgent religious sense in which he saw reflections of a deeper moral crisis in European society and culture.

Maritain wrote two works in which he gave voice to these concerns, *Dialogues*, a series of reflections on art, literature and morality, and *Art and Faith*, a collection of letters exchanged with Cocteau during the height of their friendship and Cocteau's brief return to the sacraments. Of certain interest to the Cocteau student, these texts are also important in assessing Maritain's complex view of modernism, especially in its aesthetic and ethical aspects. In conjunction with other writings, including his seminal *The Peasant of the Garonne*, they help shed light on the reasons for his consistent objection to modernism's formative ideas and their ideological expression in what he termed "absolute Machiavellianism."

The first part of this paper is accordingly aimed at understanding the concepts that formed modernism, and what Maritain found problematic in them. Of particular interest is Maritain's definition of aestheticism that entails a critique of the Kantian concept of the aesthetic that goes beyond the domain of fine art, and shows how aspects of modernism distort human life. The second part considers his relationship and correspondence with Cocteau in that context, and explains why Cocteau drew Maritain's attention in the period prior and subsequent to his conversion. Finally, the third part examines Maritain's ambivalence toward modernism, and identifies the modernist aspects of contemporary art and popular culture.

2. The modern mind

At the heart of Maritain's well-known call on the modern mind to return to the study of being and abandon the errors of rationalism and agnosticism is a notion that applies directly to Cocteau and his milieu. Maritain frames it clearly in *Angelic Doctor*, his biographical study of St. Thomas, published in 1931. There he speaks of the replacement of "speculation and logical discernment" by "a sort of refined play of instinct, imagination, intuition, visceral emotions" a consequence of which is the lack of "courage to form a judgment," to recognize the actuality of good and evil.[1] When truth is not ordered to God and to being, imaginary and subjective realities dominate human life and undermine moral virtue.

Maritain describes prophetically the advent of "a false humanitarian mysticism, pseudo-Buddhist, theosophical or anthroposophical, a false region of the heart which claimed to install itself at the expense of the mind, in contempt of the Word which creates and forms Its laws."[2] He continues with a penetrating foresight about the rise of European totalitarianism that will form the basis of his 1939 *Twilight of Civilization*: "it is from a pseudo-spiritualism and a pseudo-mysticism that we may expect the greatest dangers of deviation in our time."[3]

---

[1] Jacques Maritain, *The Angelic Doctor: The Life and Thought of Saint Thomas Aquinas* (New York: Dial Press, 1931), pp. 114 and 130-31.

[2] Ibid., pp. 77-78.

[3] Ibid., p. 78. "We are face to face... with a demonic *paratheism* or pseudo-theism," he writes in *Twilight*. He offers this analysis of National Socialism: "Racism is existentially related to this demonic pseudo-theism, since, in its reaction against individualism and in its thirst for communion, it seeks that communion in human animality, which, once separated from the spirit, is no longer anything but a biological inferno." Jacques Maritain, *The Twilight of Civilization*, translated by Lionel Laudry (New York: Sheed & Ward, 1943), pp. 20-21.

Thirty-five years later, in The *Peasant of the Garonne*, he remembers Cocteau in a similar context whose relevance to their relationship will become clear later in our discussion. Intimating that charity presupposes an intellect committed to supernatural truth, he tells Cocteau, who signed his correspondence with a heart, that in a world "full of dried up hearts and flabby minds," "*we must have a tough mind and a tender heart.*"[4]

The same commitment is required of art. According to St. Thomas, beauty enters the intellect through the senses as brilliant form and is perceived as such only by those who discern in beautiful things the Wisdom of God.[5] Charity and beauty presuppose an intellect joined to God and being. Without this connection, art is a mirage.

The notion that European civilization is in decline (a view also held by Pope Benedict XV)—"Europe has killed her *past*" (Maritain's emphasis)—and incapable of generating the vital forms of beauty and the values that embraced the Church for centuries, preoccupied Maritain in the 1920s.[6] His discussion of art in that context betrays an incisive grasp of the reasons behind modernism's passion for decomposition and fragmentation. In *The Things That Are Not Caesar's* (1927), Maritain writes of the anguish and alienation of contemporary youth, "strolling in its own humanity as in a museum," indifferent spectators eager to destroy "too many masterpieces" because they cannot create their own. "All the fragrance of beauty, the forms and values, the very pictures by which our ancestors lived, which made nature fraternal to them and the universe familiar...have suddenly become remote from us." "We are exotic to our very selves," Maritain observes, "is it surprising that nothing should strike us as exotic and

---

[4] Jacques Maritain, *The Peasant of the Garonne: An Old Layman Questions Himself about the Present Time* (New York: Holt, Rinehart and Winstaon, 1968), p. 80, Maritain's emphasis; Raïssa Maritain, *Raïssa's Journal: Presented by Jacques Maritain* (Albany: Magi Books, 1974), p. 182.

[5] Jacques Maritain, *Art and Scholasticism and the Frontiers of Poetry*, translated by Joseph W. Evans (New York: Charles Scribner's Sons, 1962), pp. 24-26.

[6] Jacques Maritain, *The Things That Are Not Caesar's*, translated by J.F. Scanlan (New York: Charles Scribner's Sons, 1931), p. 102.

that every human form indifferently should excite our curiosity—or merely bore us?"[7]

The modern imagination is caught in a parade of images. The artist dreams, hallucinates and creates her own myths. This fascination with sights and spectacles of all kinds draws from the aesthetic as Kant defined it: fleeting, subjective, detached and unaffected by the objective conditions of its experience. For Maritain, modern art displays the Kantian dissociation of morality from being, which serves only to "narrow the real and consequently impoverish the materials of art," by rendering it blind to the "whole truth of the universe of good and evil."[8] A work bereft of this truth, of "what is most real in the world," remains invisible to a "darkened soul," which lives in a world of illusion and easily convinces itself that art can dictate morality. Maritain calls this "an absurdity."[9]

In the *Peasant*, he sees with trepidation a post-Vatican II Church vulnerable to modernist ideas. Of the term, he writes this: "The word modernism has aged, but I do not know a better, and to have aged makes it especially good: for nothing ages so quickly as fashion, and those theories which make truth or its conceptual formations a function of time."[10] He warns about the coming of an "*interior*, truly visceral Christianity," an empty and superficial faith, attractive because of the false euphoria it generates, an imaginary and symbolic religion of the heart, indifferent to natural and supernatural truth.[11] He considers dangerous the rejection of truths established in the Church over the centuries, especially the supra-historical truths of Thomism,

---

[7] Maritain, *The Things That Are Not Caesar's*, p. 103.

[8] Maritain, *Art and Scholasticism and the Frontiers of Poetry*, p. 147.

[9] Ibid., p. 146.

[10] Maritain, *The Peasant of the Garonne*, p. 5, footnote #6. For a discussion of the reaction caused by the book, see Brooke W. Smith, *Jacques Maritain: Antimodern or Ultramodern? An Historical Analysis of His Critics, His Thought and His Life* (New York: Elsevier, 1976), pp. 21-28, 106-17.

[11] Maritain, *The Peasant of the Garonne*, pp. 7-8.

by theologians who in the name of renewal "would like us to return to a zero point so that we can begin all over again."[12]

Maritain levels against them the same criticism that he has for the modernist experiment in art. Like many avant-garde artists, theologians are "anxious to serve the idols of the times," the fashionable Romantic notion of a pure, undiluted Christianity. Among Cubists, Surrealists, Constructivists, and Dadaists the quest for purity and primitive authenticity would lead to artistic and moral supremacy over their tradition.

In *Dialogues,* first published in 1928 in the series *Le Roseau d'Or* in which Cocteau was a collaborator, Maritain is critical of artists who embrace the Nietzschean notion of the spontaneous purity and aesthetic quality of the human act and its indifference to moral qualification. "A *sincere* priest," he writes rather acerbically of this false naturalism which Cocteau as we shall see embraced, "would mount naked to the altar, as in the black mass."[13] "The purity of the human being," he goes on, as if counseling Cocteau on his well-known search for inspiration in opium, "is to recognize the law not of the plant, but of man."[14]

Maritain sees the art and literature of his contemporaries defined by a paradox. The contraries that define the modern spirit, he explains, making it at once "Rousseauist and Manichean" are "the adoration of nature and the hatred of nature," the simultaneous exaggeration of instinct and fantasy.[15] Maritain has Oscar Wilde in mind when he writes: "Beauty has not come to the end of its submission to the shameful ascendancy of the god Aesthetics taken as the ultimate end of human life."[16]

---

[12] Ibid., pp. 159-60.

[13] Jacques Maritain, *Art and Poetry*, translated by E. de P. Matthews (New York: Philosophical Library, 1943), pp. 42-43.

[14] Ibid., p. 144.

[15] Ibid., p. 42.

[16] Ibid., p. 41.

Beauty separated from the good and elevated to an autonomous virtue, as an end in itself and a self-subsistent reality, suggests affinities between art and ideologies that exploit the intuition of supernatural life common to all human beings, by creating a theater or spectacle of the divine. Aestheticism is not benign; the "paper roses" of Wilde's aestheticism have only a deceptive purity. In essence, their charm conceals a denial of reality in the name of art, nihilism disguised as beauty.[17]

The cult of the supreme race in fascism is "breaking the natural unity of mankind;" the cult of universal community in communism is seeking to "substitute its own earthy universality for that of the mystical body of Christ."[18] Both have an aesthetic dimension. Thus, for Maritain, aestheticism is by no means confined to the domain of fine art and literature. Rather, it becomes an ontological category that denotes the falsification of human life, the domain par excellence of construed illusion, the malicious simulation of human and divine being—as in what he calls the "demonic pseudo-theism" of the Nazi state.[19]

The origins of this condition lie with Machiavellianism. It was Machiavelli, that "pure artist of the Renaissance," that envisioned politics as the art that orders ethics, with good and evil being the raw material that the statesman is called to shape, "as a sculptor handles clay or marble."[20] This "purely artistic conception of politics" introduced for the first time the notion that religion is a myth, whose end as such is to foster unity in the body politic, the ordering, in other words, of the divine to human art.[21] This ontological inversion—and perversion of being—leads, as Maritain explains, to the gradual deterioration of the Machiavellian project evident in contemporary European society and culture.

---

[17] Maritain, *Art and Scholasticism and the Frontiers of Poetry*, p. 127.

[18] Maritain, *The Twilight of Civilization*, p. 23.

[19] Ibid., p. 21.

[20] Joseph W. Evans and Leo R. Ward, *The Social and Political Philosophy of Jacques Maritain: Selected Readings* (Garden City: Image Books, 1965), p. 288.

[21] Ibid., pp. 289-90.

What starts as a refined, well-measured and reasoned art of deceit, becomes the work of "an intelligence no longer artistic but vulgar and brutal and wild."[22] Machiavellianism crumbles on its own faulty logic that seeks the art of that which by nature cannot be ordered to reason, of evil itself. But, as it crumbles, it assumes its "absolute" and final form, it becomes "a metaphysics...a religion, a prophetic and mystical enthusiasm," intent on destruction and annihilation.[23]

What in it was rational now disintegrates into the raw exercise of evil; deliberate, massive and "*boundless*" (emphasis Maritain's) in violence, injustice and lying, it "draws from this very boundlessness of evil an abominable strength." "Impetuous, irrational, revolutionary, wild" suggest the artistic genius but also the political madman, whom Maritain describes as "empty of rational personality, but open to the great collective forces of instinct, resentment and tellurian inspiration." The model for this dual figure, we are told, is the Nietzschean Dionysus. Repulsed by human suffering and the Cross of Christ, he elevates himself to a god.

The Nietzschean artist cannot plead innocent. For Maritain, this "figment of the imagination" has taken flesh and bones, in an incarnation of raw evil. He writes: "Dionysius?—the newspapers and the radio bring us news of him each morning. They have shown us how he leads his dance through the concentration camps...through a Europe delivered up to murder and starvation, oppression and enslavement, through a world set ablaze by war."[24] And he adds, "Nietzsche did not grasp that man has no choice except between two roads: the road to Calvary and the road to the slaughterhouse."

In the racial super-state, in the collective utopia and in societies subjugated to the dictates of productivity and profit, man suffers "animalization" and "paganization," the sacrifice of soul and life to lifeless images and idols.[25] The idolatry of race, the communion of blood

---

[22] Ibid., pp. 290-91.

[23] Ibid., p. 293.

[24] Maritain, *Twilight of Civilization,* p. 9.

[25] Evans and Ward, *The Social and Political Philosophy of Jacques Maritain,* pp. 159 and 161.

and myth in which the Nazi state found unity and purpose, suggest a world of simulation in which empty (totemic) forms dominate reality and reduce the human person to a nominal and expandable being, whose annihilation bears no consequence or sense. In a world of such radical ontological loss, where human intercourse is reduced to commerce with signs and human beings to tokens of utility, life and love do not have a place.

At the heart of modernism, then, is the deterioration of the aesthetic. Severed from what Maritain calls, in *Angelic Doctor*, the "natural unity" of reason and the "supernatural unity" of grace, the aesthetic has assumed an empty autonomy and has turned unavoidably into the realm of instinct and fantasy, aligning itself with false gods.[26] For Maritain, this is essentially a Kantian error. When Kant excluded intellectual delight from the experience of beauty, he shifted the focus of the aesthetic from the real to the subjective and emotional, rejecting beauty's transcendental nature.[27]

From Kant onward, beauty, and by extension art, lose their inherent presence in and dependence on being, and are dominated instead by feeling and imagination. The good in now an aesthetic value. Maritain saw clearly that the outcome of this exercise, would be "*counterfeit* ...*counterfeit* of the supernatural and of miracle...of grace and the heroic virtues," a farcical morality and faith that would create the passivity and apathy that makes human beings susceptible to demonic influence and heretical thought.[28]

Art that celebrates man made in the image of himself rather than God—the equation of truth and illusion, the fusion of dream and instinct and the estrangement of human life from the moral realities with which it is organically intertwined—is a natural complement to absolute Machiavellianism. Surrealism, with its Freudian underpinnings and idealization of an irrational primitive imagination, the purist ideals of Constructivism and Socialist Realism that served the

---

[26] Maritain, *The Angelic Doctor*, p. 90.

[27] Maritain, *Art and Scholasticism and the Frontiers of Poetry*, footnote #56, pp. 162-67.

[28] Ibid., p. 133, emphasis added, and p. 227, footnote #193.

Soviet State as ideological tools, the hyper-classical art of fascism that perpetrated the myth of a super race, give aesthetic expression to this ideological form.

This is why the artist must be held responsible and where possible turned toward Christ. Maritain is clear that when art, in an abuse of its creative power, intrudes in the domain of morality—an "imperialist invasion," he calls it—it cannot extricate itself from moral responsibility by invoking aesthetic freedom and disinterest or its rights to a childlike playfulness.[29]

The motto "art for art's sake" is therefore rejected because it assumes that artist and work can be detached from "the living forces which animate and move the human being," among which is desire, love, and moral conscience.[30] When a work that is deemed morally evil, and the judgment is true, it is the artist, his moral conscience, that needs to change, to be purified, and not the work through external means (e.g., censorship). Anything else "is not a solution, it is a fake, or an escape."[31] "There is no purity," he writes elsewhere, "where the flesh is not crucified..."[32] This last notion is at the heart of Maritain's interest in Cocteau.

3. A descent into magic

"There is no pure sin," we read in *Dialogues,* in a passage that most likely echoes a conversation with Cocteau: "the pure contour of impurity is an impure thing."[33] One brings to mind Cocteau's signature erotic sketches (many shared with Picasso), his erotic poetry (*The Angel Heurtebise*, 1925) and semi-pornographic literature (*The White Book*, published anonymously) all steeped in a calculated and obsessive

---

[29] Jacques Maritain, *The Responsibility of the Artist* (New York: Charles Scribner's Sons, 1960), pp. 64-65. Maritain, *Art and Poetry*, p. 45.

[30] Maritain, Ibid., p. 49.

[31] Ibid., p. 63.

[32] Ibid., p. 134.

[33] Maritain, *Art and Poetry*, p. 51.

language of self-professed innocence, elegance and simplicity.[34] Maritain continues with what seems an admonition:

> In making out of your sin beauty, you send it like an angel among your brothers. It kills them without a sound. However, this is not your first fault. But that of yourself within yourself for having hidden a corpse in the branches of your arteries, as if God did not see.[35]

By 1928, Maritain had good reason to think of Cocteau in such terms. In 1927, Cocteau's protégé and companion Jean Desbordes had published a book titled *J'Adore* in which he suggested that lovers in their act of union have more of the Divine Presence than does the Holy Sacrament. Maritain found Cocteau's enthusiastic endorsement of the book disturbing. He completed *Dialogues* on the Feast of the Ascension, 17 May 1928. In the endnote, written a year earlier on June 27, and published only in the 1928 French original, we read:

> I have just received the final page proofs of a book with a preface by Jean Cocteau in which he makes himself a laughing stock by celebrating the author as an Adam before the fall and by urging the young to embrace a new religion of love—a religion which proclaims all love to be pure. ...They adore, do they! God and the genitals (and the printed page). I know how puerile this is, but it is a betrayal of Christ perpetrated with the most horrible lack of awareness. I also know what tragic suffering dwells in Cocteau's heart, and I wish I could be silent. But to suffer the profanation of the Gospels, the confusion of raving sensuality with religion—that is impossible. [36]

Maritain is writing these lines only three years after Cocteau's return to the Sacraments in June of 1925, after a period of opium

---

[34] Cornelia A. Tsakiridou, "Classical Cocteau," in *Reviewing Orpheus: Essays on the Cinema and Art of Jean Cocteau*, edited by Cornelia A. Tsakiridou (Lewisburg: Bucknell University Press, 1997), p. 101, footnote #14.

[35] Maritain, *Art and Poetry*, p. 35.

[36] Francis Steegmuller, *Cocteau: A Biography* (Boston: Little, Brown and Company, 1970), p. 391. Jacques Maritain, "Dialogues," *Le Roseau d'Or* XXX, Chroniques No. 6 (Paris: Plon-Nourrit et Cie), 1928: 17-62; p. 62.

detoxification. In the Preface to the English edition of *Art and Faith*, written in January of 1947, he explains that he saw in Cocteau's conversion an effort to create "poetry for God" at a time "in which the Prince of the World was the master of Dreams."[37] Although he concedes that the "new poetry" he had hoped for did not come, he offers the letters as evidence of the "mysterious and ambiguous relations it [poetry] entertains with religion."[38] He remains gracious and gallant toward Cocteau ("I know the poets in whom I have my confidence"), emphasizing the testimonial importance of their correspondence "in the perishable day in which it has been born."

Maritain saw Cocteau's opium addiction as symptomatic of modern poetry's (and art's) fascination with "magical powers" that pull it "in the direction of the Devil."[39] "Shall I condemn the opium-smoker," he asks Cocteau in a sympathetic letter, "because he is trying to free himself from this lying life? No, but because he uses wicked means, he makes use of an evil to flee evil; he trusts a lie to escape a lie."[40] He challenges Cocteau's narcissism directly:

> Art has trouble defending itself against an impure angel that slaps it in the face, that wants to make use of everything for self-love, of the very gift the heart makes of itself, of its weakness even; even of God. We know this very well my dear Jean, we see this game everywhere.[41]

Maritain considered opium-induced mysticism and inspiration as demonic, an attempt by man to find salvation on his own terms, by creating an artificial, vegetative paradise. He described Cocteau's condition as "the poppy in the place of the Paraclete" and "Quietism in pills, sacrament of the devil."[42] Behind Cocteau's fascination with

---

[37] Jacques Maritain, *Art and Faith: Letters between Jacques Maritain and Jean Cocteau*, translated by John Coleman (New York: Philosophical Library, 1948), pp. 8-11.

[38] Ibid., p. 9.

[39] Ibid., pp. 7-8

[40] Ibid., p. 82.

[41] Ibid., pp. 86-87.

[42] Ibid., p. 82.

induced illusion he saw the modernist notion that human life is governed by raw instinctual realities and is, in that state, radically pure, with an innocence that mocks the purity of Christ. A conduit to this concealed world, a hallucinogen is rationalized as a moral regimen and instrument of salvation, nature's alternative mysticism.

Narcissism makes a caricature of the human person. In 1930, in *Religion and Culture*, Maritain wrote that the instinctual life of human beings is open and indeterminate because it has reason as its natural end and principle. Raw instinct cannot therefore ground the human person, without profoundly distorting and wounding its rational and spiritual nature. "The truly and fully natural man," he explains addressing the Romantic primitivism so much in vogue among modernists, "is not nature's man, the uncultivated soil, but the virtuous man...formed by the inner culture of the intellectual and moral virtues."[43]

The circumstances that gave rise to the Cocteau-Maritain correspondence were defined by three events: the untimely death of Cocteau's intimate friend, novelist Raymond Radiguet, in the winter of 1923, his opium addiction and detoxification two years later, in the winter of 1925, and the sustained efforts of Jacques and Raïssa Maritain to draw Cocteau into their Catholic circle.

Maritain was familiar with Radiguet's novels and admired his talent. According to Cocteau biographer Frederick Steegmuller, shortly after Radiguet's death, Maritain urged Catholic journalist Henri Massis to write a review of the young man's work.[44] Maritain's purpose, Steegmuller contends, was to counteract the attention given to Radiguet by the *Nouvelle Revue Francaise*, an agnostic and politically left journal that was hostile to Cocteau, and thus to draw Cocteau to his circle. Cocteau wrote immediately to both Massis and Maritain expressing his gratitude. Raïssa has a different explanation. Cocteau, she records in her diary in July of 1924, "came to Jacques because he

---

[43] Evans and Ward, *The Social and Political Philosophy of Jacques Maritain*, pp. 214-15.

[44] Steegmuller, *Cocteau*, p. 337.

had been told he could make him find peace again, and find God again."[45]

In his response to Maritain in August of 1924, Cocteau confesses: "Out of all youth I chose Radiguet to make him my masterpiece. Imagine his death, and me alone, half-mad amidst the rubble of a crystal-cutting workshop."[46] The remark reveals a self-centered detachment that is consistent with Cocteau's refusal to visit the dying Radiguet (who died alone) or even to attend his funeral—according to Coco Chanel he was afraid of contracting typhoid.[47] It also recalls the atelier of fluid mirrors and animated statues in his celebrated films *Orpheus* and *Blood of a Poet*, items that figured prominently in his visual idiom.[48] Both works exhibit the self-indulging, erotic, sensibility whose expression in Catholic idiom was to make Maritain so uneasy in 1927.

Cocteau's inspiration could shift easily from God to his own artistic identity and myth, all part of the Cocteau cult that he so meticulously cultivated. In his Catholic summer of 1925, he had actually entertained writing a play about the Virgin Mary and the mysterious birth of Christ, but abandoned the plan, fearing scandal.[49] The idea eventually translated into his play *Orpheus* (first performed in 1926). There, the mythical poet searches for inspiration and for his own legend only to end up decapitated and metamorphosed into Cocteau. Maritain must have suspected in that first year of their acquaintance (1924) that Cocteau was more interested in Cocteau (and his legend) than he was in Christ.

Cocteau's letters in *Art and Faith* suggest a tenuous conversion, perhaps a search for consolation in a Catholic aesthetic that would allow him to express and dramatize to a sympathetic public the impact

---

[45] Raïssa Maritain, *Raïssa's Journal*, pp. 165-66. Steegmuller and others unfairly view Maritain as an astute proselytizer of vulnerable souls who took advantage of Cocteau: see Steegmuller, *Cocteau*, p. 337.

[46] Maritain, *Art and Faith*, pp. 78-79.

[47] Steegmuller, *Cocteau*, p. 317.

[48] On this subject and on the classical in Cocteau, see Tsakiridou, "Classical Cocteau," pp. 78-108.

[49] Steegmuller, *Cocteau*, p. 349.

of Radiguet's untimely death. The most problematic is his facile identification with Christ. The suffering, devastated Cocteau seems taken by his role of roles—Cocteau *Alter Christus*:

> Jesus refuses to make a career. He wants to be born and to die every minute. Our crusade will be to shock out of love. I have never caused scandal without premeditation. I deem it indispensable.[50]

This act of appropriation, so typical of narcissism, presages the treatment of the sacred by art in the twentieth century and in our times. The phrase "shock out of love" recalls the rhetoric of Desbordes' *J'Adore*. In a footnote to this passage, he explains:

> Scandal and solitude, a kind of sensational flop, that is something hard. It is the only thing that suits me. Jesus sets the example for us. ...He always shocks, He discourages luck, He exposes Himself, He makes Himself ridiculous, He makes doors close on Him, He crucifies Himself.[51]

Readers familiar with Cocteau's style will recognize the self-portrait. This is Cocteau's "Passion," his de facto redemption and sanctification. The Maritains and their circle form his intrigued audience.

It is interesting to see how Cocteau describes his first encounter on June 15, 1925, at the home of the Maritains, with Father Charles Henrion, a contemplative priest and follower of Father Charles de Foucauld at the Sahara, who had gone into the priesthood under Maritain's influence.

Raïssa recalls an accidental encounter, for her a sign of Providence, with Cocteau waiting the arrival of a late ride to the Russian Ballet, and Father Henrion arriving just in time for Cocteau to hear him talk about a pilgrimage with the dramatist and poet Paul Claudel.[52] She writes: "I

---

[50] Maritain, *Art and Faith*, p. 46.

[51] Ibid., p. 68.

[52] Raïssa Maritain, *Raïssa's Journal*, p. 182. Cocteau recalls the evening in similar terms, noting that Maritain had mentioned to him a possible visit by Father Henrion and had informed him of the priest's background: see Maritain, *Art and Faith*, p. 37.

see Jean Cocteau standing, silent, in the embrasure of the window, *gripped* (emphasis hers)...The moment Charles came in, I am convinced Cocteau saw the sign of his destiny appear over the heart of a man. The heart with which he signs all his letters suddenly became *the heart of Jesus* (emphasis hers)."

Raïssa could not have known what went through Cocteau's mind. She noticed that he was deeply impressed by Father Henrion's appearance, especially by the red Heart displayed on his all white, desert habit. Cocteau went to confession three days later, on June 18 and to Communion the next day, on the Feast of the Sacred Heart.[53] "*Misericordias Domini,*" Raïssa wrote in her journal for that occasion.[54] This is Cocteau's version of the encounter, which might explain his silence and fascination:

> A heart entered the room; a red heart surrounded by a red cross in the middle of a white form that glided about, bowed, spoke, shook hands. This heart hypnotized me, distracted me from the face, beheaded the Arab's robe. It was the real face of the white form, and Charles seemed to hold his head against his breast like a martyr. And indeed the real head, burned by the sun, seemed a reflection of the heart, a mirage in all that African light. The cheekbones and the chin outlined the mirage's reliefs and tip.[55]

In this hyper-aestheticized image, the priest is cast as an exotic apparition, dismembered into heart, face, beard, cheekbones and robe. The order is both arbitrary and haphazard and suggestive of the visual idiom of narcissism and hallucination--perhaps of the faceted Cubist image. Cocteau is here engaging in the religious aestheticism that Maritain finds so disturbing in the *Dialogues'* endnote. Another example from his letters to Maritain describes Father Henrion as a theatrical specter and magician. It is followed by this remark: "A priest struck me with the same shock as Stravinsky and Picasso... Picasso and Stravinsky

---

[53] Ibid., p. 190; Maritain, *Art and Faith*, p. 42.

[54] Ibid., p. 183.

[55] Maritain, *Art and Faith*, p. 38.

know how to cover the paper with divine signs, but the Host is the only masterpiece Charles offers me."[56]

His detached observation of Father Henrion in both contexts is quite peculiar for a man reflecting on his religious conversion. It contrasts sharply with Raïssa's reflections and Maritain's efforts to help a man in great spiritual need—described by Raïssa as "a mission as delicate as it was difficult."[57] Cocteau himself had written to Maritain of his "lack of moral appetite" and "nauseated soul" before the conversion, adding, "Help came to me in the nick of time."[58]

The confession is sincere but the habits of the imagination too powerful to overcome. Cast as an aesthetic and erotic object—even orientalized—Father Henrion is turned into a sacred spectacle with Cocteau as spectator and director. Life and cinematography, faith and fantasy are here indistinguishable. The priest is in essence de-sanctified and desecrated, exactly as Maritain had cautioned in his criticism of *J'Adore*. Raïssa will mention Cocteau again on 15 December, 1931, describing what seems like a pathetic appearance, at a concert that she and Jacques attended: "Cocteau arrives wearing enormous thick white gloves, death enters with him. Desbordes has become quite thin and pale, he looks as if he had been iller than Cocteau."[59]

In his letters, Maritain warned Cocteau that his new life in the Mystical Body of Christ would not be free of rejection, falls and scandal.[60] But Christ's Love, he consoled him, would move him to reach out to all humanity.[61] He urged Cocteau to make the Cross the center of his temptations, reminding him of his encounter with Father Charles: "The heart that marks in red the whiteness of desert hermits' robes is the Heart of Truth."[62] The following line from *Dialogues* is most likely part of that conversation: "To choose the heart for emblem is to

[56] Ibid., p. 41.

[57] Raïssa Maritain, *Raïssa's Journal*, p. 183.

[58] Maritain, *Art and Faith*, p. 43.

[59] Raïssa Maritain, *Raïssa's Journal*, p. 214.

[60] Maritain, *Art and Faith*, p. 101.

[61] Ibid., pp. 95 and 126-30.

[62] Ibid., p. 109.

dedicate one's self to the only heart which does not lie, and it is encircled with thorns."[63]

Art "behaves like a god; it thinks only of its glory," Maritain repeatedly warns Cocteau; it's an "illusionist," a "pretty monster" that makes "beauty from dead matter."[64] "The painter may damn himself, painting doesn't care a straw, if the fire where he burns bakes a beautiful stained-glass window." But when art serves God, it becomes the "most worthy instrument" of grace that prepares the human race "for the life of the spirit."[65] For the artist, narcissism is a constant temptation. Modernism is indebted to this Romantic idolatry of (a deified) artistic self in the work of art, being oblivious, writes Maritain, to God's creative humility: "God does not adore His works...He does not cling to them, He lets them be spoiled by men."[66]

Steegmuller's contention that Cocteau was quite accustomed to conversions is valid and consistent with the aestheticism that we find in Cocteau's remarks about his life, times and art. On the surface benign and harmless, this tendency to translate experience into aesthetic form and moral value into aesthetic value had also a darker side, as Maritain cautioned.

Perhaps the most disturbing example is the period of the Vichy government and the Nazi occupation of France. Steegmuller and Frederick Brown paint an unfavorable portrait of opium addiction, opportunism and indifference. Brown is especially scathing in his judgment that Cocteau "failed to sense what categorical imperatives of shame and dignity the German occupation called into play."[67] And Steegmuller points out that Cocteau's response upon learning about the outbreak of the war and mobilization in September of 1939 was the simple question: "how will I get my opium?"[68]

---

[63] Maritain, *The Twilight of Civilization*, p. 49.

[64] Maritain, *Art and Faith*, pp. 95 and 96.

[65] Ibid., pp. 98 and 94.

[66] Maritain, *Art and Scholasticism and the Frontiers of Poetry*, p. 145.

[67] Frederick Brown, *An Impersonation of Angels: A Biography of Jean Cocteau* (New York: Viking Press 1968), p. 352.

[68] Steegmuller, *Cocteau*, p. 436

Cocteau's fascination with the aesthetic, spectacular aspects of Nazism in the presence of its conspicuous and undeniable evil is indeed troublesome. "I find these days exciting," he exclaimed of life in German-occupied France in 1940, "I am intensely curious about this unreal Paris."[69] Three years later, in *Comoedia* (May 1943), he was to praise sculptor Arno Breker, favored by the Nazi state and by Hitler himself, for his 1942 exhibit at the *Orangerie*, proclaiming that he looked forward to the day "when Breker's statues would invade the Place de la Concorde."[70] That same year, he had appeared with Breker on the cover of the Nazi propaganda publication *Signal*.

Maritain was right to find evil in art's alliance with illusion, narcissism and power and to see the demonic in their union, at a time when the world had not yet known how perversely art would turn against itself, making "beauty" out of barbarism. The colossal, lifeless, pseudo-classical sculpture of Arno Breker, Josef Thorak and of other artists who mistook fascism's obsession with racial degeneracy as a promise of cultural regeneration, recalls Maritain's remark about a civilization that is deprived of the living forms of its values and is more fascinated with destruction than creation.

Cocteau remained an admirer of Breker's art and advocated the sculptor's moral integrity throughout his life, ascribing to him the same supra-historical and supra-national status that he desired for himself, in the name of art. "I salute you Breker," he wrote in 1942, "from the high homeland of poets, a homeland where homelands do not exist."[71] Cocteau's bust, completed by Breker in 1963, stands next to his grave in the chapel at Milly-la-Foret, a testament to the moral supremacy of art and artist. As noted elsewhere, for Cocteau, it is the poet's prerogative to have no country, as it is his advantage to evade history and ignore morality.[72] For Breker, too, as he was to complain to Cocteau in 1952, his art was timeless and universal, while Nazism and his own affiliation with it were but unfortunate accidents of history.

---

[69] Ibid., pp. 438-39.

[70] Brown, *An Impersonation of Angels*, p. 359.

[71] Cornelia A. Tsakiridou, "Greece in Cocteau; Cocteau in Greece," *Journal of the Hellenic Diaspora* 26.1 (2000): 29.

[72] Ibid., p. 29.

4. Christian Culture

Modernism found in Maritain an astute critic but also a sympathetic friend. In earlier years, both he and Raïssa were especially optimistic if not excited about its prospects, and they often praised and agreed with Cocteau in that context. In an entry to her journal in March of 1919 about the purity and integrity of art, Raïssa mentioned Rouault and Cocteau as artists that have achieved "purity of intention."[73] Critical of Catholic attitudes toward modern art that at the time she considered ignorant, narrow-minded and "hard on artists," she hoped for a renewal that would reflect "the full and luminous Catholic doctrine."[74]

In 1924, Maritain described avant-garde art as striving "toward the purity of creative intelligence" and noted that "it is along this path that the promise of salvation lies: beset by death, a child of genius proved this to us by a masterpiece."[75] The "child" is Cocteau's friend and novelist Raymond Radiguet. In "The Frontiers of Poetry" (1927), Cocteau is a frequent source of commentary on the realism and spiritual character of Picasso's paintings, on the transcendent and mystical dimensions of modern poetry, and its willingness to "practice obedience and sacrifice."[76]

Maritain's choice of Cocteau quotations reveals more about Maritain than it does about Cocteau. It shows his eagerness to find in modernism signs of a spiritual regeneration. "The pitiable state of the modern world, a mere corpse of the Christian world," he explained, "makes one desire with particular intensity the re-establishment of a true civilization."[77] Anything approaching a confession of faith in Cocteau's writings drew Maritain's attention. He singles out this line: "Because Poetry, my God, it's you," and the following excerpt from a letter

---

[73] Raïssa Maritain, *Raïssa's Journal*, pp. 97-98.

[74] Ibid., pp. 95-96. Raïssa's ideas will influence *Art and Scholasticism*. Maritain indicates this in a footnote to the March 25, 1919 entry, adding that Raïssa's notebook contained extensive comments on art that were not published (Ibid., p. 98, footnote #5; p. 90). See also Maritain, *Art and Scholasticism and the Frontiers of Poetry*, p. 60.

[75] Maritain. *Art and Scholasticism and the Frontiers of Poetry*, p. 112.

[76] Ibid., pp. 131, 134, 149.

[77] Ibid., pp. 135-36, 137.

Cocteau wrote to him in 1926. Cocteau starts by quoting St. Therese of Lisieux and then offers his signature commentary on poetic sacrifice: "'To all the ecstasies I prefer sacrifice.' Poets should have these words tattooed on their hearts."[78] Tattoos and gloves were favorite Cocteau metaphors for the artist's sensual and illusory experiments

It might seem from these examples that Maritain misread Cocteau. But this is not true. Maritain knew all along that what he was detecting in Cocteau were only "certain profound desires of contemporary art."[79] Even though they pointed at the direction of a Christian renaissance, they were by no means evidence that its time had come.

Maritain's occasional ambivalence about modernism, and his optimism in the early twenties that it would deliver a renewal of Christian culture, can be better appreciated if viewed as an expression of three elements: first, his deep compassion for artists gifted by nature but tormented by their choices and by the spirit of their times; second, his commitment to hope as a Christian virtue nourished by Christ's Passion and Love; and third, the openness of the Thomist philosophy that he embraced.

Maritain's admiration of the Middle Ages was often criticized as a dangerous and sterile anachronism. His response was always consistent and valid. "Thomist philosophy," he wrote in 1931, "is a progressive and assimilative philosophy, a missionary philosophy...at the service of primary Truth...and Saint Thomas is not a relic of the Middle Ages...he is in all fullness of the expression the Apostle of our time."[80] Maritain tried to see all art through the universality of Thomism: "wherever art—Egyptian, Greek or Chinese—has known a certain degree of grandeur and purity, it is already Christian, Christian in hope, because every spiritual radiance is a promise and a symbol of the divine harmonies of the Gospel."[81] He found that promise in Cocteau.

---

[78] Ibid., p. 226, footnote #190; p. 229, footnote #209.

[79] Ibid., pp. 148-49.

[80] Maritain, *The Angelic Doctor,* pp. 97, 135-36.

[81] Maritain, *Art and Scholasticism and the Frontiers of Poetry*, p. 66. This is the kind of thinking that made Maritain such an important intellectual figure in Vatican II: see Smith, *Jacques Maritain*, pp. 24-26.

For Maritain, modernism was host to some of the worst fallacies drawn by the human mind. In the form of narcissism and nihilism, they threatened the spiritual, moral and intellectual integrity of the human person. But for Maritain that was not a final or irreversible condition. Even a decadent civilization "bears in its very substance the sacred heritage of human and divine values."[82] The antidote to the "anti-humanism" of modernity, he wrote, is the "humanism of the Incarnation."[83]

Maritain sought to ground the self-centered art of his contemporaries in a subjectivity that surrenders to Christ, and rediscovers art and beauty through His Passion. This is the direction, as we have seen, to which he wished to turn Cocteau. The Christian art that he anticipated would not be ecclesiastically prescribed. It would flourish out of this redeemed subjectivity, having been purified and re-humanized through the Cross. The true work of art remained for Maritain a rare phenomenon.[84]

To the great Christian artists from the past, such as Fra Angelico, de Zurbaran and El Greco, Maritain was willing to add Modernists such as Georges Rouault, Marc Chagall and Gino Severini. In their art, and especially in the work of Rouault, he saw the Christian spirit struggle against the forces of adversity, some human, some demonic, and emerge victorious.[85]

In the end, modernism for him was not the art of renewal, the integral art of the "true civilization" that he had hoped for. It was, rather, the art of the struggle and anguish of the human soul for redemption, a perilous passage at the end of which, purged and

---

[82] Jacques Maritain, *Art and Scholasticism with Other Essays*, (FQ Classics, 2007), p. 159.

[83] Ibid., pp. 164-65.

[84] Maritain, *Art and Scholasticism and the Frontiers of Poetry*, pp. 64-69.

[85] Maritain *Art and Poetry*, pp. 17-38. Cornelia A. Tsakiridou, "Vera Icona: Reflections on the Mystical Aesthetics of Jacques Maritain and the Byzantine Icon," in *Truth Matters: Essays in Honor of Jacques Maritain*, edited by John G. Trapani, Jr. (Washington: American Maritain Assocation, 2004), pp. 232-33.

renewed, art would one day rediscover its intrinsic order of sanctity, a sanctity modeled on the simplicity of Mary, the Mother of God.[86]

This time is yet to come. Judging from the state of post-modern art, its militant narcissism, its obsession with morbidity and nihilism, and the intrusion of aestheticism into morality, Maritain continues to be relevant. The contemporary artist is often no less confused than Cocteau, no less deprived of the true depths of art and humanity, and fascinated with illusion.

From Maritain's perspective, we are still under the modernist configuration. The threat of barbarism looms in our tolerance of what he called the "animalization" of man, the advent of a popular culture so anti-intellectual and base in its tastes that it cannot discern in life the radiance of beautiful form. But we also realize today that artists are as "hungry for beatitude" as Cocteau and other modernists were when they mistakenly sought in the rubrics of art "the mystical fullness that God alone can give."[87]

---

[86] Maritain, *Art and Scholasticism and the Frontiers of Poetry*, p. 149.

[87] Ibid., p. 36.

White Nights of the Soul:

Christopher Nolan's *Insomnia* & the Renewal of Moral Reflection in Film[1]

J. L. A. Garcia

"In this Light, how can you hide?
You are not transparent enough
while brightness breathes from every side.
Look into yourself: here is your Friend,
a single spark, yet Luminosity."

—Pope John Paul II, "Shores of Silence"[2]

"I said . . . to Eve[ning], 'Be soon'"

—Francis Thompson, "Hound of Heaven"[3]

"Insomnia is constituted by the consciousness that it will never finish–that is, that there is no longer any way of withdrawing from the vigilance to which one is held...The present is welded to the past, is entirely the heritage of the past: it renews nothing. It is always the same present or the same past that endures...

"...this immortality from which one cannot escape...a vigilance without recourse to sleep. That is to say, a vigilance without refuge in unconsciousness, without the possibility of withdrawing into sleep as into a private domain. "

—Emmanuel Levinas, *Time and the Other*[4]

---

[1] This article originally appeared in *Logos* 9:4 (Fall, 2006): 82-117 and is reprinted with permission. The author expresses his appreciation to Professors Laura Garcia and Thomas Hibbs, who helped him to look for deeper themes in movies and to think more seriously about them, although any mistakes are his own. J. Veith, V. Devendra, and Laura Garcia also assisted with citations and editing.

[2] John Paul II, "Shores of Silence," in *Collected Poems*, translated by Jerzy Peterkiewicz (New York: Random House, 1982), p. 7.

[3] Francis Thompson, "The Hound of Heaven," in *I Fled Him Down the Nights and Down the Days*, with commentary and notes by John Quinn, S.J. (Chicago: Loyola University Press, 1970).

1. Introduction

Today, most of what is called popular culture is part of our civilizational problem, not its solution. Still, renewing the civilization requires reaching people where they are, and we often spend much of our time, especially that we most prize, splashing about in television series, magazines, lowbrow websites, and motion pictures featuring Hollywood stars. Professor Fox-Genovese reminds us that, in *Art and Scholasticism*, Jacques Maritain advanced two damning statements of proportion: Literature is to Art as Vanity is to Moral Life and Poetry is to Art as Grace is to Moral Life.[5] If that is correct, then surely motion pictures must rank beneath literary fiction. Perhaps it is then perverse to scrutinize, in search of moral insight, an American-made feature film with familiar American movie stars (though a British director). Nonetheless, that is what this analysis seeks to do. We shall not claim that Christopher Nolan's work in his movie *Insomnia* constitutes artistry.[6] Susan Sontag famously wrestled with the question whether photography amounted to an art form, which surely leaves cinema even more in doubt. Even if there have been artists, even geniuses, of this most influential and impressive of media, Nolan has not produced a body of work that warrants his inclusion in that Pantheon. Still, Nolan displays fine film craftsmanship in this work, which also revolves around central moral questions. His movie depicts and perhaps affords glimpses of the operation of that Grace of which Maritain spoke.

The title of this piece makes reference to St. John of the Cross's poem "Dark Night [of the Soul]," which, in his commentary on the poem, the mystic describes as a night of "purgative contemplation"

---

[4] Emmanuel Levinas, *Time and the Other*, translated by R. A. Cohen (Pittsburgh: Duquesne University Press, 1987), p. 49.

[5] Elizabeth Fox-Genovese, Address to the American Maritain Association meeting: "The Renewal of Civilization," Atlanta, October 2004.

[6] *Insomnia*, released by Warner Home Video in 2002, directed by Christopher Nolan, written by Hilary Seitz, cinematography by Wally Pfister, edited by Dody Dorn, and music by David Julyan. Featuring performances by Al Pacino (as Dormer), Robin Williams (as Finch), Hilary Swank (as Burr), and Maura Tierney (as Clement).

following a voluntary discipline of self-denial.[7] His travel, and travail through this passage, "horrible and awful to the spirit," is guided by an inner luminosity. "This light," the saint writes, "grounded me More surely than the light of noonday/To the place where he (well I knew who!) was awaiting me/A place where no one appeared."[8] In our reflections, we do well to remember that such illumination must first penetrate the soul from without before it can serve as a lamp within. The article's title also invokes Dostoevsky's 1848 story "White Nights," set in St. Petersburg, subtitled "A Tale of Love from the Reminiscences of a Dreamer." For Dostoevsky's lonely dreamer, the nights are bright with wonders and promise. Its narrator rhapsodizes:

> It was a marvelous night. The sort of night one only experiences when one is young. The sky was so bright, and there were so many stars that, gazing upward, one couldn't help wondering how so many whimsical, wicked people could live under such a sky. This too is a question that would occur only to the young, the very young; but may God make you wonder like that as often as possible. Now, mentioning whimsical, angry people makes me think how well I behaved that day."

Recall, also, the story's last section, "The Morning", which begins "My nights were over. It was the morning after. The weather was bad. It was raining. The rain beat a gloomy tattoo against my window...Objects swam before my eyes. Fever was sneaking along my limbs." The tale ends this way: "So may the sky lie cloudless above you and your smile be bright and carefree; be blessed for the moment of bliss and happiness you gave to another heart, a lonely and grateful one. My God, a moment of bliss. Why, isn't that enough for a whole

---

[7] *Ascent of Mt. Carmel*, pp. 1578-80. According to the *Oxford Dictionary of Quotations*, 5th Ed., edited by Elizabeth Knowles (New York: Oxford University Press, 1999, corrected 2001, s.v. "Misquotations," p. 521), the phrase " . . . of the soul" was added in an English translation of St. John's "Noche Oscura" by David Lewis in his 1864 edition, *Complete Works [of John of the Cross]*.

[8] St. John of the Cross, *Dark Night of the Soul*, translated by Edgar Allison Peers (New York: Doubleday/Image, 1959, 1990), p. 34

lifetime?"[9] Can a moment of bliss given to another redeem a life, redeem it from its corruption? How does a life, how does a person, turn from good behavior to bad, and can a life suddenly reversed in this way really be thus redeemed? Is it still the same life? Can the same living human being perdure through such change? It is with such questions of morality and identity that this analysis engages through a reflection on Nolan's movie.

2. The Film and Its Background

Directed by Christopher Nolan, *Insomnia* was made in 2002, after his student film *Following* and his 2001 breakthrough hit, *Memento*. *Memento* attracted considerable attention on its release and, I think, is interesting chiefly for its complex, fractured narrative structure, running generally in reverse (like the stage and film versions of Harold Pinter's *Betrayal*) so that many episodes come as a surprise to the viewer, as they do for the protagonist (Leonard Shelby), who suffers from short-term memory loss. We understand them through a context supplied later, dramatizing for us our dependence on memory even as Shelby insists that memory is unreliable and no substitute for what he calls "facts." (The history of empiricism should remind us that there is no intelligible experience or knowledge without memory.) As a film, *Memento* is a triumph of form, but the substance of its ideas seems to this author thin and murky stuff.[10]

Nolan's *Insomnia* is an English-language remake of Erik Skjoldbaerg's Norwegian film of the same name, released five years earlier (1997).[11] In

---

[9] Fyodor Dostoevsky, "White Nights," in *Notes From Underground, White Nights, [Etc.]*, translated by A. R. MacAndrew (New York: Signet/ New American Library/ Penguin, 1980), pp. 7, 61.

[10] For an approach to that film that is more sympathetic and finds it more serious intellectually, see Michael Baur, "We All Need Mirrors to Remind Us Who We Are: Inherited Meaning and Inherited Selves in 'Memento,'" in *Movies and the Meaning of Life*, edited by Kimberly Blessing and Paul Tudico (Chicago: Open Court, 2005), pp. 94–110. Later in the article, I briefly discuss one part of Baur's interpretation.

[11] *Insomnia* (Norway), released by the Criterion Collection in 1997, directed by Erik Skjoldbaerg, and written by Nikolaj Frobenius and E. Skjoldbaerg. Featuring Stellan Skarsgaard's performance as Jonas Engstrom.

the Norwegian film, a Swedish police detective, in trouble because of a scandal where he was found in bed with a crime suspect during a police raid, goes to Norway to help solve a teenage girl's murder. Stressed by his professional humiliation, blinded by the northern fog, and disoriented by the long daytime, this detective (named Jonas Engstrom and played by Stellan Skarsgaard) accidentally kills another policeman–his Swedish partner, Erik Vik–as they close in on the murderer. Engstrom is thoroughly corrupt, groping a teenager whom he interrogates, toying with a woman detective, trying to seduce his hotel's desk clerk before she aborts the tryst. Most grievously, the killer, a crime novelist named Jon Holt, has seen Engstrom kill Vik and, to buy the man's silence, Engstrom plants evidence to frame the young girl's boyfriend for her murder. In the end, things take a different turn and Holt, who considers himself a sort of *doppelganger* to Engstrom, a kindred soul also trying to avoid punishment for an unpremeditated killing, dies. The woman detective, Hagen, gives Engstrom an incriminating cartridge-casing as he prepares to leave for home, sealing the concealment of his involvement in the policeman's death.

Nolan and his collaborators make some obvious changes, scripting the policemen as two L.A. cops, Will Dormer (played by Al Pacino) and his partner, Hap Eckhart. The two are under investigation back home and they travel to Alaska to assist in a local murder investigation. Nolan trades white and grey, museum-walled, Scandinavian-modern, urban apartment settings for rustic inns and cabins. The woman detective, Ellie Burr (played by Hilary Swank), is now an eager novice, excited to work on a big case, and avid to learn from and thrilled to work with a famous big-city detective. More important for our purposes here, the remake involves some relatively small but consequential changes in the plot and characters (in both the dramatic and moral senses of the latter term).

Where Engstrom eventually cooperates in Holt's plan to frame the dead girl's boyfriend for her murder, Dormer resists Finch's, even putting a gun to his head at one point. In his bleary-eyed, guilt-ridden condition, however, unsure even about his behavior in mistakenly shooting Hap, the detective is out-maneuvered by the clever and resourceful writer. Near the film's end, Will packs to return to L.A. in defeat, having failed to build a case against Finch and resigned to the latter's seemingly unavoidable frame-up of Randy, the boyfriend in the

American version. Dormer's conscience is also disquieted by the way in which the latter failure works to his own benefit, insuring that the threatening truth will be concealed and Finch will not implicate him in Hap's killing. Dormer tarries in Alaska only because he learns that his one-time protégé, the now suspicious and disillusioned Alaska detective Burr, has gone alone to Finch's cabin to recover evidence from him. Dormer, who alone knows Finch's murderous side, apprehends the young woman's danger. After a prolonged struggle against Finch, involving blades, blunt instruments, and guns, the detectives are alone, with Dormer mortally wounded.[12] Here Burr, like the woman detective in the original film, offers to discard evidence that implicates the visitor in the partner's killing. Unlike Engstrom, however, Dormer demurs, warning her against thus "los[ing] her way." These changes elevate the film's screenplay and narrative into the moral drama that is the primary concern of this analysis. I will try to show how, in fighting for Burr and against Finch, Will Dormer is struggling with and for his own self, the two characters representing different aspects of his past, possible futures, and versions of his identity.

Surprisingly, in a film touched by Hollywood, the relationship between Dormer and Burr remains one of admiration, requited by amused indulgence, not romantic passion or sexual opportunism. Nolan also adds, even more surprising in the switch from Europe to America, a layered moral complexity—the protagonist now benefits from the other policeman's death and has more than one reason, not all of them narrowly selfish, to feel relieved at this outcome, unexpected but not wholly regretted and only ambiguously unintended. Similarly, where the murderer Holt had vaguely invoked mathematics, perhaps intending a self-interested cost/benefit analysis to justify his and the Swedish policeman's trading cover-ups, now the "mathematics"

---

[12] This final episode delivers a special jolt because its brutal and sudden violence shocks in a film that, to this point, has dwelt more on violence's mournful aftermath than its graphic depiction.

mentioned by Finch, the American film's murderer, is explicitly a utilitarian calculus.[13]

Hilary Seitz, the remake's screenwriter, maintains in an interview that her version of the story plays in thirds: in the first, we think it a "fish-out-of-water" story about L.A. cops in Alaska; in the second, we think it's a "cover-up" story about a cop who's killed his partner; in the last, we think it's an "unholy-alliance" story about collusion between a murdering cop and a cop-admiring murderer.

3. Existential Themes: Identity and Two Personified Models

Nolan's *Insomnia* explores significant questions about the conditions of human existence and personal character. We will briefly discuss three main themes. First, there is a recurring return to the theme of identity, especially moral identity--that is, who one is--in a way that has implications for how one should act and react. The film engages this theme both directly, in the characters' talk about who they are, and also indirectly, and more dramatically, by presenting us (and the protagonist) with two characters who identify with him in different ways. These characters represent two aspects of his past, and also two future paths between which he must choose in the narrative's central drama. Second, in Nolan's hands, this matter of identity goes beyond the merely psychological found in, for example, Erik Erikson's 'identity crisis'. It also concerns evaluation, namely how good one is both *at* and *in* being what she is. In this case, the focus is on what distinguishes a good cop from a bad cop. Third and more deeply, this debate points towards the fundamental question of what makes our actions, and ourselves, to be moral and immoral, acceptable and regrettable, virtuous and vicious. Identity transforms role-assessment into moral assessment for such a person as Dormer, because his being a policeman is the role most salient in his self-image and self-conception. It is the self-description with which he most deeply identifies, the one that is most meaningful to him and that he sees as a (or even as *the*) principal

---

[13] Holt to Engstrom, contrasting devising a fictional murder and committing a real one: "When you've put all the pieces together, the account balances. Nothing is missing. You have complete control. Complete control. . . . It's all just mathematics. But it's impossible to calculate such a thing. You realize that afterwards."

source of meaning in his life.[14] Because of this, it also places at the center of his moral consciousness the traits of character that make someone good or bad in such a role.[15] Below, we shall see how this serves as an implicit rebuke and alternative to the utilitarianism and nihilism with which Finch seeks first to confuse, and then to seduce, Dormer into rationalizing his wrongdoing, into seeing things as the murderer sees them.

Interpreting Nolan's earlier movie, *Memento*, philosopher Michael Baur draws on the thought of Martin Heidegger: "Even though we are always thrown into the world with a past that defines who we are and what is meaningful for us, we are nevertheless also free to transform the meaning of the past by projecting ourselves into the future. [Quoting Heidegger's *Being and Time*:] 'Our lives are always a process of taking over who we have been in the service of who we will be.'" This analysis argues that something similar is afoot in *Insomnia*, taking the form in the film of a tug-of-war within Dormer between two modes of being, each one rooted in past incidents in his life, justified by its own moral vision, and embodied in a different character offering him divergent possible futures.[16]

Finch insists to Dormer on first meeting him, aboard a ferry, "I'm not who you think I am" (chapter 20). [17] Later encounters reveal that

---

[14] For a discussion of the importance of this in moral and political thought of the modernist epoch, see Charles Taylor's treatment, *The Ethics of Authenticity* (Cambridge: Harvard University Press, 1992).

[15] When, in the classic 1961 film *The Hustler*, George C. Scott's thuggish Bert tells Paul Newman's Fast Eddie that he (Eddie) has talent and was beaten by "character," he means a single-minded determination to win. We can agree, while allowing that it is *bad* character to which such success is owed.

[16] Baur, "We all Need Mirrors," p. 107. Baur thinks both that the film teaches that each of us is successively constituted by a variety of short-lived 'selves' and that this is correct. I will not here enter the interpretive issue, but think the imputed position plainly incoherent in raising but excluding any answer to the question who it is that is so constituted. Who is she herself? Here, I work with a more common-sense conception of identity and oneself.

[17] The DVD version of the film divides its action into discrete "chapters" (in preference to the more customary terminology of 'scenes'). This literary idiom, while affected, does serve to underscore what I judge to be the

Dormer does indeed have a stereotyped image of the killer as he brushes aside Finch's talk about the special circumstances in which he came to slay Kay, the young woman whose death has brought the L.A. detective to Alaska. Dormer tells the cop-admiring author and murderer that he no more intrigues the detective than does a clogged toilet fascinate the plumber: "you're my job." It will turn out that things are not so simple, but we should postpone that a little, for the more compelling question of identity is not concerning Finch but about who Dormer himself is. Admitting to the inn-keeper, Rachel, his feelings at the time about planting evidence a few years earlier to ensure the conviction of a child-murderer he thought a jury would otherwise acquit, Dormer says even then he knew, "This was gonna catch up with me. I don't do things like that" (chapter 27). This confession is accompanied by a flashback to an image of Dormer staring mournfully into space as he rubs incriminating blood into the clothing of the child-murderer Wayne Dobbs.

In a revealing sequence deleted from the film's theatrical version, Dormer and Rachel talk in a bar after he has found her emptying Hap's hotel room just after he mistakenly shot him. Dormer tells her that he and Hap had been partners for five years. Dormer says in his work he frequently deals with people who have "lost someone." Dormer finds that their feelings are often ambiguous, more complicated than expected, and discloses that he himself felt "embarrassed" as a boy over his brother's death in a fire.[18] In this conversation, still early in the murder investigation, Dormer tells Rachel that he'll stay in Nightmute as long as it takes "to find this guy," adding, "Not long." Perhaps it is himself whom Dormer has lost and now needs to find, though he does not yet fully realize it.

---

exceptional literacy, esp. moral literacy, of its screenplay. References herein to numbered chapters are to the DVD version of the film, except where otherwise noted.

[18] In the DVD's commentary, Nolan describes this as the only time till the last sequences where Dormer is fully honest with someone. He suggests that it was omitted in the theatrical version in part because the scene would come too early in the character's development for such straightforwardness, and perhaps also too early for Dormer to be so clear and accurate in his vision of himself.

I think that Dormer's character embodies a version of what is called the ethics of identity or, in the terminology of philosopher Charles Taylor, the 'ethics of authenticity'—better yet, the ethics of integrity. Though unaware of his project, Dormer strives toward a Kierkegaardian "purity of heart": a state of harmony, concord, and consistency across his general resolution of will, preferences, particular choices, actions, as well as his backward-looking attitudes (that is, an ability to look back over his choices and reactions with neither shame nor guilt). However, the possibility of people whose character is as corrupt as that of Finch should remind us that this inner consonance is not morally sufficient; there must also be harmony with natural human compassion for *each* person, not simply for *all* persons or for some such abstraction as 'humanity'.

In addition to these more direct (though not always explicit) invocations of identity in Seitz's screenplay (or, at least, in the movie's dialogue, since actor's improvisation may have played some role), Nolan's film also poses the problems of Dormer's identity indirectly and more dramatically by presenting him and the viewer with two additional characters, each of whom offers a model of the detective himself in some portion of his past and a possible future. These characters pose Dormer's, and the film's, central choice: between twin doppelgangers who illuminate contrasting aspects of the detective's distant and more recent past conduct.

The murderer, Finch, identifies himself as the L.A. detective's "new partner," beginning with the message he leaves for Dormer in their first personal contact, which also introduces his character to the viewer. Indeed, several times and in slightly different terms, he alleges a "partner[ship]" between himself and Dormer. Finch, a novelist of murder mysteries, reveals that as a younger man he tried to become a policeman. Now, he too applies procedures of professional inquiry to solve murders, though only those of his own fictional invention. He also sees himself as like Dormer in trying to understand criminals' minds, to get inside those forms of mentality, try them on, and work them through. Moreover, Finch thinks that this has given him psychological insights that extend beyond forensic psychology. There is now a deeper similarity, which Finch deems a bond. In his desperation and confusion, exacerbated by his sleeplessness, Dormer tries to pin Hap's killing on Kay's murderer (who turns out to be Finch).

Just so, Finch plans to frame Kay's abusive (but not homicidal) teenage boyfriend Randy for her murder. Most important, Finch thinks his crossing from fictional killings to real has both given him insight into what he now considers the artificial, even illusory, character of the moral difference between right and wrong, and also enables him to perceive the deeper affinity between those who commit crimes, even murders, and those who do not. On these bases, in his conversations with Dormer, Finch insists that he and Will share a similar situation, secret, and awareness, constituting a "partner[ship]" between them.

The L.A. detective fights against such involvement with Finch and repudiates any similarity between them. "Don't talk to me about us," he bluntly rebukes the writer. Alaska police investigator Ellie Burr embodies another alter ego for Dormer, representing a different aspect of him, this time a central and defining part of his more distant past as a police professional, where Finch reflects Dormer's more recent turn to planting evidence and framing a suspect. Burr has studied Dormer's cases in her academy training and wants to be more like him. She is his admirer, a fan, almost palpably delighted with this unexpected opportunity to work alongside, study, and learn from one of her professional heroes. In a different terminology, she might be called Dormer's *protégé* (protected one). Even though it is himself whom he jeopardizes, Will admonishes the novice to put more care into investigating the circumstances of Hap's death before filing her report on it. It is in fact Dormer's final and fateful choice to shield her from Finch, rather than Finch from her, that seals his fate and secures him a kind of redemption (chapter 30).

Like Dormer, Finch also had a young female admirer, Kay Connell, who relished his writing. Where neither Dormer nor Burr shows sexual attraction, Finch tells Dormer that he became sexually aroused while comforting Kay after an argument with her boyfriend and describes how he slapped her, first to "teach her a lesson" after she laughed at his arousal (presumably, erection) and then to silence her screams, finally killing her. He was unable to cope with her quick transition from the inferior's admiration to the superior's derision at a moment he describes as one of his own "vulnerab[ility]." Detective Burr, similarly, becomes disillusioned with Dormer, catching him in lies about what she realizes were his efforts to cover up some of the facts about Hap's death, and even questioning whether it was an accident. Dormer must decide whether to try to protect her and again become worthy of her respect. Here, the philosophically-minded viewer may glimpse an insight central to Kant's moral theory but that Aristotle and his followers seem to have missed. Moral deliberation and action do not arise to identify means to one's own happiness, but arise from concern lest we be unworthy of happiness. Both these men have killed and know what it is like, but Finch simply assumes that he and Dormer have experienced the same emotional reactions and have drawn a similar conclusion.

4. The characters' characters: What makes 'good cops' good?

Identity especially matters in moral assessment because someone's moral virtues, vices, and responsibilities are ones she has *as* this or that person, as being a parent, or citizen, or friend, or partner, or fellow, etc., and so to situate a person is to talk about what and therein who she is. Plainly, for Will Dormer, it is his status, his identity, as a policeman in which he is most deeply invested.[19] Thus, the question: "What does it take to be a good policeman" or as it is sometimes put, a "real cop?" is central for him. This question becomes a stand-in for a larger inquiry into the grounds of ethical assessment and the nature of virtue: what makes some conduct to be good conduct? What makes some among us good people? In what does being a good person consist? It is Ellie Burr and Walter Finch, I think, who personify in their lives, and in their encounters with Dormer, two ways of answering this question.

The day of their arrival in Alaska, Dormer allows, in conversation with Hap about the L.A. police internal examination, that, although he thinks himself a good cop, together the partners have committed misdeeds that the investigation will likely uncover. In a more hostile phone conversation after Hap's death, Dormer snarls to the Internal Affairs investigator Warfield that officers like Warfield and his fellows in I.A. "suck the marrow out of real cops." At this point, Dormer is still desperately and confusedly casting about for a way out of his dilemma. Later, as he proceeds with his cover-up of the truth about Hap's killing, the film provides a graphic illustration of the depths to which Dormer

---

[19] The detective shares his life with no spouse or children.

has sunk. He fires a bullet from Finch's gun into a dead dog he comes across in a filthy alley, planning to retrieve the bullet and switch it for the one with which he mistakenly shot Hap as the two visiting detectives pursued the fleeing Finch in fog-shrouded woods. Here we see how Dormer has descended from the white gloves he used in (what we learn was) an earlier episode of planting evidence to frame a guilty man he thought would otherwise go free to the bloody hands (though encased this time in translucent gloves) he gets recovering the bullet from the dog's slimy corpse.

Like the Darwinian bird who is his namesake, Finch is the one who has adapted to survive. It comes as little surprise that, for him, the good way to live is one that manifests successful strategies for survival. This is the implicit nature of the "partner[ship]" he offers Will. Finch will enable him to survive with his career and reputation intact if Dormer cooperates in Finch's plan to escape punishment for Kay's death by framing her young boyfriend, Randy. After Dormer blows up at him during a police investigation, Finch tells the Alaskan detectives that if Dormer is indeed a good cop, as they insist, then he (Finch) would "hate to see a bad cop" (chapter 24).

Dormer is upset (and draws on this real anger when he feigns an uproar to abort an initial inquiry into Hap's death) that he (and the local police) did not, but should have, known about the tunnel that the murderer used to escape from the trap into the fog whose shrouding density led to Hap's death. However, the truth is that human beings cannot anticipate and specially plan for every contingency. That is one reason we need to develop character traits, dispositions–virtues–to see us through unexpected turns of events.[20]

While still dazzled by her hero-worship, Ellie quotes to Dormer a remark of his that she had found in her police academy research on his

---

[20] John Doris's book *Lack of Character* (Cambridge: Cambridge University Press, 2002) argues that in general people do not have the kind of character traits that would count as virtues. Let us here set aside flaws in the psychological experiments and philosophical reasoning that purport to show the virtues' infrequent instantiation. The chief moral issue, however, is whether we should strive to cultivate and retain them, whether they are possible, achievable, and important. Not whether they are common.

cases: "A good cop can't sleep because a piece of the puzzle is missing. A bad cop can't sleep because his conscience won't let him." Dormer is at this point himself the bad cop. He has descended from framing one murderer for crimes from whose punishment he'll otherwise escape to attempting to frame another for a killing that Dormer himself committed, to a desperate struggle to spare himself from Finch's offer to help pin Kay's murder on her teenage boyfriend Randy. Dormer only half-remembers Ellie's quotation as a remark made by his own earlier self. He responds, "Yeah, that sounds like something I'd say." This manifest distance from himself, at least from an earlier and better self, poignantly invokes the film's theme of moral identity. It shows starkly his own migration from good cop to bad. He seems to flirt with a familiar moral skepticism, condescending to the supposedly immature young man who could pronounce on things in such simplistic, black-and-white terms. Yet, he knows that the younger Dormer's views, while more innocent, were not therefore immature, and that the contrast he drew should not have been dismissed as simplistic, but bore the clear simplicity of truth.

The chief moral danger Dormer faces is that he will adjust and adapt as Finch has, that he will come to sleep soundly, no longer troubled by a strangled or wearied conscience. That is the temptation Finch offers as a model and "partner." It is instructive to recall that Aristotle talks of persons linked in some forms of friendship as "other selves." Dormer's inability to sleep leaves him struggling day and (indistinguishable) night with the choice between being Ellie's good cop and Finch's adapted, adjusted bad cop. Though he longs to sleep, it is his constant wakefulness that provides him with the unwanted but needed opportunity to struggle for his identity, his self. The old saw is wrong: the wicked can rest. Aquinas affirms, paradoxically, that the pleasures of sin are part of God's way of punishing the sinner. His point is that the Lord sometimes makes it harder for us sinners to save ourselves, or to reform, by providing us pleasing distractions. Eventually, sin's soothing delights take on a horrifying visage. As we shall see below, though Dormer does not recognize it, his sleeplessness is less a curse than a blessing.

5. Images and Symbols

Dormer's sleeplessness, which is disturbed by insistent intrusions of light, indicates his troubled soul and gives Nolan's film its central motif, the one from which it borrows its title. Our awareness of this central symbol is aided by an array of additional metaphors and symbols, to which we should now turn, beginning with some of the movie's striking visuals. As the opening credits start, a small plane flies in and out of dense banks of clouds, the camera sometimes outside capturing the scene, sometimes inside the cabin with three men, a pilot and his two passengers. The elusive lucidity and unclarity of the fog continues through the pilot's ominous warning to his passengers, L. A. Police detectives Hap Eckhardt and Will Dormer, entering rural Alaska, "It's gonna get rough." It will, indeed, for both men, though in very different ways. This initial haze subtly introduces the film's continuing themes of longing for peace while fearing truth and clarity. Under the credits, we get images of (1) dark blood, spreading outward on a white cloth, permeating a rectangular weave of silvery fabric in (receding) close-ups, interspersed with (2) craggy, unforgiving peaks of icy mountain spires, and with (3) the plane coming into and out of fog, the screen bleaching white as it enters the fogbank. At the end of this sequence, with the pilot's warning, his plane suddenly crosses almost unimaginably lush, verdant forest—hinting at the possibility of an inner peace to match this idyllic glimpse—then plunges into impenetrable fog. This theme is resumed a short time later in the film. Having set a trap for the killer, luring him to a rustic cabin to retrieve some evidence, the detectives suffer a setback when a policeman clumsily knocks over a megaphone alerting the suspect. The detectives rush the cabin and, finding it empty, plunge through its broken flooring only to find themselves instantly enveloped in thick fog, stumbling over slippery rocks in their pursuit (chapter 8). That pursuit is not only unsuccessful, but sets the stage for Dormer to shoot into the beclouded scene where his bullet finds his partner instead of the killer, Finch.

Several times during the movie, we come across a bright glare, which might eventually facilitate vision but at first only blinds and dizzies both the characters and us viewers. This painful light serves as a symptom of Will's temporary insomnia, helping to disorient him during a phone call from Finch, who offers the once-good detective his

Faustian trade of cover-ups (chapter 22). (The proposed trade may recall the memorable "criss-cross" proposed, and unilaterally begun, in Hitchock's *Strangers on a Train*.) This luminosity seems to unsettle Will in ways that go beyond the physiological, perhaps threatening to illuminate an ugly fact about his past conduct, and an unambiguous one about recent actions, both of which he desperately wants hidden. For the same reason, however, this light also indicates Grace seeking Will Dormer, who may well here represent our own wills. The light will uncover the truth and, frightening and painful as the process may prove, it is only the truth that can set Will free. Significantly, such a glare seeps around and under a window-shade in Dormer's Alaska hotel room with an insistence we want to call merciless, as Dormer desperately tries to block it out just prior to his final conversation with Rachel about his past catching up with him (chapter 27). The light is not merciless, however, but indicates a Mercy that will not be deterred.

The fog and the light serve to blind and confuse, threatening Dormer and his fellows with losing their way.[21] As his sleeplessness and moral confusion combine to addle Dormer's mind, his car scarily spins out of control on a winding Alaska road (Chapter 28). Again, in a scene to which we shall return below, Dormer warns Ellie in the film's final lines, "Don't lose your way. . . . Just let me sleep" (Chapter 30). This pairing of the need to maintain the right path with Dormer's longing for rest links the film's two most important and pregnant themes. In fact, the L.A. detective will find tranquility only when he has regained the right path and rests, as they say, in peace.[22] The theme of dangerous, unsteady footing recurs. Rachel tells Dormer and Hap, upon their first arrival at the hotel she operates, that people like them, from the "lower 48," reveal themselves in their gait: "I can tell by your walk...Unsure." More dramatically, broken, perilous flooring marks both the trapdoor in the cabin beneath and near which the first chase

[21] An Alaska mental health clinician whom I met at a London medical ethics conference confirmed in conversation with me that the sleeplessness the state's long days can cause newcomers sometimes triggers both auditory and visual hallucinations, as Dormer's character experiences.

[22] We shall not rest till we rest in Him, as Francis Thompson's poem "The Hound of Heaven" vividly reminds.

ensues and the flooring in Finch's other cabin, where the film's action culminates and ends.

The motif of treacherous footing is memorably visualized in the movie's most harrowing sequence. Dormer quickly identifies the mystery-writer Finch as a suspect and goes to his home to investigate. Finch returns home, realizes that someone has entered and is still inside his apartment, and flees. Will gives chase through streets and down to the waterfront where Finch lures the detective out onto a run of logs in the river. The scene is as beautiful and majestic as it is terrifying, handsomely shot both from above and, apparently with hand-held cameras, at the level of the actors' bodies. Having impetuously continued the chase onto this new terrain, over which Finch nimbly speeds, the L.A. cop soon discovers himself over his head literally as well as figuratively. The camera again is at the level of the character's head, which is, more than once in the short sequence, nearly crushed between crashing logs as he surfaces for air. Through the camera's lens, we even peer up from depths at both the detective and the logs above him.[23] Plainly, the scene is rich in metaphorical significance. This is where Finch's ability to adapt, like the bird whose name he bears, is most effectively manifested. Both characters' upright posture on the riverbound logs calls to mind logrolling and, of course, in political slang 'logrolling' is a term for the cynical trades wherein politicians help each other to the public detriment (chapter 18). Finch proposes just such a deal to Will, a swap wherein Finch will help frame Randy for Hap's death at Dormer's hands, provided Will helps him frame Randy for Kay's death at Finch's. That Finch knows his way around in a way that Dormer does not, that entering the logs places Will in mortal peril, certainly points to the moral stakes of playing along, 'cooperating in evil' as the theologians call it. For, should he follow Finch, Will's soul is no less in jeopardy than is his body on the fast moving logs in the rushing river.

The water here, in the plunge through the floating logs, is turbulent. In several other scenes, we spy water washing, foaming, enveloping,

---

[23] Nor should we slight here the work of the sound engineers in skillfully amplifying the river's roar and the crash of the colliding logs in the air and then muffling them when the camera submerges beside Dormer.

and churning, for example, in the foam behind the ferry where Finch outlines to Will the 'logroll' (deal) he envisions. In such scenes, the water's turbulence parallels the troubled state of Dormer's mind and conscience. There is, however, sometimes a very different view of water, especially in the placid waterfall shown as the plane moves towards its landing in the opening sequences. There, water seems to offer hope, perhaps symbolizing purgation, cleansing, even baptism.[24]

Finally, we should note a few of the other optical motifs that the film skillfully (and not always visually) offers. Dormer says at the beginning of the investigation, as he examines the victim's corpse, that the killer "crossed a line and didn't *blink*." He adds, "You don't come back from that," explaining his belief that this killer will strike again and more viciously. Later, the film recalls Dormer's stare as he finished planting evidence to catch an earlier case's murderer. This stare, accompanying his narrated recollection that he knew this wrongdoing would catch up with him, seems the functional equivalent of the blink that Finch never made. It is the fact that Dormer can still save himself, can still "come back," that provides the film its central ethical drama.

The need for moral clarity may lie behind a different optical motif: Dormer's eyes play tricks on him as his sleeplessness waxes and his conscience becomes more guilty. They offer him images of the living Hap as he pretends to join the search in the woods for his partner's killer and again, later, in his hotel room's chair. Sometimes, the optical symbolism approaches the didactic. Near the film's end, Dormer feels himself outsmarted by Finch and is close to a despairing surrender. As he struggles with palpable desperation to block out the creamy yellowed sunlight that bleeds through and around his room's feeble window shade, the hotelkeeper Rachel comes in response to complaints about the noise caused by Dormer's frenzied rearrangement of the room's sparse furnishings in his losing battle against the insistent light. Though we might expect her to upbraid the detective when she confronts him, she instead lives up to her surname. (The symbolism of the names of various characters is treated in the next section.) When

---

[24] When I presented some of this material at a University of Notre Dame conference, one member of the audience suggested a possible allusion to Lady Macbeth in this motif.

he pitiably pleads to her, "It's so fucking bright in here," she gently corrects him: "No, it's dark in here."

Perhaps most vividly, near the film's close we learn that what looks at the beginning like someone's rubbing a shirtcuff to remove a bloodstain is actually Dormer's rubbing blood *into* the clothes of a murderer, in the course of which process he pulls the shirt partly on. This reversal of what we have seen, giving it a new and unexpected meaning and significance, pointedly demonstrates what Dormer is becoming and whose side he joined when he decided that his high-minded goal of convicting the guilty justified his planting evidence.[25] What we read as one crime turns out to be a transgression of a different kind.

6. Names

The richness of symbols used in the film is not limited to the guiding motif of sleeplessness and the visual and thematic elements we have just examined. Many of the names in the English version of *Insomnia* are likewise symbolic, even allegorical. Indeed, some critics complained of excesses here. First, the action is set in the town of Nightmute, Alaska, which is perhaps too obviously allegorical a name. Enveloped in a long 'silent night' where all is "bright" through daylight hours that stretch long into night, not all is "calm" in Nightmute. Russia's white nights showered Dostoevsky's young dreamer, who was mentioned at the beginning of this analysis, with dazzlements and astonishment that people could be wicked in such a world. His later recollection of them offers the satisfied, if deluded, recollection that he behaved well. The film's main character, Detective Will Dormer, is not young. In contrast with Dostoevsky's dreamer, Dormer is old, weary, and cynical, and all too aware that he has not behaved so well. Alone with his conscience, where sleep might have brought "heavenly peace," the daytime brings Dormer bleary-eyed hallucinations and the night dream images of a past sin that constitutes a hellish torment.

---

[25] This small but consequential reversal recalls the slight auditory change and pivotal reversal of meaning at the end of Coppolla's great 1974 film *The Conversation*, where "He'd *kill* us if he got the chance" shifts to "He'd kill *us* if he got the chance," transmuting the poignantly prescient fear of the perceived victims into the cool rationalization of the actual victimizers.

The characters' names are similarly fraught with symbolism.[26] Patently, Detective Will Dormer is not a name the filmmakers have picked at random. In fact, the protagonist's Christian name may be as important as his surname, introducing the theme of choice and images of sleep and sleeplessness. He knows how badly he has behaved, and what he experiences is not a "moment of bliss," but one of long delayed rest and peace. It is enough "for a lifetime" in that it redeems a life gone bad. Like John of the Cross, Dormer undergoes a reflection that proves purgative. The cinematographer, in one of the DVD's interviews, mentions the mirrors in the police offices, and the crucial scene, glimpsed several times, in which Dormer turns out to be planting evidence, is mainly seen in a reflection. Unlike Saint John, however, Dormer's purgative nights are involuntary, nudged along by his insomnia, his guilty conscience, and troubling new entanglements.

Detective Hap Eckhardt, Dormer's L.A.P.D. partner, has cut a deal, promising to cooperate in the investigation into police misconduct, thus threatening not only Dormer's reputation but also the convictions and incarcerations built on it. He dies, shot by Dormer in blinding fog, in an accident whose status as such Dormer himself comes to doubt. Hap's first name may hint at the chanciness of causal chains, an aleatory characteristic that serious moral theory recognizes as rendering them unsuitable to bear the weight of differentiating right from wrong actions. Some philosophers, notably Bernard Williams and Thomas Nagel, speak of "moral luck" both in the consequences of someone's actions and in the circumstances and choices she comes to face.[27] Character traits can constitute a hedge against moral luck, girding us to hew to what is virtuous and decent even in times of adversity and not just from the good fortune of an easy life.

---

[26] I will suggest that several, particularly those of the women, are charactonyms, indicating traits of personality or character of those who bear them. Others, such as Finch and Warfield, I suggest, have a deeper significance.

[27] See Thomas Nagel, *Mortal Questions* (Cambridge: Cambridge University Press, 1979), ch. 3, and Bernard Williams, *Moral Luck* (Cambridge: Cambridge University Press, 1981), ch. 2.

Detective Ellie Burr heads the investigation for the police force in Nightmute, Alaska. She (in French, *elle*) is a 'thorn in the side' as Dormer's youthful admirer. She helps provide the 'prick' of conscience, 'needling' Dormer, not letting him rest. Perhaps she represents what some have theorized is a woman's distinctive moral voice.[28]

Walter Finch is the young girl's killer, who witnesses Dormer shoot Hap and Hap's pained death as he accuses Dormer and struggles to get away from him. Finch later offers to Dormer to trade help in matching cover-ups. What of this name? The finch is a songbird, and perhaps this directs us to attend to his utterances. More important, finches were one of the species whose survival in different environments through differential adaptation (esp., of beaks to varying food sources) inspired Darwin's evolutionary thought.[29] Finch is a writer of murder mysteries, who has come to Alaska, adjusted over time to the nighttime sun and, having struck Kay in a fit of passion, killed her. Rapidly adjusting once again, he has calmly cleaned her body and covered up the crime. Now he schemes to manipulate Dormer into helping him avoid capture. Finch is, at one point, described as Kay's "familiar": an odd phrasing that calls to mind the term "familiar" as used for an animal inhabited by a spirit (often a malign one) accompanying someone. Is Finch

---

[28] See Carol Gilligan, *In a Different Voice* (Cambridge: Harvard University Press, 1993).

[29] "The remaining land-birds form a most singular group of finches, related to [and differing from] each other in the structure of their beaks, [etc.] . . . [T]wo species may be often seen climbing about the flowers of the great cactus-tress; but all the other species of this group of finches . . . feed on the dry and sterile ground. . . . The most curious fact is the perfect gradation in the size of the beaks in the different species . . . from one as large as that of the hawfinch to that of a chaffinch . . . Seeing this gradation and diversity structure in our small intimately-related groups of birds, one might really fancy that from an original paucity of birds in the [Galapagos] archipelago, one species had been taken and modified for different ends." Charles Darwin, "Journal of Researches" (a.k.a. "Voyage of the Beagle," 2nd ed., 1845, in *Darwin on Evolution*, edited by T. F. Glick and D. Kohn [Indianapolis: Hackett, 1996], pp. 28-29). From this and similar observations on the *Beagle*'s 1831-1836 voyage, Darwin came not just to "fancy" but to hypothesize that the different bills evolved on different islands as adaptations to the islands' differing food sources.

Dormer's "familiar" in this sense of the term? Finch is metaphorically an animal (bird namesake, human predator), a malign spirit who "accompanies" the reluctant Dormer, phoning him, meeting him, haunting his nights.

Rachel Clement, the keeper of the Alaskan motel where Dormer and (briefly) Hap stay, is not exactly the scriptural weeping Rachel. Still, she refuses to judge or condemn when Will confesses to her, only listening sympathetically and offering him merciful (clement) words, as we discussed above.

As for the minor characters, Detective Warfield is absent and unseen, although often mentioned, and he is once briefly heard on the phone. Warfield is the L.A.P.D. Internal Affairs investigator. Surely, this is one of the film's pregnant, if admirably understated, tropes: the field of battle where the moral struggle occurs is an internal affair, something within the agent's soul, not a matter of results in the external world—not even the number of lives lost and saved. We will examine this and related points in the next section. Randy is the physically abusive and unfaithful (i.e., randy) boyfriend of the dead girl, Kay Connell.[30] Finch tries to frame him for Kay's murder. Dobbs, the child-murderer whom Dormer (and Hap?) framed some years earlier, is never seen or heard. He is visually indicated only by flashback scenes of Dormer 'daubing' Dobbs's clothes with blood to frame him.

Even some of the story's animals and books are given resonant names. Finch has two dogs. According to the jacket of one of his books that the viewer glimpses, one of them is named Lucy (light), a gesture towards the film's chief theme. We also come to know of three mystery novels that Finch has written. Shown, or mentioned on the glimpsed jackets of other books, they are titled *Otherwise Engaged*, *Blood Shack*, and *Murder...[at?] Sunrise*. Each of these titles seems to prefigure one or more episodes in the screenplay. First, Dormer investigates an Alaskan

---

30 Might it be significant that the dead girl's name is phonically indistinguishable from a mere letter? Is this, perhaps, meant to underscore the ease with which she can be reduced to anonymity, as when Finch urges Dormer to abandon his duty to bring her real killer to justice, invoking "the other Kays" who will be endangered if catching her killer sets other killers free?

murder in order to flee being investigated in LA. We also recall Dormer's secret agenda of covering up his killing of Hap while catching Kay's murderer. In addition, there is Finch's reversal of roles from suspect to unwanted partner. All of these episodes suggest covert forms of engagement beneath the public ones. Second, the violent attacks on Ellie and Dormer near the film's end, set in a rustic cabin, along with the mention and glimpses of Finch's painstaking cleaning of Kay's corpse in the same place, give substance to the description "blood shack." Finally, the early morning gunplay at the film's end reminds us that the third title, "murder at sunrise," almost finds a referent in the script's events.[31]

7. Moral Insight

The first moral issue we should treat is the one roughly captured in the question raised by the screenwriter herself: what circumstances make an event into an accident. The matter here is not merely of terminological significance, but ethical significance as well: which factors serve to mitigate or erase someone's culpability for her behavior? More deeply, what can justify a course of action? These questions are tied to the issue of moral identity, noted earlier. Finch thinks—at least, he repeatedly maintains—that he is not who and what Dormer initially thinks him to be. That is, he is not a vicious murderer who deserves to be caught and punished, because he killed his young admirer Kay Connell only by accident. But, his own account of the event belies this description. As he comforted her after a fight with Randy, he reveals that he became sexually aroused and began to slap her when she found this ridiculous, laughing at him. He insists to Dormer that he "never meant to do it," that he killed but never murdered the girl. Her killing was not premeditated, but his assault on her was intentional and, as it continued, so may her death have been intended. Even if it was not, Finch is reasonably held to account for the foreseeable effect of his unjustified and immoral behavior. Finch compares his lethal attack on Kay to Dormer's shooting Hap in the thick fog. But the analogy is faulty. The detective was justified in firing to hit a fleeing suspect who had just shot one of the Alaskan policeman pursuing him, and hit only by mistake. (Quite literally: in the fog,

[31] There is, to be sure, a homicide but, just as surely, it is justified defense.

Dormer took Hap's figure for that of the suspect.) Finch, however, had already exceeded his rights in striking Kay. That he lost control and beat her to death cannot excuse his conduct, but it makes his crime manslaughter, that is, a kind of murder. The calm meticulousness with which he then cleansed her body to remove forensic evidence only heightens the contrast with Will's inner torment.

The truth matters little to Finch, who weaves fictions by trade. In a revealing exchange between the two principals, Dormer asks, "Is this an accident?" pointing his gun at Finch's head. Finch replies, "If you want it to be" (chapter 25). *Pace* Finch's claim, however, shooting a man doesn't become an accident simply from wanting it to be one, but only from not wanting and meaning it be his shooting. Aquinas rightly held that it is the agent's intentions that fix the moral status and species of her actions. Anscombe reminded us that there are objective and realistic limits on what we can intend any action to be. To think we can make our actions whatever we want, simply by our wanting itself, is to deny any objective truth to these matters at all, especially to deny that there can be truth and falsehood in moral judgments. In the next section, it is argued that what Finch presents principally as a consequence-based moral theory in fact masks a deeper moral nihilism.

The fact is that ethics proceeds from the outside in. Anyone's self-knowledge is limited; a person's own past motives are sometimes unclear, even opaque, to her, and not just in the minute details. Still, the partial indiscernibility of motives does not make them wholly undetectable, nor unimportant. Finch, the author, holds forth to Dormer, on the importance of motives: "It's all motivation. What did you feel [when Hap died]? Guilt? Relief?" Contrast Dormer's professed skepticism about the significance of motivation, when he sneers at Finch: "Reasons for doing what you did? Who gives a fuck?" (chapter 20). Human action, as such, is done for reasons and with intentions, a fact that the late philosophers Donald Davidson and Elizabeth Anscombe affirmed.[32] The particular reasons for which someone acts will not always serve to vindicate her action, as Dormer rightly insists.

---

[32] See G. E. M. Anscombe, *Intention* (Ithaca: Cornell University Press, 1957); Donald Davidson, *Essays on Actions and Events* (Oxford: Oxford University Press, 1980).

To think otherwise is to succumb to the error that good ends can suffice to justify any means. Still, as Aquinas affirmed, it is someone's plans for realizing an objective that determine the moral character of her actions. They do that insofar as they show how the agent is in acting responding to the various valuable (and disvaluable) possibilities in play in her situation. It is in intending objectives that we 'own' them, make them ours, and thus identify with them, investing them with our identity and investing our identity in them.

For Finch, at least as he puts it to Dormer, the problem is one in what some have called moral mathematics. Finch challenges Dormer to consider the consequences for other cases if he secures Finch's conviction for the murder of Kay Connell. For then, Finch will convincingly reveal Dormer's own morally suspect part in Hap's death, thereby discrediting him, which will likely free many of the killers that Dormer's past testimony and investigations helped convict. "What about the other Kay Connells?" Finch challenges the compromised detective. "Do the math. You're a pragmatist; you've got to be [as a cop]" (chapter 21).

Do the ends justify the means? Machiavelli famously thought so, the utilitarians agreed, Finch has argued their case, and Dormer himself appeals to this old saw to rationalize the past conduct whose exposure now threatens him and whose moral meaning that peril is forcing him reluctantly to face. In his sleepless, addled state late in the movie's action, he recalls the feel of Dobbs's clothing, the texture of his own descent from grace. This memory comes to him as he packs his own clothes to leave Alaska, thinking he has failed to catch Finch and must accede to the latter's framing of Randy. He offers his rationale to the merciful Ms. Clement, his voice now stripped of its conviction, betraying the purported reasoning for a rationalization. "Dobbs needed to be convicted. The end justifies the means, right?" (chapter 27).

The true mark of moral commitment, however, is not that to which one is committed but that which one refuses to do.[33] In contrast to the

---

[33] Those interested in an introduction to some of the problems in utilitarian moral theory might profitably consult Sterling Harwood's "Eleven Objections to Utilitarianism" in *Moral Philosophy: a Reader*, 3rd ed., edited by Louis P. Pojman (Indianapolis: Hackett, 2003), pp. 179–92.

utilitarians' emphasis on desirable results, the traditions of Kant and the theorists of virtue focus on the rights and 'inviolability' of prospective victims. This is progress, but the film digs even deeper in a way reminiscent of the famous suggestion of one of Graham Greene's compromised characters that matters of good and evil go deeper than those of right and wrong.[34] The issue is not merely one of somebody's conduct and its effects, but of what fits with who she is.

If the agent's ends do not justify her chosen means, what does? In the words of the British philosopher Sir David Ross, what makes right acts right? The argument of this author, which requires further development at another time, is that moral justification proceeds from within the agent, from her motives and choices, to the action she performs, not from the action's effects in the outside world. While the movie, of course, does not explicitly articulate a moral theory, there are hints within it of a similarly input-driven account of right and wrong. "What the hell's wrong with you?" a pedestrian shouts to Dormer when he starts his car and almost runs her down. This incident unfolds just after he has switched the bullet he fired from Finch's gun into the dead dog with one from Hap's corpse (chapter 13). There is, then, never merely wrong or right action, but always something wrong or right *with us.*

It is character that is central, the usual site and source of the moral motivations and choices that determine our actions' moral status and significance. Because character itself—at least, good character—involves and requires a certain integrity, that is, an integration of the self, its motives, and its projects, there is support for Kierkegaard's pronouncement, borrowed from Scripture, that moral consistency demands "willing one thing." We find Dormer, however, in his moral confusion, acting at cross-purposes, covering up one killing while investigating another; trying to frame Finch for one death (Hap's) and to build a legitimate case against him in another (Kay's). This is antithetical to genuine integrity (that is, the moral virtue of integrity) and it is in this, rather than in Finch's distracting numbers game, that moral substance lies.

---

[34] My reference is to Pinkie in Greene's *Brighton Rock.*

Character involves facts about both actual and counterfactual situations: what is, but also what would be. In a related way, several of the movie's characters debate the moral significance of both what was done and what would have been done. Thus, Dormer charges that Finch would have slept with Kay, as if it does not matter that he did not. Similarly, Finch insists that Randy would have hurt Kay worse if she had lived, as if it did not matter that Randy did not in fact kill her and that he could be licitly punished for it as if he had.[35] In such implicit reasoning, both go too far. Still, both Dormer and Finch are right to say that people's inclinations (as shown in counterfactuals) do reveal something morally important about them, if not about their actions. Their dispositions to act and react, their traits of character and their commitment all entail facts about what they *would* do in various circumstances. In short, it is there we find their virtues and vices (chapters 23, 25). Often, the most important effects of a course of action are not on others and their happiness, but on the agent herself and her character. The late Pope John Paul II stressed the reflexivity of action, its effects in helping shape and confirm the agent's own traits. Some dialogue in the film also invokes this theme. "You're tainted forever. You don't get to pick when you tell the truth. Truth is beyond that," Finch tells Dormer, correctly pointing out that people will lose trust in Dormer once some of his frame-ups are discovered (chapters 20, 25).[36]

But is this not comparatively minor stuff? Can concern for the agent's motives and traits really serve as an adequate replacement for a focus on the happiness and suffering of other people? No, it cannot do so entirely. Agents must concern themselves with others' well being, and that is a principal mark of their virtue. It does not follow that the moral judge or ethical theorist must do the same. In any case, the

---

[35] Compare the plot of Stephen Spielberg's 2002 film, *Minority Report*, wherein police apprehend people and have them charged for "future crimes." Someone who will certainly decide to do evil unless impeded should be dissuaded, even prevented. But she cannot be punished, not legitimately, not even intelligibly.

[36] On "taint," note our surprise, which was mentioned earlier, when we learn at the end that the unidentified hand was not rubbing the blood out of the white fabric but rubbing it in, polluting. Dormer's corruption has already sunk deep by the time the film's main action begins.

problem here is not one of magnitude, as the movie's dialogue handsomely affirms. In a revealing conversation between detectives Dormer and Burr, when they first meet, the L.A. veteran instructs the Alaskan neophyte not to ignore what she considers minor matters. He reminds her that "small things" display character. "People give themselves away [in small things]," he cautions, employing an intriguing ambiguity. "It's all about small stuff. Small lies, small mistakes. People give themselves away the same in misdemeanors as they do in murder cases. It's just human nature" (chapter 6). We should consider the ambiguity between the epistemic and ontological/juridical senses of 'giving oneself away': both unintentionally informing others about oneself ("betraying" one's character, as we sometimes say) and also losing (alienating) one's soul/self. We do well here to attend to a deleted scene on the DVD where Will and Rachel discuss people who have, in his words, "lost someone." The larger question is, having thus lost oneself, given oneself away (or sold it for the whole word), how do we regain our selves? What is crucial is not the magnitude of an action's benefits and harms, but rather to what extent a person is invested in her actions and their effects, and thus what motivates her to perform them, what it is in her that they make manifest. These are what determine whether she stands to lose herself in the bargain.

One way of framing the point is that the movie offers itself to interpretation as an essay in what can be called an ethics of identity, according to which the moral life is essentially an internal affair. Can an action's *intentions* and motives matter morally, even more than its *effects*? Warfield, recall, was the L.A.P.D. Internal Affairs officer investigating corruption. It was he who had secured Hap's cooperation against Dormer in events just before the film's action. In the work's most pregnant metaphor, internal affairs are the moral *battleground* (that is, the field of warfare) where the story's chief drama plays out. This deepens the metaphor of internal affairs, calling to mind the spiritual writers' talk of "the interior life."[37]

---

[37] Compare the shallower metaphor in the 1990 film *Internal Affairs*, which featured Richard Gere and Andy Garcia. There, 'internal affairs' involved only the 'mind games' that Gere's crooked cop played on Garcia's honest one, especially playing on the latter's insecurities and marital problems.

Perhaps what is ultimately at stake, what the protagonist is (and we are) capable of, is indicated in a brief conversation from the original Norwegian film that, unfortunately, has no parallel in the American remake. When the Norwegian detective, Engstrom, pays a hospital visit to a local policeman wounded just before the chase that resulted in the other Norwegian policeman's 'accidental' death, the wounded cop, alone in the room, doesn't pay attention to Engstrom's entrance, thinking at first it is just a hospital worker in the room. However, he soon looks up and says, "I thought you'd come to put out the light." Indeed, Engstrom does have reason to put out the light of this man's life, as he may be the only witness to the cop-on-cop killing. (As it turns out in both versions of the story, the wounded policeman saw nothing of the fatal shooting, but the murderer they'd hunted did.)

8. Moral Nihilism

We observed above that Finch tells Dormer, even while the detective holds a gun to the writer's head, that shooting him—and, by implication, any action—can be turned into an accident just by wanting it to be one. This denies the reality of our actions, deprives them of any internal nature or essence and thus of any inherent moral stature. In a late night phone conversation with the agonized and sleepless Dormer, Finch is more explicit about what philosophers would call his moral anti-realism. "You and I share a secret. We know how easy it is to kill somebody. That ultimate taboo? It doesn't exist outside our minds." As Finch sees it, even the most serious moral proscription is mere taboo, nothing more than a local convention of disapproval (chapter 22).[38] Finch, however, offers no explanation of how he achieved this supposed insight, nor why he thinks himself justified in affirming it. That life is fragile, and the moral proscription against its violation easy to break, does not show that proscription is a mere figment of thought, so that nothing really counts as breaking it. Nor does the fact that Finch might well get away with murder prove that neither it nor anything else is really good or bad but is only popularly *thought* to be

[38] The French Jewish philosopher Emmanuel Levinas stressed the proscription against unjust homicide as the paradigmatic, original, and gravest of moral norms, conceiving it as an inescapable imperative confronted in the Other's face. See Levinas, *Basic Philosophical Writings*, edited by Adriaan T. Peperzak, et al. (Bloomington: Indiana University Press, 1996).

so. It is hard to see how it even lends support to that thesis. Finch's murder fills him with a self-perception that he is one of the elite, a member of the *cognoscenti* who see through the illusions that cloud lesser minds, those of the common run of mankind. However, he offers no reason for this new identity, and if he is right to think himself an unusually thoughtful murderer, he is no less vicious for that.[39] We reasonably see him as both perpetrator and victim of self-delusion along with other crimes.

The filmmakers, we may assume, do not share Finch's arrogant delusion, but neither is it clear that they see through it. It is disappointing that one of the film's main moral suggestions, put in the mouth of one its most sympathetic characters, is in fact not so different from Finch's. To Dormer's pathetic entreaty for vindication, his plea that she agree that his end justified his framing of Dobbs and by implication his capitulation to Finch's seemingly inevitable framing of Randy, Rachel Clement replies, "I guess it's about what you thought was right at the time, then: what you're willing to live with."[40] But what about how to act, not just now, but also "at the hour of our death," which Dormer must decide? It is not evident how, or even that, her proposed solution can address that question. More important, the film's narrative dramatizes a deeper problem with the simplistic formula to which Rachel gives voice. Some of us are able to adapt to, and thereby to "live with," almost anything, like Darwin's finch, from whom I think the name of Robin Williams's character is borrowed. By

---

[39] For a helpful refutation of the assumption that the reality, objectivity, and seriousness of moral features can somehow be rejected in a way free of normative implications and without making substantive moral claims, see Ronald Dworkin's "Objectivity and Truth: You'd Better Believe It" in *Philosophy & Public Affairs* 25 (1996): 87–139.

[40] The audio is indistinct here and it may instead be that what she says is "I guess it's more about what you thought was right at the time than [about] what you're willing to live with." In either case, we should perhaps recall Aristotle's suggestion, in his *Nicomachean Ethics*, that the voluntary and the involuntary are distinguished in the agent's later reactions.

his life and example, Walter Finch proves the inadequacy of Rachel's shallow ethic.[41]

The real issue is not whether the locus and source of morality are in our minds. Even if it is, Finch's conclusion that it is illusory is premature. Many philosophers have thought ethics "only in our minds" without thinking it therefore empty. That giant of the Enlightenment Immanuel Kant took moral duty to consist in commands of pure reason. His contemporary Adam Smith construed duty and virtue as conformity with our approval as idealized spectator/judges. Smith's friend David Hume saw virtue as based in natural human tendencies to sympathetic feelings.[42] In our time, John Rawls saw social justice as rooted in our agreement behind an imaginary veil of ignorance—and so on. The issue, rather, is what we are saying in making a moral judgment and whether the relevant part of the world really is like that or is only thought to be. So, moral judgments, reactions, and relations may be "only in our minds" but also accurate, well-grounded, objective (at least, intersubjective), and therefore non-illusory, *pace* Finch's assumption.[43]

Perhaps what Finch is trying to articulate is that morality has no sting. Even if its rules and principles are somehow real, or at least objective, they have no sanction to enforce them. Why be moral, live virtuously? Epicurus, Jeremy Bentham, and John Stuart Mill all thought morality's sanctions needed, in somewhat different ways, to be socially contrived. Of course, Christians hold that our immorality can wreck our

---

[41] The moral philosopher will also want to ask the pointed question, how can its being thought right (by its agent) be a right-making feature of an action? What plausible theory of moral justification supports such a claim?

[42] *New Yorker* magazine film critic David Denby seems confused about this in his review of a book on the Scottish Enlightenment; he attributes to Adam Smith and David Hume the view that morality is a human invention. See Denby, "The Scottish Enlightenment," *New Yorker*, Oct 11, 2004, pp. 90–98.

[43] We should bear in mind that Finch's dismissal of taboo is uninformed. The Christian philosopher Alasdair MacIntyre, in his provocative *Whose Justice? Which Rationality?*, reminds us that even Polynesian "tabu" started out as intelligible restrictions on harmful and ignoble action, and only later (under Western influence) degenerated into arbitrary, manipulated restraints as social control by the more powerful over the less powerful.

immortality; unrepentant sinners live eternally, but in the torment of damnation. One problem is that this seems to be no less an external sanction than are Bentham's, even if more certain. More recently, Robert Nozick has suggested that immorality has an internal value-cost: it makes the agent's life a lesser one, whether or not she knows or cares.[44] The French Jewish philosopher Emmanuel Levinas goes deeper, and the Polish Catholic Karol Wojtyła joins him.[45] For them, it is only in and through committing ourselves to other persons, and therein to the moral virtues, that our personhood is known and brought to its fulfillment. This may well be where the film points in its linkage of morality to identity and the way in which, in fulfilling official duty, the good cop therein fulfills his or her self.

9. Conclusion

The scene between Dormer and Rachel in the hotel room on his last night brings to culmination his long battle, mentioned above, against the insistent light that always finds its way around or through every window shade, every obstacle. The American poet E. E. Cummings famously found love to have smaller fingers even than the rain, which can work its way into and saturate heavy fabric, even stone.[46] But it is in the verse of the English Catholic Francis Thompson that we find a closer prefiguration. His eponymous "Hound of Heaven" seeks out the sinner who flees Him, insinuating himself into and undermining every

---

[44] Robert Nozick, *Philosophical Explanations* (Harvard University Press, 1981), ch. 5.

[45] See Levinas, *Basic Philosophical Writings* and Karol Wojtyła (Pope John Paul II), *Person and Community: Selected Essays,* translated by Teresa Sandok (New York: Peter Lang, 1993).

[46] " . . . your slightest look will easily unclose me/though I have closed myself as fingers,/you always open petal by petal myself as Spring opens/(touching skillfully, mysteriously) her first rose/or if your wish be to close me, i and my life will shut very beautifully, suddenly/ . . . nothing which we are to perceive in this world equals the power of your intense fragility . . . /(i do not know what it is about you that closes/and opens; only something in me understands/the voice of your eyes is deeper than all the roses)/nobody, not even the rain, has such small hands" E. E. Cummings, "somewhere i have never travelled" (1931) in *Complete Poems 1904-1962,* edited by George Firmage (New York: Norton, 1994).

distraction into which flight is taken, turning it into a signpost back to the God from whom the narrator tries with increasing frenzy to escape.[47] In just the same way has the Light, the light of Grace and the light of Truth, thwarted each of Dormer's efforts to elude it. He seeks mental oblivion in slumber, but he is not ready for it.[48] At this point still, his would be that sleep of reason that produces monsters. First, he must learn a lesson from Scripture: "Let us throw off the works of darkness and put on the armor of light; let us conduct ourselves properly as in the daytime..." (Romans 13: 12)

In the movie's penultimate scene, Dormer looks into the water, through the hole in the floor of Finch's cabin, and sees Finch's face looking up at him as if it is his own reflection (chapter 30). Has he become Finch? Then, slowly, Finch's face fades away as his corpse sinks. It is as if Dormer is being released from this option, this part of himself. Dormer then goes outside into the fresh air, beneath a cold grey sky, to spend his last moments with Ellie, his other option and *alter-ego* (alternative self). He devotes them to helping her, admonishing her "not [to] lose [her] way," receiving a sort of absolution from her, and finding the peace for which he asks. "Let me sleep. Just let me sleep..." he says, not imploring this time, not desperate, but hopeful. At last he is ready to receive the rest for which his pursuit had become increasingly frantic. Now he is at peace, at home within himself, ready to slumber even surrounded by the light he has fled throughout most of the film. "From a chalice/Lucent-weeping out of the dayspring./So it was done:/I in their delicate fellowship was one . . ."[49]

"Don't lose your way," Dormer warns. This is the injunction by which we must all live, recalling C. S. Lewis's conception, in his *Abolition of Man*, of Lao Tsu's *Tao* as The Way, the natural law written in our hearts.[50] How should we walk this way? "Once you were darkness, but now you are light in the Lord. Walk as children of Light" (Eph. 5: 8). The

---

[47] "Fear wist not to evade as Love wist to pursue . . . /'Naught shelters thee, who wilt not shelter Me'" (Thompson, "Hound of Heaven").

[48] "Therefore stay awake! For you don't know on which day your Lord will come" (Matthew 24: 42).

[49] Thompson, "Hound of Heaven."

[50] C. S. Lewis, *The Abolition of Man* (New York: Macmillan, 1955).

Christian, presumably, will not need to be reminded to bear in mind the more authoritative injunction, "Sum *via, veritas, vita.*"[51]

We have here undertaken what might be called a close moral reading of Nolan's remake of *Insomnia.* Godard wrote, in the screenplay for his 1960 film *Le Petit Soldat*, "Photography is truth. Cinema is truth twenty-four times a second."[52] There are places where Nolan's *Insomnia* approaches moral truth—at least, surprisingly serious and sensible moral reflection—in whatever today's digital analogue is to twenty-four times a second.[53] It provides glimpses of the grace that, as we saw at the start, Maritain thought perfects moral life as poetry does art. That is to say, grace brings the moral life to its highest realization. Still, we can do better in closing than quote Godard and invoke Maritain. Let us turn in the end to Jesus' instruction to Nicodemus on the timeless contest between illumination and obscurity. It could serve as a commentary on Detective Will Dormer's flight from light and his final redemption:

"For God sent His Son into the world not to condemn the world, but so that through Him the world might be saved...On these grounds is sentence pronounced: that though the light has come into the world

---

[51] "I am the Way, and the Truth, and the Life" (John 14:6).

[52] The indicated time was that of the speed of frames through a movie projector. I had taken this to be a claim that motion pictures go beyond photography by insistently bombarding us with the repetition of reality and by closely recording its changes over minute portions of time. Critic Michael Wood has recently suggested a different nuance, finding in the French a suggestion that viewing a film may intensify and magnify our experience of reality. He offers this as a more literal translation: "'the cinema is twenty-four times the truth . . . each second.'" (See Michael Wood, "Taking Reality By Surprise," *New York Review of Books* 51, no. 17 [November 4, 2004]: 53.)

[53] Contrast Nolan's with the morally superficial film *Changing Lanes*, released around the same time in 2002, where Ben Affleck's character rejects the way of the Church he walks out of and instead decides to blackmail his corporate bad-guy bosses into doing the–materially, objectively–right thing. The viewer has little reason to think this arrangement can last much past the credits, and the silly 'kick-ass'-resolution shows that the scummy character has changed only his ends, not his means, and that therefore he has not grasped the broader importance of means (the quality of any intentions, will) nor their internal connection to ends and character.

men have shown they preferred darkness to the light; because their deeds were evil. And indeed everyone who does wrong hates the light and avoids it, for fear his actions should be exposed. But the man who lives by the truth comes out into the light" (John 3: 19-21).[54]

[54] Other works consulted: J.L. Austin, "A Plea for Excuses," and "Three Ways of Spilling Ink," in *Philosophical Papers,* 3rd ed. (Oxford: Oxford University Press, 1979), pp. 175–204 and 272–87. Thomas Hibbs, "A Neo-Noir Filmmaker Echoes a Philosopher's Quest for Truth," in *Chronicle of Higher Education* (November 14, 2003). Jonathan Weiner, *Beak of the Finch: Evolution in Real Time* (New York: Knopf, 1994).

PART III:

Civilization, Christian Morality and Christian Culture

Christian Identity and Scholarly Vocation in a Secularized Society

Carlos A. Casanova

The Western World is an inheritor of Greek philosophy and Hebrew prophecy through the action of the Christian Church. The barbarian tribes who invaded the Western Empire were transformed into Latin Christendom. In this civilization universities were born, with a degree of freedom from political powers to develop science, art, philosophy and theology. The Church was a representative of the spiritual sphere of humanity and its relationship to God; while the Emperor or kings were representatives of "secular" power. Thus, through a unique process briefly and skillfully described by Eric Voegelin in *The New Science of Politics,* the West also became a place of unique freedom of the spirit. A similar view is expressed by Orestes Brownson, in *The American Republic.*[1]

Tensions between the Emperor, the Pope and the kings escalated as the secular powers of the West became increasingly civilized. This resulted in jealousies, creating tensions between the Emperor and the Church. Different political communities included in Latin Christendom longed to become the sole *Corpus Mysticum*, to the exclusion of both the Roman Church and other political communities. So, the earthly *Leviathan* began a claim for a cult beyond Christ's motto "Give to Caesar what is Caesar's and to God what is God's." Later, the *Leviathan's* claims for such a cult took two different forms: the "divine right of Kings" and the "sovereignty of the People."

The closer to the start of the simmering jealousies, the more the inertia of Christian customs and morality kept the consequences of the idolatry of nationhood in check. Thus, the different "states" that resulted from the dissolution of Latin Christendom during the wars of the 16th and 17th centuries respected the freedom of the spiritual

[1] Eric Voeglin, *The New Science of Politics* (Chicago: The University of Chicago Press, 1952), especially pp. 102-17. Orestes Brownson, *The American Republic* (New Haven: College and University Press Publishers, 1972), pp. 72 ff. and 86 ff.

sphere, allowing universities and the newly founded "Academies" to search for truth with a large degree of freedom. As Tocqueville observed, even among modern absolutist monarchies, the power of Christianity more often than not kept kings and princes from gross violations of human dignity.[2] Concerning Latin Christendom *before* the age of absolute monarchy, the efficacy of religious deterrents from gross violations of human dignity is even clearer, as noted by Manuel García Pelayo, who studied the phenomenon in his work *El Reino de Dios, arquetipo político.*[3] Moreover, thanks to the strength of existing institutions and customs, the Classical and Hebrew-Christian traditions also manifested themselves in the rise of rationalistic theories of natural law. Although often opposed to the Catholic Church, these secured a place for freedom of spirit through declarations of natural rights.

Later on, however, as the destruction of Christianity progressed, various revolutionary governments succeeded in obtaining a divine cult. The Nazis destroyed every liberty, including the freedom of universities, as the Communists have done and still do in the Western world, including Spain and Spanish America, and in the East. The extent of the enmity between sectarian secularism and Christianity is large because the first regards the second as a rival religion.[4] Ironically,

---

[2] Alexis de Tocqueville, *Democracy in America* (New York: Alfred Knopf, 1953), Vol. 1, pp. 326-27.

[3] Manuel García Pelayo, *El Reino de Dios, arquetipo político* (Madrid: Revista de Occidente, 1959). G. K. Chesterton has interesting remarks about this point in his *The Return of Don Quixote*, in *Collected Works* (San Francisco: Ignatius Press, 1999), Vol. 8, pp. 197-98.

[4] The last two paragraphs provide a mere outline. The history of this process can be seen to some extent in Eric Voegelin's works, especially in *From Enlightenment to Revolution*, *The New Science of Politics*, and his several studies on what he called for a long time "Gnosticism." The author develops these topics at greater length in *Racionalidad y justicia. Encrucijadas políticas y culturales* (Caracas: UCAB-ULA, 2004), especially chapters 2 and 3. Sometimes, the apparently ecumenical intentions of the most extreme secularists can be misleading. Under the pretense of ecumenical discourse, it is not difficult to find the will to power and the attempt to form a new "People" or its "vanguard" out of one's own Nation so as to impose one's own creed on the world. For instance, Condorcet wanted that power for the French intellectual

in many Western or Western-influenced countries, the secularist ideology of our time uses the language of "individual rights" as its weapon.

1. The current situation in the United States

The tendency of the modern State to demand a political cult and to make void traditional freedoms of the Western World is becoming apparent even in the USA. Some self-branded "liberals," who are actually secular extremists, attempt to convert every institution, public and private, into a model of the public ethos that they wish to impose on society. Freedom of association will not be respected; and no spiritual institution will be able to escape the clutches of these extremists. Presently, their methods consist mainly in well-orchestrated propaganda and social pressures. Those who stand for a principle opposed to the secularists' creed become the target of charges of "irrationality," "authoritarianism," and even of "Nazism." This kind of prejudice manifested itself in some criticisms of Mel Gibson's movie *The Passion of the Christ.* But its lack of success, despite the influence secularism enjoys in the mainstream media, shows to what extent cultural elites in United States are often distanced from the people.[5]

(see *From Enlightenment to Revolution* [Durham: Duke University Press, 1975], pp. 130-32) and the Soviet Union followed Bakunin's plan (given to Czar Nicolai I) for the conquest of a great empire (see *The New Science of Politics*, p. 177).

[5] The author felt this kind of pressure recently at the University of Notre Dame. "The Observer," an independent newspaper edited there, published a story about some students wearing armbands at a football game to contest "Notre Dame's No. 1 Princeton Review ranking for intolerance of 'alternative lifestyles,'" that is to say, of the lifestyle of gays and lesbians. Wanting to respond to a student demand for wider discussion of the issue, the author wrote an article arguing that homosexual marriage is not possible in accordance with natural law, and that to say this does not imply discrimination against anybody. "The Observer" published the article, but included a drawing of a man beating and raping a student wearing an armband, all against the background of the Irish clover. This was a true instance of symbolic language! These are all elements of this kind of tactics. Such elements lie very far from the use of rationality and very close to

A multitude of examples of such prejudice could be given. But let us turn our attention to a paradigm case—the reception of *Uncle Tom's Cabin* by critics in the United States. Abraham Lincoln reportedly said that the book "made this great war."[6] In the edition by The Modern Library (New York: 2001), we find a survey of opinions of different critics since 1852. In the beginning, many people saw the novel as a revolutionary work. In the South, some greeted it as an evil and unscientific one, while in other circumstances it was seen as a noble and encouraging work. But a recent critic, Hortense J. Spillers (1989), sees in the book nothing less than a *summa* of evil and a piece of reactionary rubbish. Why? Because it did not find "a path to radical social revision" (Marxist feminism), and because it has "at its heart" a "theological terror" (the fear of eternal damnation.) The novel is, according to Spillers, "an opportunistic deployment of the ideologies of a kerigmatic gospel." In the eyes of some secularists, the Christian character of this book transforms its revolutionary significance into reactionary rubbish.

Something is truly amiss among cultural elites of the United States. History and all reality are approached with cynicism and strong prejudices. Eric Voegelin, quoting Hooker, says of it, "the attitude is psychologically iron-clad and beyond shaking by argument."[7] Voegelin found a strong trend of irrationality in the United States when he stayed here for two years on his first visit. This trend can be seen clearly in current secular thought. John Rawls is arguably an instance, and the fact that the praise for his work has been completely unaffected by the many contradictions that it contains is a clear indication of an even greater problem.[8] The roots of this irrationality appear to lie in the fear of drawing the last consequences of intellectual theses. Secularist thinkers want to arrive neither at the nihilism of a Nietzsche or of Hume's sophistical arguments, on the one hand, nor at

---

manipulation and abuse of power. Of course, this personal anecdote is only a marginal and unimportant instance, although a very graphic one.

[6] See a group of early critics of the novel in *Uncle Tom's Cabin*, pp. 641-48.

[7] Eric Voegelin, *The New Science of Politics*, p. 137.

[8] See the author's *Una lectura platónico-aristotélica de John Rawls* (Pamplona: Cuadernos del Anuario Filosófico, 2003), pp. 15-16; see also the last section of this paper.

the Absolute of a true religion, different from the cult of their beloved 'People' or 'Nation,' on the other.[9] In such a context, it is not difficult to discover ancient tactics used again in our times.

From the Puritan revolution in England, some very effective ways to destroy a human institution, or institutional order, are well known. As noted by Eric Voegelin:

> ...in order to advance the "cause" the man who has it will, "in the hearing of the multitude," indulge in severe criticisms of social evils and in particular of the conduct of the upper classes. Frequent repetition of the performance will induce the opinion among the hearers that the speakers must be men of singular integrity, zeal, and holiness, for only men who are singularly good can be so deeply offended by evil. The next step will be the concentration of popular ill will on the established government. This task can be psychologically performed by attributing all fault and corruption, as it exists in the world because of human frailty, to the action or inaction of the government. By such imputation of evil to a specific institution the speakers prove their wisdom to the multitude of men who by themselves would never have thought of such connection; and at the same time they show the point that must be attacked if evil shall be removed from this world. After such preparation, the time will be ripe for recommending a new form of government as the "sovereign remedy to all evils."[10]

In light of Voegelin's account, one cannot fail to see the similarity in the use that secularist critics of the Catholic Church have made of the sexual scandal in New England, the echoes of the scandal in fictional movies made in Spain and Mexico, and the present efforts for the "democratization" of the Catholic Church.

Opinion in some academic settings is now ripe to accept the dogma that every institution, both public and private, has to be "liberal" and

---

[9] See Eric Voegelin, *On the Form of the American Mind* (Baton Rouge: Louisiana State University Press, 1995), pp. 41, 43-44, 245, 281-82.

[10] *The New Science of Politics*, pp. 135-36. For other features of the Puritan's tactics, see also 136-37.

"democratic." No moral opposition to homosexuality and no tenet against the use of contraceptives or against abortion as ways to the liberation of women can be tolerated. No authority will be recognized besides the assembly of the people, in Church or State, except, that is to say, the *natural rights* discovered and imposed by the "liberals."

In academic Catholic or Christian communities, some of these steps have already been taken. In more secular settings, there is an even more advanced state of corruption: no reference to the Christian past of this country or of Europe will be allowed, except in order to ridicule it; no "what" questions; no talk of God or the soul. Karl Popper was afraid to state this kind of question in the academic medium of the 1970s, a time already thoroughly affected by a scientistic and anti-metaphysical ideology.[11] He appears to reject "*what*" questions, questions about the essence, but he reintroduces them in a hidden way in a footnote, in order to avoid the censure of his readers. John Searle provides us with two other significant examples. Benjamin Libet once told him "that in the neurosciences, 'It is okay to be interested in consciousness, but get tenure first.'"[12] Materialist thinkers claim that the problems of freedom of the will and of consciousness will be solved when talk about them disappears.[13]

In philosophical circles, but perhaps not yet in neuroscientific circles, it can be enough to show that an author has a religious affiliation to avoid considering his arguments. For example, John Searle himself holds a materialistic view of the "mind" based only on the argument that a "dualism" would violate the scientific picture of the world that "we" have built with so much effort during the last four hundred years.[14] As regards John Eccles, the great "dualistic"

---

[11]Karl Popper, *The Self and Its Brain* (New York: Springer International, 1977), pp. 9, 100, 172, 175, 193 and 553.

[12] John Searle, *The Mystery of Consciousness* (New York: A New York Review Book, 1997), p. 193.

[13] See John Searle, *The Rediscovery of the Mind* (Cambridge, Massachusetts: The MIT Press, 1992), pp. 29 and 250. The latter passage contains an explicit reference to Richard Rorty as one author of these claims.

[14] See, for example, *The Mystery of Consciousness*, p. 194; *Minds, Brains and Science* (Cambridge, Massachusetts: Harvard University Press, 1984), p. 98; and *Mind. A Brief Introduction* (Oxford: Oxford University Press, 2004), chapters 1-5.

neuroscientist, Searle dispatches him with a brief phrase: he "... has a religious commitment with the existence of a soul ..."[15] Thus, Searle provides an example of the anti-religious pressure. We should keep in mind that he also shares in the orthodoxy of secularism, where one can speak about "consciousness," but not about "soul."

The issue of secular orthodoxy is becoming grave. There is social and legal pressure to hinder both private and public persons from expressing religion, Christianity in particular, in the public square. These attacks against the expression of religion often take the mask of an alleged constitutional principle of the separation of Church and State. According to secularist thinkers, this principle means that God has to be progressively and completely evicted from public life, in order for the State to be open to human beings of every creed. Of course, this interpretation and its grounding are preposterous. The interpretation is absurd because, on the one hand, this country mentioned God and Christ in the very text which is invoked in favor of the separation of Church and State.[16] On the other hand, the way in which things evolved during the nineteenth century made it clear that every creed could be practiced in the United States, if it did not endanger the public order of this society. This view is also absurd, because its real effect is for the secularists to impose on public life their own pseudo-religious belief, even when the majority of the people may disagree with it.

This latter point deserves careful analysis, because it reveals that the secularist religions are apt to be non-democratic, and contrary even to the already false maxim that the "assembly of the people," ought to be sovereign.[17]

---

[15] *The Mystery of Consciousness*, p. 136. See also p. XIII.

[16] So the text of the Constitution ends: "Done in Convention by the unanimous consent of the States present the seventeenth day of September in the year of our Lord one thousand seven hundred and eighty seven." Indeed, this country invoked God even in dollar bills!

[17] Leo XIII, in *Immortale Dei* (nn. 2, 10, 13, 17 and 23), showed that the maxim of the sovereignty of the people is anti-Christian and ought to be distinguished from the problem of political regimes, which is entirely different.

2. The Secularization of the Church as a Movement Akin to the Divinization of Society

Let us turn our attention to the effects that this process of secularization has had within the Church. The pseudo-religious forms of secularism are enemies of true religion. They want either to destroy any trace of religion or to transform the remaining traces into mere instances of the general secular spirit that they intend to impose on society. At the same time, the eternal temptation before the soul of a Christian can lure her into the vanity of pleasing the world or of enjoying the pleasures that the world in its turn offers. Should a Christian yield to this temptation, he would lose his identity and would become what the secularists want him to be. A share in the honors or powers or pleasures of "this world" is received in exchange for the soul.

The loss of identity is happening within Catholic colleges and universities through the influence of some scholars, including theologians. Ralph McInerny argues that, in large measure, the yielding to secularism was initiated in consequence of the occasion for dissent provided by the encyclical *Humanae Vitae.* This, in effect, caused the exertion of a will to power over the faithful. The sexual issues with which the Papal document deals, and the confusion that followed after the Second Vatican Council, allowed room for certain theologians to substitute their own authority for the authority of the Church.[18] We might add that not only Christian colleges and universities are being secularized, but also religious orders and, considering the number of canonical "annulments" of marriage granted every year, the Church courts.

Within the Church in the United States, one of the main temptations to error has to do with the very powerful cultural and political myth of "democracy." Many people strive to substitute the concept of absolute "democracy" for the hierarchy of Christ's Church. In the face of this distortion, the most obvious experiences are denied. For example, even in political society it is very clear that there is government and it does

---

[18] See Ralph McInerny, *What Went Wrong After the Second Vatican Council* (Manchester, New Hampshire: Sophia Institute Press, 1998), pp. 108-09 and 136-37.

not merely execute the will of the governed subjects.[19] But, in the distorted view, God is replaced by a new idol, *the People*. Of course, in reality people are always actually subject to authority. What the Catholic advocates of "democracy within the Church" want, as seen by McInerny with lucidity, is simply to replace the *Magisterium*.[20] It is not difficult to discern in this the familiar 'will to power' that probably moved Satan since the beginning of time.[21] This can be immediately noticed in the key documents that McInerny considers in his analysis of the Church in the United States.

Charles Meyer, for example, tells us; "If there is an underlying fallacy in the statement of the [dissenting] theologians [of the Curran statement], it is perhaps that truth can be attained more readily through a democratic process than by an authoritarian decision."[22] In "the most outspoken statement" against *Humanae Vitae*, written by Monsignor George Schlichte, we discover this real core of the problem with ease:

> The Holy Spirit is present first of all in the community of God's people, and those who fail to reflect the consensus of this community damage the effectiveness of the Church's mission.[23]

One wonders if that "Holy Spirit" is not, by any chance, the *Volksgeist* of Hegel and the post-Hegelians instead of the Eternal God, sovereign of every nation.

An old Papal document can be of use one century after its publication for understanding the mechanisms with which this secularization of the

---

[19] See *The New Science of Politics*, p. 38: "ruling power is ruling power also in a democracy, but one is shy of facing the fact." James Madison stated already in *The Federalist Papers* (XIV, originally published on November 30th, 1787), that the Republic of the United States is not a democracy, but a republic.

[20] See McInerny, *What Went Wrong After the Second Vatican Council*, pp. 91-92.

[21] See Saint Augustine, *De Trinitate*, book 13, chapter 13.

[22] McInerny, *What Went Wrong with Vatican II*, p. 98. The Curran statement was published by *The New York Times* on July 30, 1968 and in pages 60-64 of McInerny's book. Charles Meyer is quite right in pointing to "democratism" as the main fallacy.

[23] McInerny, *What Went Wrong with Vatican II*, p. 77.

Church works! An important point to be emphasized here is that this analysis reflects an attack upon the very sources of Christian wisdom. The Scripture and the Fathers are submitted to textual criticism. Not every kind of textual criticism is problematic, of course. But it becomes so when it can be "rightly called *agnostic, immanentist, and evolutionist*" as *On the Doctrines of the Modernists* observes.[24]

Once an entire discipline is formed with underlying principles that are not judicious, the situation of young scholars becomes difficult. If they want to be regarded as "serious intellectuals," they cannot disregard the hermeneutical web developed in the tradition of such a discipline. But it is then difficult to distinguish between what is true and useful for a sincere study of the sources and what is a consequence of a philosophy incompatible with Faith. This situation is made even more difficult because historians and critics of the Christian tradition have formed "a close alliance" so that:

> If one of them makes any utterance, the others applaud him in chorus, proclaiming that science has made another step forward, while if an outsider should desire to inspect the new discovery for himself, they form a coalition against him. He who denies it is decried as one who is ignorant, while he who embraces and defends it has all their praise... The domineering overbearing of those who teach the errors, and the thoughtless compliance of the more shallow minds who assent to them, create a corrupted atmosphere which penetrates everywhere...[25]

Other key points of the secularist attack include those alternative philosophies with which one could answer critics' claims about religion and "rationality." One such tradition is scholastic philosophy. Against her, "they use the weapons of ridicule and contempt."[26] Inextricably united to the attack against the philosophical tradition of the Church, the encyclical argues that "To bring contempt and odium to the mystic Spouse of Christ, who is the true light, the children of darkness have been wont to cast in her face before the world a stupid calumny, and

[24] See "On the Doctrines of the Modernists" (*Pascendi Domini Gregis*, 1907) (Boston: Saint Paul Editions, 1954), #34.

[25] Ibid.; see #34.

[26] Ibid.; see #42, p. 53.

perverting the meaning and force of things and words, to depict her as the friend of darkness and ignorance, and the enemy of light, science and progress."[27]

All of this is reinforced by more general tactics.

> There is no species of insult which they do not heap upon [Catholics who fight the battles of the Church], but their usual course is to charge them of ignorance and obstinacy. When an adversary rises up against them with an erudition and force that renders them redoubtable, they seek to make a conspiracy of silence around him to nullify the effects of his attack... For them the scholarship of a writer is in direct proportion to the recklessness of his attacks on antiquity and of his efforts to undermine tradition and the ecclesiastical magisterium.[28]

Moreover the document observes that such persons "seize upon professorships in the seminaries and universities..."[29]

The causes of the fall of many churchmen as a consequence of these attacks are also pointed out by the Successor of Peter: "They are possessed by the empty desire of having their names upon the lips of the public..."[30] "When a Catholic layman or a priest forgets the precept of the Christian life which obliges us to renounce ourselves if we would follow Christ and neglects to tear pride from his heart, then it is he who most of all is a fully ripe subject for the errors of Modernism."[31] "The

---

[27] Ibid., #42, pp. 54-55

[28] Ibid., #42, p. 55. It should be noted that not everyone who makes use of Modern philosophical doctrines or scholarly tools in theological research can be charged with the characterization made by Pius X over one hundred years ago. Some scholars, for example, do not have other intellectual tools, and they use them honestly and in the best way they can. Moreover, some modern doctrines (phenomenology, for example) are better suited for a proper use by theologians. What I am trying to uncover is the fact that the manipulation of Catholic consciences described by Pius X is still very active, even though, of course, it is not the only active phenomenon among Catholic scholars who use "Modern" philosophy.

[29] Ibid., #43, p. 55.

[30] Ibid., #43, p. 56.

[31] Ibid., #40, p. 52.

young, excited and confused by all this clamor of praise and abuse, some of them afraid of being branded as ignorant, others ambitious to rank among the learned, and both classes goaded internally by curiosity and pride, not infrequently surrender ..."[32]

I think that the Pope was completely right in the analysis of the crisis and its causes. As already indicated, I must add that today in the United States many churchmen—lay and clerics alike—have derailed the cult of God and built the cult of *their* people. This is the cause of their conceiving that absolute *democracy* has to be established in the Church: it is not God but the people—led by them, of course—that is the source and object of faith and cult.[33] This is also often the cause of their ignorance and isolation from the life of the Church outside the United States.[34] Thus, both from outside and inside the Church, the old methods of carrying about a revolution have been used. Such methods include showing the miseries of the members of an institution and attributing such evils to the institution itself.

Even though Pius X saw well the nature of the disease and most of the contemporary ways of its spreading, he could not stop it, because the only measures at his disposal were of a kind that is unable to vivify an institution. As Maurice Hauriou argued, norms and regulations, sanctions and punishments are dead without a preexisting spirit animating the institution.[35] In the Church, that spirit is the living Faith that heals and elevates human reason. The Pope did what he could and

---

[32] Ibid., #42, p. 55.

[33] An example of this spiritual disorder, *ethnolatría*, can be found in William L. Shannon's "Eucharist, Understanding Christ's Body," published by *Catholic Update* (Cincinnati: Saint Anthony Messenger Press, 1998).

[34] Some bishops are reducing the course of studies of seminarians and taking out the study of Latin. This move is misguided for two reasons. First, one of the greatest dangers for the Church in the United States lies in its isolationism and the country's general ethnocentrism. Second, another great danger is activism that causes neglect of study, prayer and contemplation. To throw young men to work in parishes without a strong inner life, under the presupposition that workers are needed urgently, is a grave mistake. Give us men with a rich inner life and we will have an abundance of fruits.

[35] Maurice Hauriou, "Teoría de la institución y de la fundación," *Obra escogida* (Madrid: Instituto de Estudios Administrativos, 1976), pp. 257-96.

should have done, but that was not enough. The Church needs the sound attentiveness of Catholic intellectuals both to the Word of God and to reality. Thinking Catholics have to understand, first, and show, later, that reason does not belong to the so-called "rationalists." Reason is not in opposition to God. Reason, without God, is condemned to absurdity.[36] As J. M. Bochenski stated, "Sartre is the most intelligent and the sharpest of all atheists. He perceived that, real being in the world could only be explained by God. But Sartre is not willing to recognize God; he thinks that He is a contradiction, and therefore he quite logically deduces that all being, particularly man, is absurd, senseless."[37] We can say even more: reason is not opposed to faith. "God's foolishness is wiser than human wisdom, and God's weakness is stronger than human strength."[38] Reason is very poor in theoretical resources concerning the most important aspects of the position of human beings in the universe, and weak in its control of the irrational aspects of life, without faith and grace.

For Catholic colleges and universities in the United States, this is a matter not only of fidelity to Revelation. It is also a matter of justice. The faithful entrust their children and their money to these institutions in the belief that students will be formed intellectually in The Faith and the money will be dedicated to furthering that very Faith. When colleges and universities act as secularized institutions, they are committing a fraud.[39] Do they want to be secular? No problem! But they should be honest. They should stop receiving money on behalf of their lost Catholic identity.

For young scholars, this might be a matter of eternal salvation. Do they want to have a "brilliant career" within the current state of such

---

[36] Friedrich Nietzsche understood this very well. For this reason he stated that we have no choice but to believe in God, as long as we still believe in grammar.

[37] I.M. Bochenski, *Philosophy: An Introduction* (Dordrecht, Holland: D. Reidel Publishing Company, 1962), p. 107.

[38] 1 Cor. 1: 25, New Revised Standard Version.

[39] This is what lies behind the powerful article of Susan Biddle Shearer, "Notre Dame Has a Duty to Uphold Church Teachings," *South Bend Tribune*, 18 March 2005, B5.

institutions? They should be ready, then, to exchange their soul for that career. Do they want to do something really important, to preserve and to transmit the treasure of The Faith and authentic religion to future generations? Do they want to help in the fight against the powers of darkness and against the menaces of the cult of the earthly *Leviathan*? In that case, they should be ready to use their inventiveness in the design of new institutions or, when necessary and possible, in providing a new spirit to the existing ones. In doing so, they have to commit themselves to an enterprise that will take decades and maybe centuries to blossom.[40] This is what our forefathers did to preserve The Faith from any degradation of human doctrines and to build Christian civilizations. This is the call that God is shouting to young Catholic scholars.

---

[40] And they should be ready, also, to dedicate hours to true meditation on the Word of God, because without prayer and contemplation there is no hope of doing anything for God. In order to spend hours in meditation, the young Catholics of the United States need to overcome a very powerful tendency of their culture to overestimate practical activity and underestimate the value of contemplation. Eric Voegelin found this tendency often in his study *On the Form of the American Mind* (see pp. 35-36, 62-63, and 219, for examples). Pius X refers to it as the principle of the "Americanists:" "the active virtues are more important than the passive, and are to be more encouraged in practice" (#38, p. 48). This principle has many incidences in academic life. Among them, for example, the quantity of books read is often more valued than the meditation needed to discern truth from error.

CHRISTIAN MORALITY:

A MORALITY OF THE DIVINE GOOD SUPREMELY LOVED ACCORDING TO JACQUES MARITAIN AND JOHN PAUL II

Denis A. Scrandis

This paper argues that Christian moral philosophy proposes a morality of the Divine Good supremely loved. Jacques Maritain takes this position in his historical and critical survey of the subject, published in English under the title *Moral Philosophy*, in 1964.[1] John Paul II defends a similar viewpoint in his encyclical letter *The Splendor of Truth*, which was issued in 1993.[2] The following brief analysis is intended to show the agreement between these two authors on the subject of Christian moral philosophy. The development of the authors' respective positions on this subject matter will be deferred to a later time.

Western philosophical thought began with Greek speculation concerning nature, being, and happiness. Moral philosophy in the West was given its first definitive shape by Socrates, Plato, and Aristotle. Aristotle articulated a view of man as a being that seeks ends through the actualization of his powers, and in having a rational nature he determines himself in the pursuit of happiness. Human beings, who naturally seek fulfillment through rational choice, must therefore face the question of discovering their final end.

Maritain outlines Aristotle's position in regard to the end of man for two reasons. Aristotle offers a doctrine that Maritain finds to be both largely correct on its own merits in spite of some flaws, and it also serves as an historical point of departure for Christian moral philosophy. Since Aristotle does not employ specific religious teachings in his writings, he speaks in Maritain's estimate in a singular way for *human reason*, which leaves his doctrine religiously unencumbered, yet

---

[1] Jacques Maritain, *Moral Philosophy* (New York: Scribner's Sons, 1964).

[2] John Paul II, *The Splendor of Truth* (Boston: St. Paul Books and Media, 1993).

remarkably apt for union with *faith* in the Christian solution to the end of man.

Part One: Reason's Definition of the End of Man

1. Aristotle Identified the Good and Happiness

Aristotle taught that human nature has a natural tendency to seek happiness. Man thus seeks by nature to discover what good or goods, the possession of which, yields happiness. Maritain concludes that Aristotelian happiness (*eudaimonia*) consists in the perfect fulfillment of human nature.[3]

Aristotle found among the multiplicity of human goods both a hierarchy of goods and a supreme or sovereign good that exercises authority over subordinate goods.[4] Happiness consists of interior and exterior elements. Interior elements include wisdom, virtue, and pleasure, where contemplation is superior to action and life lived virtuously (owing to its fruition in good and beautiful actions) is superior to living for wealth, honor, or pleasure. Elements exterior to the soul include friendships and wealth.[5] Yet, happiness is more than its parts. The art of living rightly is the "art of ordering one's life in such a way as to attain the supreme end: happiness."[6]

2. Seeking Equilibrium Between The Choice of a Good Action and Happiness

In Maritain's interpretation, Aristotle's ethics faces a major difficulty. A contemplated choice must be measured by reason in two ways. On the one hand, reason must find a concrete and virtuous action (that, say, is a mean between two extremes). On the other hand, the contemplated concrete action must also be a means to the long-term goal of happiness. Reason measures one and the same moral action both as to how it attains the plenitude and beauty proper to a human

---

[3] Maritain, *Moral Philosophy*, p. 31.

[4] Ibid., p. 32.

[5] Ibid., p. 34.

[6] Ibid., p. 33.

action (that means it is good in and for itself) and as to how it serves as a means to happiness (that means it tends toward the ultimate end).[7] Maritain says that Aristotle gives primacy to the finality of life as a whole: "for Aristotle, what dominates the whole field of ethics and the way in which specific virtues are to be determined, is the consideration of the ultimate End, the primacy of the Supreme Good, or the happy life."[8]

Yet, Maritain sees a problem:

> All this amounts to saying that the equilibrium sought by Aristotle was not decisively attained. I fear, moreover, that a kind of vicious circle is implied in his procedure: the fact is that virtue appears herein as essentially a means toward the...blessed life; and yet virtue is also an integral part of that blessed life.... The means to the end (virtue) thus enters into the very notion and [constitution] of the end to which it is directed.[9]

The Aristotelian theory thus has a problem.

3. The End Has Two Faults

Aristotle's happiness consists of several elements and is a complex whole that motivates reason's entire grasp of the moral life. Yet, Maritain laments "Our whole moral life, all our effort and striving toward rightness and virtue are suspended from an end which, in fact, vanishes within our grasp."[10] Although tailored to the aspirations of human nature, Aristotle's sovereign good embraces so many ends and conditions that few can approach it.[11] Maritain concluded that Aristotle's happiness is neither practically accessible nor practically constraining.

Another difficulty comes from the eudaimonist conception itself and from a failure to distinguish between the good and happiness, which Aristotelian metaphysics itself understood. Maritain explains:

---

[7] Ibid., p. 36.

[8] Ibid., p. 35.

[9] Ibid., p. 36.

[10] Ibid., p. 48.

[11] Ibid.

> Aristotle, in agreement with Socrates and all the Greeks, identifies the sovereign Good and Happiness. Now Happiness is, so to speak, the subjective side of the Good; in the concept of Happiness the notion of Good refers back to the subject. If there is no good, which is desired and loved more than happiness, it is inevitable that happiness should be desired and loved for the sake of the subject it beatifies.[12]

According to Aristotle's conception of happiness, man loves many things in and for themselves. Yet, once they are subsumed under happiness, i.e., once happiness becomes the supreme and presiding end, the desire for and love of this end is for the sake of the person it fulfills. Maritain concludes that:

> [Aristotle's] moral teaching leaves us enclosed in love of ourselves. It is *my* good that I love and will in willing and loving Happiness as the supreme Good supremely loved, that is to say the Good taken subjectively, the Good as a perfection of the subject ... or as a fulfillment of human life.[13]

Maritain also tells us that the Stoics, responding to this problem in Aristotelian ethics, replaced the criterion of happiness with a new one, i.e., with the notion of accomplishing the Natural Law. That replacement removed the vicious circle.[14] In sum, Maritain thought that Aristotle had discovered the right approach to moral philosophy even though his solution involves the problems cited.

Part Two: Christianity's Definition of the End of Man

1. The First Impact of Christianity on Moral Philosophy: Redefining the End of Man

For Maritain, Christian teaching on the end of man confronted human reason with surprises:

---

[12] Ibid., pp. 48-49.

[13] Ibid., p. 49.

[14] Ibid., p. 37.

> It came as a strange novelty to learn that the final End of human life—not only as supreme Value good in itself and for itself, but as the supreme Object the possession of which constitutes human happiness—is God Himself, the infinite Good, self-subsistent Being. God in His intimate life, the uncreated Glory itself is the end in which our appetite for happiness will be satisfied beyond measure.[15]

The end of man is now understood as God and not merely natural happiness. Human happiness is no longer seen to be limited to the satisfaction that comes from a full life virtuously lived; it is rather achieved in the possession of God, which is accompanied by saturating joy. In discussing the end of man, Maritain distinguishes three things.

1. God in His infinite goodness and lovability is the absolute ultimate end.

2. Man's possession of the absolute ultimate end, through which man enters into the divine fullness, is man's subjective ultimate End.

3. The possession of God and the fulfillment of all aspirations in the love of God produce joy in the soul, which is the joy of God Himself.

Maritain insists, not only on these three distinctions, but also on their mutual relationship. Desire for beatitude (the subjective ultimate end) is inseparable from love of the absolute ultimate end, while desire for God's joy is inseparable from desire for beatitude. However, desire for joy and beatitude are subordinate to love of God. Beatitude is loved, but God is loved more. Beatitude, as union with the Supreme Good, can only be loved truly (and subordinately) in and for the love of the subsistent Good loved supremely for itself.[16]

The egocentricity of eudaimonism is overcome. Man's primordial love for himself is torn away and directed toward God whose good we wish for more than our own. This is possible and even easy, not in the order of nature, but in the order of charity. Christian hope causes me to wish that God be mine, neither for myself nor by means of myself, but because I love God more than I love my happiness and myself.[17]

---

[15] Ibid., p. 75.

[16] Ibid., p. 78.

[17] Ibid., p. 79.

With Christianity, a new order of being—one that perfects the order of nature--discloses itself and involves a created nature in the life of God. St. Paul (I Cor. XIII, 13) identified three such supernatural principles: faith, which is the adherence of the intellect to things not seen, hope, which is confidence in one more powerful than oneself, and charity or love of God above all. These three humble dispositions, which are too weak to function as virtues in the natural order, constitute virtues in the divine order once they are ordered to God and exercise precedence over the powerful, natural (or *cardinal*) virtues.[18] Moral life thus embraces both the theological virtues and rules, which are proportional to the divine life, and the moral virtues and rules, which are proportioned to the life of reason within the order of nature.[19] The theological virtues need the natural virtues and the perfection of human life depends on charity.[20]

2. The Second Impact of Christianity on Moral Philosophy: Love of Friendship between God and Man

Christianity's second most significant impact on moral philosophy was to recast the relations between God and man: love is now possible. In the order of nature, a man loves the first cause by nature, but does not love God as his friend. Love between friends is a mutual relation between equals and man is not God's equal. Yet, in the order of charity, grace raises man to the supernatural order by sharing the very life and goods of God with man and by producing a community of life and goods, which involves a kind of equality that is a condition of friendship. This notion of communion with God is well beyond the reach of human reason and a scandal for pagans of every age.[21]

Christian moral philosophy, Maritain says, makes charity "the keystone of the whole edifice of morality."[22] Charity extends principally to God and secondarily to all men. The whole moral life of man depends on charity, i.e., this undivided love of God and love of neighbor. The

---

[18] Ibid., p. 80.

[19] Ibid., p. 81.

[20] Ibid., p. 80.

[21] Ibid., p. 81.

[22] Ibid.

whole law consists in the precept to love God with our entire soul and the precept to love all men as our brothers.[23]

Charity impacts human life and conduct in ways that no pre-Christian moral philosopher could have imagined. In fact, Maritain sees charity as reversing values in regard to the perfection of human life. The Christian saint, for example, opens his very weakness to grace and draws his life from charity, which is unlike the Stoic hero of virtue. It is the saint's humility that receives grace and is paradoxically exalted.[24]

3. Reason Alone Articulates Only Part of Moral Philosophy

Christians and pagans both exercise the cardinal virtues. Yet, a man's moral experience that has been nourished by faith and its life of communion with God is different in ways that challenges the moral philosopher. Maritain says that if the moral philosopher fails to recognize them, then "he is leaving out things, which form an integral part of that human reality which he intends precisely to elucidate on the level of reflection" and that he "causes moral philosophy to quit the soil of existence and fly off into the void."[25] The entire enterprise of moral reflection is at stake.

Maritain says that reason and faith are two sources of morality, namely, natural law and the divine law, which includes the Old Law of Sinai and the New Law of the Gospels. Maritain says that the "precepts of the Decalogue are essentially a revealed formulation of the principles of natural law."[26] Yet, Maritain believes that it would be a mistake to lose sight of the Divine origin of the Ten Commandments.

Maritain fears that both natural morality and revealed morality are set at risk by transferring the prohibitions and prescriptions of the Decalogue to seemingly equivalent natural law rules. Although Maritain does not explain the risk, it is possible (in light of man's need to live in a conscious relation to God) that the Decalogue (being an account of how God requires men to love God and neighbor) must

---

[23] Ibid., p. 83.

[24] Ibid.

[25] Ibid., p. 86.

[26] Ibid., p. 87.

remain highlighted in human consciousness as a divinely inspired set of rules precisely because those rules constitute a minimum that serves, not just the common good of human society (which is the domain of natural law) but, the good of the Kingdom to come. In other words, to lose sight of the Ten Commandments as divine expectations risks losing participation in the divine community now and possibly forever.

Part Three: John Paul II On The End of Life

1. Human Nature's Quest for God

In the First Chapter of *Veritatis Splendor*, Pope John Paul II analyzes the meaning of the dialogue between Jesus and the "rich young man" that is reported in the 19th Chapter of Matthew. The outline is:

> Question: What must I do to have eternal life?
>
> Answer: Keep the commandments.
>
> Question: All these have I kept; what still do I lack?
>
> Answer: If you wish to be perfect, sell all you own, give the proceeds to the poor, and come, follow me.[27]

John Paul II interprets the young man's questions to be about the full meaning of life. This inquiry is not just that of a single individual, it is moreover the searching of man in response to the "absolute Good which attracts us and beckons us; it is the echo of a call from God which is the origin and goal of man's life."[28] John Paul II says "the man who would understand himself thoroughly...must appropriate and assimilate the whole reality of the Incarnation and Redemption in order to find himself."[29]

2. The Objective and Subjective Ultimate Ends of Life

John Paul cites scripture to establish the truth of the revelation that God alone is good in an unqualified way (Mt. 19:17 "There is only one

---

[27] John Paul II, *The Splendor of Truth*, s. 6.

[28] Ibid., s. 7.

[29] Ibid., s. 8.

who is good;" and Mk. 10:18 "No one is good but God alone"). This uniquely and unqualifiedly good God is uniquely and unqualifiedly worthy of being loved, according to Mt. 22:37 "with all one's heart, with all one's soul, and with all one's mind."[30] This same good and lovable God "is the source of man's happiness ... is goodness, fullness of life, the final end of human activity, and perfect happiness."[31] God is the objective ultimate end of man and the source of perfect happiness, which is the subjective ultimate end of man.

3. God Answers the Question: What Good Must I Do to Have Eternal Life—To Be Perfect?

John Paul II teaches that God has communicated to men what goods lead to eternal life. (Recall that Maritain emphasized these included observance of the natural law and the Decalogue, as well as living the life of grace.) Firstly, God has created man with wisdom and love and ordered him through natural law to his final end. Secondly, God taught what must be done and avoided in his ten commandments. And thirdly, Jesus' kingdom of Heaven is a participation in the very life of God.[32] For John Paul, the commandments of the Decalogue, especially the prohibitions of murder, adultery, theft, and false witness, represent a first necessary step in the journey toward freedom from sin. They are only the beginning of freedom—not its perfection.[33] Jesus referred the young man to the two commandments (love of God and love of neighbor) as conditions required for eternal life.[34]

Beyond this baseline of eternal life and the moral perfection required for it, Jesus proposed yet another condition of a higher form of moral development. He does so in the form of a challenge: "If you want to be perfect...Come, follow me." This is starkly simple, but it requires the plenitude of God's gift of grace.[35] In addition to natural law and the Decalogue, and the two-fold law of love, Jesus also proclaimed a

---

[30] Ibid., s. 9.

[31] Ibid.

[32] Ibid., s. 12.

[33] Ibid., s. 13.

[34] Ibid., s. 14.

[35] Ibid., s. 17.

"new commandment," i.e., to "love one another even as I have loved you," which requires also that we follow him perhaps even to our own cross.[36] John Paul II and Maritain agree on the basic goods that God has communicated to man that will lead to eternal life.

4. Conclusions

Reason, represented by Aristotle, defined happiness as a composite final end for man that consisted of the best things of human life, i.e., wisdom, virtue, friendship, etc. So defined, happiness suffered from several faults. Focused on the fulfilled soul, reason fell into egoism. Stoics substituted the notion of accomplishing the natural law, which, though it sought to graft the dictates of reason onto the dispositions and passions of the soul, redirected attention from self to something transcendent, namely, to the natural law. All of this occurred in the realm of reason and without interaction with faith.

Christianity, as understood by Maritain, redefined the end of man, distinguishing an absolute or objective ultimate end, which is self-subsistent Being, from a subjective ultimate end, which is a vision of the essence of God. This possession of God fulfills all the aspirations of the soul and produces a joy that is the joy of God Himself. Egoism is avoided since beatitude—as union with the Supreme Good—can only be loved *truly* in and for the love of the subsistent Good loved supremely for itself. Charity extends principally to God and secondarily to all men. The whole moral life of man depends on charity, i.e., the whole moral life of man rests on this undivided love of God and love of neighbor.

John Paul II teaches that God is unqualifiedly good and lovable. God is the source of fullness of life and of man's happiness. The love of God and neighbor is a condition of perfection, but adherence to the Decalogue is a minimum condition for eternal life. Thus both Maritain and John Paul rest Christian morality on charity that loves God to the fullest, and we conclude that Christian morality for them is a morality of the Divine Good supremely loved.

---

[36] Ibid., s. 20.

St. Thomas on Love of Self and Love of Others

Patrick Lee

1. Introduction

According to St. Thomas Aquinas, beatitude, or happiness, is the ultimate end of each person's deliberate actions. Different persons, and even the same person at different times, may identify beatitude with different conditions: one person may identify his beatitude or his ultimate end, as wealth, another as power, still another as union with God. But, all agree, say Aristotle and St. Thomas, that each person is acting for the sake of happiness or beatitude, conceived as an ideal condition. This position is at the core of Thomas's ethical theory.

Various critics of Thomas have for a long time argued that this "eudaimonistic position" logically implies that other people are viewed only as mere means in relation to the perfection of one's nature. In other words, Thomas's position that the ultimate end of all one's actions is one's beatitude seems to imply that one cannot act for the sake of someone else's good for their own sake.

The present analysis examines this objection: How does Thomas's theory avoid egoism? Before answering this question, we must first briefly examine Thomas's notion of love as a disposition, and his distinction between love of concupiscence and love of friendship.

2. Love as a Disposition

According to Thomas, desire, in the broad sense, is an act of tending toward a good. If such a tendency follows upon a natural form it is a natural appetite. Desires that follow upon sense knowledge are acts of the sense appetites, and desires that follow upon intellectual knowledge, that is, tendencies toward understood goods, are acts of will.

Prior to these acts of loving there is in the sense appetite or will a favorable disposition or proportion toward the sensed or understood good. One senses or understands a good, and this good attracts the sense appetite or will, that is, this known good disposes the appetite toward it. This disposition or modification of the appetite to be favorably disposed toward a good, produced by the known good, is love. Thus, Aquinas describes love as follows: "the desirable (*appetibile*) moves the appetite, introducing itself, in a way, into its intention, and as a consequence the appetite really tends toward the desirable, as the goal of its motion...Therefore the first change in the appetite produced by the desirable is called love..."[1] So, for example, one smells a hamburger, this sensed good affects one, that is, moves one's sense appetite, disposing it favorably toward itself. Or if one gets to know someone, his goodness may move one's will to be disposed to his good, not for one's own sake but simply as his good—a disposition produced in one's will by the known good, this time an understood good. The disposition toward a known good (on either level) is what Aquinas means by love.

3. Love of Concupiscence and Love of Friendship

In speaking of the act of loving, Thomas distinguishes between two types. To love (as an act) is always to will good to someone. So, one can speak of loving that which one wills to a person. For example, one loves wine or health if one wills those to another or to oneself. This, says Thomas, is love of concupiscence. Or one can speak of loving the person to whom one wills good: thus, willing food and health to one's children is to love one's children. And this is love of friendship or love of benevolence. One can love other persons with either type of love. If one loves another because he is good company, or because one can learn from him, then one loves him with a love of concupiscence. On the other hand, to will good to another for his own sake and not just as a means toward some benefit to oneself is to love him with a love of friendship. Some critics of Thomas, in effect, interpret him as saying, or implying, that we love ourselves with a love of friendship, but all others, God included, only with a love of concupiscence.

This, of course, is a misinterpretation. Aquinas clearly teaches that we ought to love God and our neighbor, not just with a love of concupiscence, but with a love of friendship. Charity is a supernatural friendship with God, in which both God and neighbor are loved with a love of friendship, whereas irrational creatures are loved only with a

---

[1] *ST* I-II 26.2.

love of concupiscence.[2] Indeed, Thomas teaches that, even on the natural level, that is, even before one brings grace into the picture, we should love God more than ourselves; otherwise our love is deficient. Answering the objection that one's love of God is for the sake of enjoying him, and therefore one's love of God is based ultimately on one's love of self, Thomas says:

> That a man wills to enjoy God pertains to that love of God which is love of concupiscence. Now we love God with the love of friendship more than with the love of concupiscence, because the Divine good is greater in itself than our share of good in enjoying Him.[3]

Thus, for Aquinas it is quite clear that God is to be loved for his own sake, not merely for the sake our perfection;[4] indeed God should be loved wholly and without measure (that is, one cannot love God too much).[5]

In fact, Thomas calls love of concupiscence love only *secundum quid* while love *simpliciter* is love of friendship: "For that which is loved with love of friendship is loved *per se* and *simpliciter*; that which is loved with a love of concupiscence is not loved *simpliciter* and according to itself (*secundum se*) but is love for another (*alteri*)."[6] Love of concupiscence relates to its object as accidental, and what is accidental must be reduced back to what is substantial. Of course, nowhere does Thomas say that the only substance one can love in the manner of a substance is oneself; on the contrary, everywhere he teaches the opposite.[7]

---

[2] *ST* II-II 25.3.

[3] Ibid., 26.3 ad 3. See also the previous objection and its answer: "The part [that is, the human person as a member of the community of the whole universe] does indeed love the good of the whole, as becomes a part, not however so as to refer the good of the whole to itself, but rather itself to the good of the whole."

[4] Ibid., 27.3.

[5] Ibid., 27.5.

[6] *ST* I-II 26.4.

[7] Ibid.

Critics could reply, however, that while Thomas in many places affirms that we should love others for their own sake, his position that every deliberate action is for the sake of one's happiness is incompatible with that claim. One might reply that Aquinas's Christianity led him to affirm genuine disinterested love of others and of God, but that his philosophical notion of beatitude is logically inconsistent with that position. To see that this view is mistaken we must explore further Thomas's notions of love of neighbor and love of God.

4. Love of Neighbor and Love of Self

The distinction between love of concupiscence and love of friendship can be misunderstood. The Swiss Lutheran theologian Anders Nygren made famous the distinction between *eros* and *agape*. According to Nygren, *eros* is the acquisitive drive, that is, the drive toward self-perfection. Greek philosophy, said Nygren, held *eros* to be supreme and the fundamental law or pattern of reality and life. But, according to Nygren, the Christian idea of *agape* is radically different. *Agape* is the desire for someone's else's good. It is pure, disinterested love. In *agape*, one transcends *eros* and wills good to another for his own sake, with no concern for oneself.[8] Now, on first reading of Thomas on love, one might be tempted to identify his love of concupiscence with Nygren's *eros*, and Thomas's love of friendship with Nygren's *agape*.

But that would be a mistake. Thomas does not say that love of concupiscence is love of self and love of friendship is love of another. Rather, love of concupiscence is found in every act of love: it is not a distinct act, but an aspect of every act of love. In every act of love, I will a good (that's love of concupiscence) to a person (whether another or myself, and that's love of friendship). So if I will health to another, my love of that health is love of concupiscence. If I will health to myself, my will's relation to the person to whom I will that good—namely, myself—is love of friendship. And so Aquinas does not think love of concupiscence is bad, something we have to set aside, to attain love of friendship. Rather, in every act of love, there is both love of concupiscence and love of friendship.

---

[8] Anders Nygren, *Agape and Eros*, translated by Philip Watson (Philadelphia: Westminster Press, 1953).

How is it possible for human beings to love others with a love of friendship? Aquinas's answer is that good is the cause of love, which, of course, means a good that is proportionate to the one who loves. "Now the proper object of love is the good; because, as was said, love denotes a certain connaturality or complacency of the lover toward the one loved. Now to each thing that is a good which is connatural and proportionate to it."[9] This is not to say that the good is only my individual perfection—in fact, he has just denied it in the text in question (I-II, q. 27, a. 1). Rather, the sort of object which is "connatural and proportionate" to me moves or attracts my will. If that object is (or would be) instantiated in a distinct subject, then I am inclined toward the good of another.

One might ask: which type of love is Aquinas speaking of here—love of concupiscence or love of friendship? The answer is, both. What is connatural and proportionate to me moves or affects my will, so that I have a favorable disposition toward it. To will the proportionate object as a substance is to love *simpliciter*; to will a proportionate object as an *accident* is to love (something) as directed to someone, that is, to that person whose fulfillment it is. One can will the existence and actions of other substances as means toward one's own perfection—loving them with a love of concupiscence. But one can also will the being and perfection of substances other than oneself, precisely as substances—and that is to love them with a love of friendship.[10] Thus, there is no sharp split between love of concupiscence and love of friendship: one wills the being of oneself and of those connatural and proportionate to one.

But Aquinas's explanation of our love of others becomes clearer when he explains that similitude also is a cause of love. A person naturally loves himself, but also those who are similar to himself, because insofar as they are similar they are united to him.

---

[9] *ST* I-II 27.1.

[10] Also, my life, that is, my substantial being, is connatural and proportionate to me, and so I will it to me—here, of course, I am willing my substantial being as though it were an accident in me—life is good to or for me, but really, my life just is me.

> Therefore the first kind of similitude [whereby they both have the same form in act, rather than just in potency] causes love of friendship or benevolence. For, from the fact that two things are similar, having as it were one form, they are in a certain way one in that form, just as two human beings are one in the species of humanity...And therefore the affection of one tends toward the other, as it is one with himself, and he wills good to him as to himself.[11]

On Aquinas's view, each agent acts for its own good—that is its nature. But the agent's natural tendency or love does not stop at his own individual perfection. One's love also naturally extends toward those who are united with oneself. Then, one wills good to these others as to oneself. They are, as it were, "other selves." One must recall that for Thomas, "similitude" means a union or unity together with difference.[12] Two things are similar just in case they are one, or have the same form, in one respect, but differ in other respects. Thus, one naturally loves oneself, and those with whom one is in communion. This same point is made earlier in the *Summa Theologiae,* where Thomas is speaking of an angel's love of another:

> As was said above, it is true of both angel and man that he naturally loves himself. But, that which is one with a thing, is (in a way) that very thing. Hence everyone loves that which is one with himself...Hence it should be said that one angel loves another with a natural love insofar as the other is one with him in nature.[13]

Aquinas also at times refers to this similarity or union that grounds love of another as a "*communicatio.*" There are different types of friendships, and they differ as being based on different connections or unions. Thus, he distinguishes between a friendship of "consanguinity," a friendship between co-citizens, and one between co-workers.[14]

---

[11] Ibid., I-II 27.3.

[12] Ibid., ad 1 and ad 2.

[13] *ST* I 60.4c.

[14] Cf. *DDN*, chapter 4.

This union, which is the basis of the extension of one's love of self to others, must be distinguished from the union which love itself establishes. When Aquinas asks whether union is an effect of love, he says that one must distinguish between the ontological union that precedes and grounds love (of friendship) of others and the union in affection, which is an effect of love. As a consequence of love of friendship, the other is related to oneself as another self: one's affections are related to him just as they are to oneself. But preceding this union of affections is the love itself, and preceding the love itself is the ontological union—of one sort or another—that grounds the love.[15]

So, one can say that while Thomas certainly holds that every agent acts for its perfection or fulfillment—the self for whose fulfillment one acts is not an isolated individual, but a being with real ontological connections or unions with others.[16] Every agent acts for his own fulfillment, but not just for his merely individual fulfillment. Rather each person acts—or should act, for there are defections from this, of course—for the fulfillment of himself and of those with whom he is ontologically connected.

5. Love of God and Love of Self

The importance of unity in Thomas's explanation of love of others is further clarified when he examines the relationship between love of God and love of self. In several places, Aquinas argues that it is natural for us to love God more than ourselves, and this, of course, with a love of friendship. But he explains how this is so in a way that maintains a fundamental harmony between love of God and love of self.

He argues that now, because of the wounds of original sin, we need grace to enable us to love God more than ourselves. That is, one of the effects of original sin is a disorder in the natural inclination of one's will. Still, it is natural for the creature to love God more than itself. This inclination, he explains, is part of the creature's natural inclination to its own perfection. The following passage sets out the argument in syllogistic form:

---

[15] *ST* I-II 28.1c and ad 2.

[16] See Aristotle, *Nicomachean Ethics*, Bk. VIII.

> Now, in natural things, everything which, according to the nature of that which it is, is of another [*secundum naturam hoc ipsum quod est, alterius est*] is more principally and strongly inclined to that of which it is, than toward itself...For we observe that the part naturally exposes itself for the sake of the preservation of the whole, as, for example, the hand is without deliberation exposed to a blow for the sake of the preservation of the whole body...Therefore, since God is the universal good, and under this good are naturally contained both angel and man, and since every creature, according to that which it is, [*secundum id quod est*] is of God [*Dei est*], it follows that by a natural love both angel and man love God more, and more principally, than themselves.[17]

Thomas returns to this explanation frequently, explaining that each creature is, in a way, a part of the whole universe, and on that basis it is natural for the creature to love the good of the whole universe, which is God (for the universe is the expression of God's own goodness) more than one's particular self.[18] Of course, this should not be read in a pantheistic way. Nor does he mean that a person is merely a part of the whole of creation. Each person is a whole in his own right, that is, a substance.[19] Still, a person is a member of the larger community: this belongs to a created person according to what he is. So, his perfection consists in being a constituent or part of the good of the universe.

This argument has, of course, been interpreted in various ways. I believe Aquinas is making two distinct but related points here. First, each creature's good is a participation of--that is, a finite replica of some aspect of--God's universal good. Whatever goodness is in each creature pre-exists in God in a higher manner. Each creature is naturally inclined to its own good. But that good is found in God in a higher manner. Therefore, the creature's natural inclination in some way will be toward God even more strongly than toward its particular good. This is why in the above passage he speaks of the universal good, under which the creature's good is contained. Similarly, when

---

[17] *ST* I 60.5.

[18] See *ST* I-II 109.3; II-II 26.3.

[19] Cf. *ST* I 29.1.

presenting this argument in his *Commentary on the Divine Names*, he says, "For that which is superior among beings is compared to the inferior as the whole to the part, insofar as the superior possesses perfectly and totally that which the inferior possesses imperfectly and particularly..."[20] So, the good to which a creature is naturally inclined (its own) is found more perfectly in God, and as a consequence, the creature's natural inclination extends, in some way, to God. What this means exactly for non-rational beings is difficult to understand. It seems that, applied to them, it can only mean that they tend toward what is *in fact* an imitation of some aspect of God's perfection. In rational beings, however, it seems to imply a conditional inclination: *if* one knows that God exists, then one will have a favorable disposition toward him and his plan.[21] In any case, while Thomas holds that the love of self is the root of the love of other created persons, it is *not* the root and cause of love of God. Rather, his position is that an ingredient in one's basic natural inclination is an inclination toward the universal good of which one's proper good is a participation or imitation.

Second—and I think more clearly—it belongs to what a creature is ("*secundum hoc id quod est*," Thomas says) to be a member of the whole universe. So, if the creature inclines toward its fulfillment, then it must incline toward cooperating with other members in its community, and, ultimately, in the largest community of all, the universe. As a good basketball player is not just one who scores baskets, makes rebounds, and so on, but is, by the nature of the case, one who also plays well with his teammates and contributes to the good of the team; likewise, the perfection of any creature includes as an essential component his contribution to, and, if he is a rational being, his caring for, the fulfillment of the good of the whole universe, not just his own individual good.[22]

---

[20] *DDN*, chapter 4, lecture 9 (#406). *III Sent.* d 29, a 3.

[21] Note also that, since this is a natural inclination, it is toward God as the author of nature, not toward God as personally present, that is, as offering personal communion with him. *ST* I 60. 5 ad 4; I-II 109.3 ad 1.

[22] Cf. *ST* I-II 109.3: "The reason why [it is natural for man to love God above self] is because it is natural for everything that it desire and love something, according as it is naturally apt to be [*secundum quod aptum natum est esse*], for

This point could also be stated as follows. To love oneself is to will what is really good to oneself. But, caring only about oneself diminishes oneself. Caring only about oneself, acting as if one were the center of reality and everything and everyone else a mere means toward one's own perfection, severely detracts from one's perfection. So, to love only oneself is not to love oneself. The sinner, says Thomas, does not properly, or genuinely, love himself. True, he has a disordered love of self, but he does not will what is genuinely good to himself.[23] To will what is genuinely good to oneself requires that one be a person who cares for others for their good as well as for oneself.

And, expressed in still another way: if you love yourself, then you will want to be morally good and have friendships, real friendships. Someone might object that this makes caring for another a means in relation to one's individual perfection. But the point is that only if one genuinely—that is, not as a mere means—cares for others for their own sakes, is one an upright, good person. One cannot, coherently, want to be morally good merely as a means toward an end, and one cannot will to have a friendship in the full sense of the term, unless one is morally good for its own sake and unless one cares for one's friend for his own sake, and not as mere means toward one's own perfection.[24] Caring about even one's own individual perfection logically entails caring about other people's perfection for their own sakes.

We can now return to the question whether Thomas's position on beatitude is compatible with his position that we ought to love God and neighbor for their own sakes. The fundamental answer to this objection is as follows: true, every act is for the sake of one's own good—otherwise, the action does not flow from within, but is imposed from outside. However, this does not mean that every act is for the sake only

---

'each thing acts according as it is naturally apt to be,' as is said in the Second book of the Physics. Now it is clear that the good of the part is for the sake of the good of the whole. Therefore also by a natural appetite or love, each particular thing loves its own proper good for the sake of the common good of the whole universe, which is God."

[23] *ST* II-II 25.4.

[24] Aquinas says that so-called friendships of utility and friendships of pleasure are not friendships in the full sense of the term: *ST* I-II 26.4 ad 3.

of my own individual good. Rather, as we have seen, Thomas is quick to point out that I am inclined toward my perfection according to the sort of thing I am. And I am not just an individual. First of all, I am in communion with other people in various ways: family members, co-citizens, co-students, co-employees, and all other human beings. These different ontological unions ground different types of affective unions. Second, as a creature, my good is a reflection—vague and inadequate, but real—of the universal and infinite goodness which is God. Thus, my natural inclination is toward my good, but not as if it were the center, or the only good, in the universe. It is toward my good as a part of, or a constituent of, the good of the universe as reflecting the universal good, the fulfillment of God's plan. And so beatitude, for Thomas, cannot consist in my own individual fulfillment in isolation. It is essentially social.

Thomas takes over Boethius's definition of beatitude: "the state perfected by the possession of all goods."[25] Aquinas holds, of course, that the essence of true beatitude is vision of the divine essence as it is in itself. This is a *supernatural* condition, that is, one which is more than the actualization of our natural capacities. In addition, however, beatitude will include the fulfillment of all of our natural capacities, since in creating us God directs us to our natural fulfillment. God is the author of our nature, that is, the natural inclinations in us as directing us toward our fulfillment are from God. The fulfillment of our natural capacities—which in the early questions of the *Prima Secundae* Thomas says will come about by an "overflow" (*redundantia*) from the beatific vision itself, is our natural fulfillment. So, there will be supernatural fulfillment (union with God) and natural fulfillment (actualization of natural capacities) as components of complete beatitude.[26] Neither of these components, however, should be conceived individualistically. Communion with God is by the nature of the case social, a communion with the three divine persons, but also a supernatural communing with all the other saints, all the other friends of God.[27] Natural fulfillment also will include friendship, the fulfillment of our social nature. So, our

---

[25] See *ST* I-II 2.1.

[26] St. Thomas speaks of the "*bene esse* of beatitude." See *ST* I-II 4.5.

[27] Ibid., 4.8.

friendships will have both natural and supernatural components or levels. Therefore, acting for the sake of beatitude is not aiming merely at one's individualistic perfection, but is aiming at a condition that is communal. My beatitude includes more than my individual fulfillment. Thus, one could express Thomas's thought by saying that one's ultimate end in life should be the glory of God, understood as the fulfillment of God's plan for creation, and one's own good as a constituent—not a mere means, nor the end to which everything else is a mere means.[28]

6. Objections

Let us now consider just one objection regarding Thomas's position. Although not mentioning Thomas Aquinas by name, Dietrich von Hildebrand criticizes his position that solidarity, or union, is a basis of genuine love of another. While von Hildebrand concedes that we often do have solidarity with others, and that this can ground a type of caring about them, this type of caring should not be confused with love. Wherever solidarity is the basis for interest, according to von Hildebrand, one views the other as a part of oneself, or as one's possession. For example, solidarity may ground the interest of a husband in his wife so that he may resent people insulting her or mistreating her, even though he himself frequently abuses her, or a master resents someone mistreating his servants, despite the fact that he mistreats and abuses them.[29] In the same way, John Crosby speaks of solidarity that grounds taking an interest in others, but only "on the basis of absorbing others into ourselves, or considering others as extensions of ourselves. But, surely there is no self-transcendence in attaining to the other by abolishing him or her as other!"[30]

On the contrary, there are three points to make in reply. First, Aquinas's claim is that the *love of friendship* for oneself is extended to

---

[28] Cf. Germain Grisez, *The Way of the Lord Jesus, Volume 1: Christian Moral Principles* (Chicago: Franciscan Herald Press, 1983), ch. 19.

[29] Dietrich von Hildebrand, *The Role of Human Love*, translated by Jan Van Jeurck (Franciscan Herald Press, 1977), pp. 9-11

[30] John F. Crosby, *The Selfhood of the Human Person* (Washington, D.C.: Catholic University of America Press, 1996), p. 180.

another on the basis of that other's ontological union (same nature, same city, same family etc.), not a mere love of concupiscence. Why assume, as do von Hildebrand and Crosby, that, in effect, such an extension is impossible, that instead, the solidarity allows one only to view the other as a possession or a part? No argument has been given for this assumption.

Second, while there certainly are possessive husbands and abusive masters who view other persons as one with themselves, these are not the types of unions causing the love that Thomas refers to as love of friendship. He explicitly distinguishes this sort of case from a case where an ontological union causes an extension of love of friendship. In his commentary on Dionysius's *On the Divine Names*, he explicitly distinguishes between loving another as *a part of oneself*—the kind of love based on the union that is evidently referred to by von Hildebrand and Crosby—from loving another as *for his own sake*.[31] In other words, Aquinas explicitly recognizes that in some cases an ontological union (solidarity) grounds only a love of concupiscence. But he also claims that in other cases an ontological union grounds a genuine love of friendship of another.

A third point in reply to the claim of von Hildebrand and Crosby is that they evidently did not look hard for possible counterexamples. Certainly the love of a mother for her child (or of a father for his child) in some way grows out of the maternal (or paternal) relationship itself. This love is as it is, not *only* because of the intrinsic degree of goodness in the child—although that of course is also present, as Thomas insists. Rather, it is clear that this love for one's child is based, in part, on his nearness to, or unity with, oneself. A mother loves her child very intensely, not simply or only because he is very good—there likely are other children better than he—but because he is her child. And yet most instances of maternal love are not cases of viewing the child as a part of oneself or as a possession. So, Thomas roots one phenomenon (genuine love of another) in another (natural inclination toward one's fulfillment). This is quite different from saying that one is just a disguised form of the other.

---

[31] *DDN*, chapter 4, lect. 9.

7. The Significance of Thomas's Answer

We might ask ourselves why Thomas takes such pains to root love of neighbor in love of self, and why he insists that the inclination to love God is an ingredient in our natural inclination. Also, we might ask, is this insistence necessary? Why not simply say that when we perceive someone who merits our love, then we love him? Why not simply say that when we love another for his own sake we are transcending our natural inclination toward self-perfection? Why, in other words, does Aquinas resolutely align himself with what Pierre Rousselot called "the physical conception of love," and why should we do so?[32]

Indeed, the position that the will is able to act outside the direction of its natural inclination was strongly championed by Duns Scotus. Scotus argued that, while there is in the will a natural inclination toward the perfection of the agent, an inclination he calls an "*affectio commodi*" (affection for the advantageous), the will also has the ability to transcend its natural inclination and render to the object what is due *it*. This ability he calls the "*affectio iustitiae*" (affection for justice). According to Scotus, then, in order to act morally one must transcend one's inclination toward self-perfection, and thus will to the object what is fitting to it, irrespective of its relation to oneself.[33] On this view, "acting according to nature" is not yet acting in a morally significant way. The morally significant acts occur when the will is able to set aside its natural appetite, and act according to *its affectio iustitiae*.[34] Something like this position is proposed by von Hildebrand and many of his followers.

Aquinas considers a position that in some ways is similar to Scotus's when he considers the teaching of William of Auxerre. William taught that our nature inclines us to love ourselves more intensely than God, and that only with the supernatural gift of charity do we love God more

---

[32] Pierre Rousselot, *The Problem of Love in the Middle Ages*, translated by Alan Vincelette (Milwaukee: Marquette University Press, 2001), first published in French in 1908 in *Beiträge zur Geschichte der Philosophie des Mittelalters*, VI, 6 (Muenster: Ashendorff, 1908), and then in book form again in 1933.

[33] On Scotus's ethics, see: *Duns Scotus on the Will and Morality*, translated by Allan B. Wolter (Washington, D.C.: Catholic University of America Press, 1986).

[34] John Duns Scotus, *Opus Oxoniensis*, Book II, distinction 6, question 2.

intensely than ourselves. Thomas's answer is significant: "[I]f it were natural to love oneself more than God, it would follow that natural love would be perverse, and it would not be perfected by charity, but destroyed by it."[35] The *affectio iustitiae* of Scotus is not supernatural, and so Scotus's position differs from William's. Still, like William, he holds that the will's natural appetite or inclination is simply toward one's own individual perfection. Indeed, according to Scotus, to love any other person for his own sake involves acting outside or beyond the natural tendency in one's will. So, like the position of William of Auxerre criticized by Thomas, this position implies that one's natural inclination is self-centered or egoistical. Genuine love of others requires setting aside one's natural tendency. To act morally one must ignore one's natural inclinations and act instead on the basis of the merits of the object itself.[36] In turn, this position implies that the goodness of the self is in tension with the goodness of God. On this view, then, something of human nature, indeed something quite central—the basic natural inclination to fulfillment—must be set aside or suppressed to make room for love of God.

However, this position has profound difficulties. It is a fundamental metaphysical truth that each agent acts for its own perfection; this is simply a manifestation of its distinctness, of its being a distinct agent or distinct being. If there were an inclination in the will which is outside its natural appetite, then it would have to be either preternatural, if it were not against or contrary to the will's natural appetite, or violent, if it were against the will's natural appetite. Such an inclination would have to be something coming to it solely from an *extrinsic* agent, and, to that extent, not natural.

To this, one might object that it is just the nature of the will to tend toward good as such, not toward the agent's good. However, the good is fulfillment, so the object of a tendency must be *someone's* or *something's*

---

[35] *ST* I-II 60.5.

[36] This in turn produces a dualism between one's natural self, or the natural side of oneself, and one's moral self, similar to the dualism in Kant between the phenomenal self and the noumenal, or moral, self. On this point, see Jean Rohmer, *La Finalité chez les Théologiens de Saint Augustin á Duns Scot* (Paris: Vrin, 1939).

fulfillment. What this objection would be saying, in effect, is that the will's nature, or natural appetite would be, not toward its own good (that is, the good of the agent, this human being) but toward the good of the whole, or perhaps, the good-of-every-person-known. But that cannot be the whole story. For in that case the will would be by nature *only* a part; it would have no more tendency toward its own good than toward anyone else's. It would not have a specific or individual nature. Suppose you have a whole, W, composed of x, y, and z. Now suppose x tends toward W's good, and that x's relation to its own good is just the same as its relation to y's good and z's good. And suppose this is true, analogously, of y and z also. Well, that is incoherent. For in that case x, y, and z, could not be different beings. For the actions of a thing follow its being, and if the tendencies of x, y, and z, are no different at all, then x, y, and z are not different. That is, for any x and y, their inherent tendencies cannot be exactly the same (or: have the same logical ordering); for, since action follows being, x and y would not be distinct beings.

It is not incoherent to say that x has a tendency toward W's good (the good of the whole, or more precisely, the universal good, of which x and y are participations) as an integral part of its tendency toward its own good, because it is by nature a part (as a member of a community) of W—that is Thomas's position. You could even say that it tends toward the good of W more than its own good. Still, its relation to y's good and z's good must be different than its relation to its own good. Specifically, the logical order of its natural interests must differ; x's tendency to y's good and z's good must be based and patterned on its more original tendency to its own (x's) good.

Also, x's tendency toward y's good or z's good must be a specification of its basic natural tendency toward its own good (which can include its tendency toward W's good, since x is a participant of or image of W); otherwise, the tendency toward y's good or z's good is preternatural or violent (to be preternatural rather than violent there would have to be first a union of y's or z's nature with x's). So, x can tend toward y's good or z's good, but only if z's good or y's good first comes under the umbrella or formality (*ratio*) of x's good. What is at stake in this issue is the metaphysical distinctness and distinct goodness of each creature, as opposed to its absorption in the being and goodness of the Absolute. The creature's good or fulfillment cannot consist only in being for another. It must possess an inherent being and tendency; additional tendencies, unless they are preternatural or violent, must be in some way specifications of, within the rubric of, those inherent, natural tendencies.[37]

The relationship of love of God and neighbor to love of self is *analogous* to the relationship of grace to nature, or, even more generally, of God to creatures. Just as there is no dichotomy between grace and nature, so one must be careful not to create, in one's theory, a dichotomy between the divine good and the human good, or between love of God and love of self.

Part of who you are is the fact that your love follows an order, so that you love more those who are nearer to you, nearer to your self, than those more distant. You love your father more than other men not because he is objectively better than they, but because he is your father. For Aquinas, this is entirely right, proper, and morally good. In Aquinas, there is no bifurcation between an ethical, universalistic standpoint, and a natural, particularistic one. The universal standpoint is achieved, but one arrives at it by extension, by extending one's interests, not by setting aside those which are, after all, bound up with one's deepest personal identity.[38] So, one could rightly call Thomas's distinctive position on love *personalistic,* since it safeguards against reducing or absorbing the identity of the person.

Thomas avoids egoism, but he also avoids viewing genuine love of self as an alternative to, and so in fundamental tension with, love of God and love of neighbor. According to Thomas, we are called to love God and dedicate ourselves to doing our part in the fulfillment of God's plan. This is indeed the grand vision of the *Summa Theologiae.* Every agent acts for its own good. But its own good is a likeness of God's infinite goodness, willed by God, conserved in being by God, and moved

---

[37] This applies also to supernatural tendencies. While they dispose the creature to fulfillment, which transcends its own nature, still, the natural tendencies of such a being must be open to such addition. The will's orientation to understood good makes that possible.

[38] Cf. Christine Sommers, "Philosophers Against the Family," reprinted in *Analyzing Moral Issues with Reasoning, Reading, Writing, and Debating in Ethics,* edited by Judith Boss (New York: McGraw Hill, 2005).

toward attainment of its proper end by God, an end that is at the same time a component in the implementation of God's Providence, God's eternal Plan. So, working for the attainment of one's own good, or the good proportioned to one's nature, and working for God's glory—these are not antithetical. Rather, there is a genuine harmony between one's own fulfillment and the love of God or the fulfillment of his plan. One must not make oneself the center, reducing all else to a mere means toward one's own good, since one's own good is only a part of the whole, the whole being the common good of the whole universe. On the other hand, one's genuine good—which means one's real fulfillment, including first-order goods such as knowledge, health, and artistic development—is neither a competing (perhaps distracting) alternative, nor an extrinsic means in relation to the fulfillment of God's plan. Rather one's genuine fulfillment is an intrinsic constituent of the good that God plans. So, one ought to love oneself, that is, will to oneself what is genuinely good for oneself, but as part of the fulfillment of God's plan.

ANALOGY:

MISCHIEF, MALICE, AND METAPHYSICS

James G. Hanink

Anecdotal evidence more than suggests that college graduates entertain comic memories of Philosophy 100. The comedy can become explicit in *Dilbert,* a daily strip exploring corporate vagaries. A recent example comes to mind. "Wally," a veteran wage-slave, is trapped, mind adrift, in a meeting. Wait, now! Has Wally, tilting forward, fallen asleep? No, Dilbert explains; he's had a "paradigm shift." (My sincere apologies to Thomas Kuhn, long a victim of popularizers.)

Yet often the comic is a defense against the tragic. The negative thesis of this essay is that one of the tragedies with which we must now contend is that much of our public discourse muddles the language of analogy, and that too often the muddling is malicious. The positive thesis of this analysis, on the other hand, is that a realist metaphysics, of the kind rarely found in Philosophy 100, can help us put matters right. The essay argues, in addition, that such a realist metaphysics must continue to contest a perennial foe: an eviscerating nominalism that, if unchecked, would evacuate reason itself.

1. Mischief and Malice

Perhaps the reader will find the negative and critical thesis seems unduly severe. Often enough, it is only mischief, not malice, which muddles our public discourse—especially when it takes on a commercial accent. As a longtime "Emeril wannabe," I recently joined the Good Cook Book Club. We ought not to complain too much about the Club's warm e-mail welcome to its cyberspace "community of readers," even though the missive comes with easy to follow "let's get down to business" steps for efficient online payments.

But, mischief can range from the mild to the mystifying. My academic colleagues speak of "changing the culture," not of academe, but of our small college of liberal arts. Journalists write about the "community" of millions of Latinos in the Los Angeles area. Publicists extol the "family" of Wal-Mart employees. We might ask, to be sure, how much this mischief truly matters. Perhaps we can allow some leeway for the vagaries of "socio-babble." Nobody would confuse it with, say, *science* and its sober demands. Another clip from *Dilbert* captures the difference. Our not so dynamic duo, Dilbert and Wally, are called to a meeting with their "pointy-haired boss." Grimly, the boss announces that the CEO plans to change, not the company's corporate culture, but its DNA. "This," says the fearful boss, "sounds medical."

But when malice becomes midwife to mischief, we'd best be on alert. In some institutional quarters, legal and even ecclesiastical, we are now instructed to speak of the "marriage," not only of a husband and a wife, but of those with same-sex attraction. And recently organizers of the Rose Bowl Parade, with their theme "Celebrate Family," looked for homosexual "families" to enlist. Nonsense on stilts gives way to fantasy on floats, and somewhere along the line it's time to draw a line.

What's going wrong? At one level, the problem is "inflationary" language that ignores basic distinctions. There is a place for verbal exuberance, even extravagance. But we should largely reserve this space for sports writers—and the financial reporters who monitor our *plunging*, *soaring*, or *wildly oscillating* stock markets. If philosophers, however, want to help form a responsible citizenry, they would do better to speak of the *tone* of a small liberal arts college, of the Latino *population*, and of an *association* of Wal-Mart employees. My college, after all, is far too small and derivative to have its own culture, and the millions of Latinos in the Los Angeles region are far too many and disparate to be a community.[1] (In contrast, reports of a San Pedro "tattoo community" are suspect if only because its denizens are far too few and too transient.[2])

In several contexts, indeed, linguistic license can put us in peril. Wal-Mart employees who confuse their employer with their parents do

---

[1] Here I can only acknowledge the importance of T. S. Eliot's discussion of culture understood analogously. He distinguishes among the culture of the individual, of the group, and of society as a whole. For an analysis of this, see Tracey Rowland's *Culture and the Thomist Tradition after Vatican II* (London and New York: Routledge, 2003), beginning with pp. 20-21.

[2] "Tattoo You," by Joshua Stecker, *Long Beach Press-Telegram's San Pedro Magazine*, July, 2005, p. 26.

so at their own risk. Another pair of examples implicates familiar hazards. In the 2002-2003 school year, teacher and staff absenteeism in the Los Angeles Unified School District cost taxpayers more than $432 million. What's the explanation? The district identifies a "culture of entitlement" as the culprit, and thereby neither explains nor remedies anything.[3] And the London-based petrochemical firm, BP, has of late been under investigation for its poor safety record. OSHA, citing employee lapses, observed that BP managers at a Texas refinery "don't have a culture of safety that looks at all the details."[4] This diagnosis is more likely to obscure than to expose individual worker negligence.

A variety of reasons can explain why people resort to inflationary language and ignore basic distinctions. Simple laziness, no doubt, is one. Other reasons are more sinister: the world, and an appetite for its attention; the flesh, and our desire for its excitement; and the devil in his role as the Father of Lies. But the analysis of such reasons seldom falls to the philosopher. My focus in what follows will be the way in which inflationary and referentially un-tethered language disregards distinctive structural realities. Far too often, we speak of culture, of community, and of family in an analogically attenuated way without respecting what constitutes these fundamental human realities. Nor can we honor what constitutes them, much less recognize why it is honorable, unless we grasp the kind of reality that only a *primary* culture or community or family can fully exhibit.

Malice predictably and eagerly plays midwife to mischief when some deliberately misuse the flexible language of analogy to advance their partisan interests. Often, too, such malice recruits and enlists disordered emotions in exploiting a species of logical confusion about primary structures. This maneuver is transparently at work in the critical case of marriage. Whatever its trials, marriage has a profound appeal. The wellspring of this appeal is the complementarity of its "two-in-one-flesh" communion. Yet, articulating the full structure of

---

[3] "Teacher absenteeism costs school district millions," by Melissa Milios, *Daily Breeze*, June 24, 2004, A13-14.

[4] See "An Oil Giant Faces Questions About a Deadly Blast in Texas," by Chip Cummins and Thaddeus Herrick, in *The Wall Street Journal*, July 27, 2005, Section A, p. 1.

primary marriage makes philosophical demands, especially if one's philosophical vocabulary is impoverished. Thus, it becomes easy enough to coin a same-sex imitation of marriage. Left unchecked, this false currency further devalues our public discourse.

2. Metaphysics

My first and negative thesis, then, is merely diagnostic: examples are ready at hand to show how public discourse muddles the language of analogy, and sometimes with malice aforethought.

But my second and positive thesis, to which I now turn, is constructive. A robust, realist metaphysics can help counteract muddling, and even mischief. In the analysis that follows, I explore two resources for such a realist metaphysics. For the first of these resources, we are indebted to the "early" John Wild (later he was to make a "phenomenological turn"). Wild's analysis appealed to what he termed an "end-ordered" noetic reality. His analysis of social groups in light of such a reality is of critical interest. Neither reductive nor inflationary in his thinking, Wild understands the nature of a group in terms of "*a single end, rationally held in mind by the different members.*"[5] A realist account of community, I argue, might well begin with Wild's proposal, although it should go beyond it. The second resource is what W. Norris Clarke, S.J., presents as the category of "system." Treating it as a necessary supplement to Aristotle's categories, Clarke identifies system as an accident that occurs in many subjects at once. As such, it is an irreducible mode of unity.[6] A successful realist account of marriage and its sexual complementarity, I will argue, can make good use of Clarke's analysis of "system," although it does need further specification.

In fashioning a realist account of community, we might usefully start by contrasting it with a pair of sharply divergent, and badly flawed, opposing views: reductive individualism and, its theoretical

---

[5] John Wild, *Introduction to Realistic Philosophy* (New York: Harper & Brothers, 1948), pp. 180-89.

[6] W. Norris Clarke, S.J., *The One and the Many: A Contemporary Thomistic Metaphysics* (Notre Dame, Indiana: University of Notre Dame Press, 2001), pp. 135-36.

opposite, a kind of quasi-ontological reificationism. The individualist view, on the one hand, is that a community is nothing more than the individuals who compose it. The reduction is ontological. The individualist, moreover, often keeps company with the egoist, who, in turn, insists that we act, or should act, only out of self-interest. Given the views of such an alliance, any group, however noble, will upon inspection reduce to converging individual interests.

This reductive individualism, however, faces its own problems. The first is that it dissolves community by undermining the social character of the human person. The communities in which we live shape who we are. We do not habitually, much less inescapably, cobble together our communities simply to advance our private interests. (Doubtless on occasion our behavior is thus indictable, but no one supposes otherwise. Human failure does not constitute a philosophy.) Second, this reductive individualism erodes the moral dimension of community. Some social structures markedly advance, while others dramatically imperil, our flourishing. We are responsible for both sorts of structures; but they can nonetheless reach, with a cumulative perplexity, beyond our individual actions. The logical analysis of this cumulative dimension can prove elusive, but our experience of it is only too familiar. The enduring legacy of racism, with its polymorphous perversity, is but one example.[7]

On the other hand, a quasi-ontological reification of community is as flawed as reductive individualism. Such reification is especially ominous when it makes an idol of the nation as a community. A sense of individual powerlessness is one source of this idolatry. Because a community is often temporally prior to its members, its power and scope frequently extend beyond that of its individual members. But whatever its source, such reifying of community is badly mistaken.

It is mistaken, first, because any group can act only insofar as its individual members act. It is mistaken, second and more pointedly, because social sin is the sin of flesh and blood human beings. In speaking bluntly about the "structure of sin," John Paul the Great underscored the indispensable role of personal agency.

---

[7] For a theological analysis of racism, see *Brothers and Sisters to Us: U.S. Bishops' Pastoral Letter on Racism in Our Day* (United States Catholic Conference, 1979).

> It is a case of the very personal sins of those who cause or support evil or who exploit it; of those who are in a position to avoid, eliminate or at least limit certain social evils but who fail to do so [...]; of those who take refuge in the supposed impossibility of changing the world, and also of those who sidestep the effort and sacrifice required, producing specious reasons of a higher order.[8]

John Paul's judgment emphasizes that no social structure can dissolve individual responsibility. While it is a mistake to see a group as nothing but its individual members, it is also a mistake to suppose that a group could itself be an ontological "super" person or could somehow take moral priority over the person. Both errors distort human nature by misreading human agency.

How, then, might we develop a satisfactory and realist account of community? Let's turn, for the moment, to a full statement of John Wild's proposal. "*The human group is a set of diverse, individual activities made one by their common reference to a single end, rationally held in mind by the different members.*"[9] Note well: Wild presents the group (and not, say, a heap or a herd) as a distinct reality; it is one which is made so by an intelligible and shared end. But since he chooses to define a *group* rather than a *community*, we need to recognize some critical distinctions between the two.

One distinction is that not all groups are communities, at least not in the morally relevant sense. In our ordinary conversation we readily recognize this important difference. Members of a particular group frequently recognize that they fall short of being a community; and, for just this reason, they struggle to become a community. Such a group, as it happens, might fall short of being a community, and even have no prospects of becoming one, in at least two different ways. First, the group might pursue an already disordered end. A business cartel, for instance, might be negotiating to put together a greedy and exploitative monopoly. Second, another group, with a distorted notion of how to achieve its goal, might pursue a legitimate end and yet do so

---

[8] John Paul II, "Apostolic Exhortation: *Reconciliatio et Paenitentia*," (December 2, 1984), AAS 77 (1985): 217.

[9] Wild, *Introduction to Realistic Philosophy*, pp. 185-86.

in a badly mistaken way. An advocacy group, as an instance, might oppose a wrongheaded scheme for commercial land development. The group's end is worthy. Yet the group might seek its goal in a distorted way, for example, by blocking low-income housing. In contrast to both such groups, an authentic community, in the morally relevant sense, shows that it shares as its transformative good both a worthy end and a right understanding of how to achieve it. Thus, for a welcome and familiar example, a local community of advocates for the homeless might come together in a series of Habitat for Humanity projects.

At this juncture a further distinction, important in the literature of community, is in order. *Not* every community, in the morally relevant sense, need be what sociologists, following Ferdinand Tonnies, term a *gemeinschaft.*[10] The logically specifying difference is that while we can and often do come together to form a community, for example, of "concerned citizens," the fashioning of a *gemeinschaft*, in that it is an affective phenomenon, never begins with calling a meeting, setting an agenda, and identifying a shared goal. On this point, I find myself parting company with Jacques Maritain's distinction between a community as "more of a work of nature" and a society as "more of a work of reason," insofar as it implies that there is no such thing as an intentional, in contradistinction to a natural, community.[11]

What, then, do these various distinctions suggest? Taken together, they help to suggest that a community involves the shared and dynamic pursuit of an emerging common good rather than merely a fleeting convergence of individual interests. The following definition satisfactorily reflects this understanding: *A community is an alliance of persons who share a unified pattern of activities and a reflective pursuit of a common good.* Not surprisingly, though, some further clarification is in order.

Note that on this proposed definition human persons are prior to their activities. John Crosby, in carefully rejecting Max Scheler's notion of community as "quasi-personal," speaks to the point at issue. Against Scheler, with whom he is often in sympathy, Crosby rightly insists that:

---

[10] See Ferdinand Tonnies's classic *Gemeinschaft und Gesellschaft* (Leipzig, 1887).

[11] Jacques Maritain, *Man and the State* (Washington, D.C.: Catholic University of America Press, 1998), p. 2.

"[A] collective person presupposes individual persons and exists only in and through them and apart from them is nothing at all (though of course it is more than the sum of them)."[12] This something "more," we are to understand, is a moral reality rather than a substantial reality.

And what is "the common good" to which the proposed definition would refer us? This common good is the whole range of material and cultural preconditions that enables us to pursue the basic personal and shared goods, taken together with the integrated realization of these several goods.[13] Unlike the narrowly utilitarian good, the common good integrates rather than maximizes. For this reason, we dare not abstract the common good from flesh and blood persons. Thus, Jacques Maritain's "law of redistribution" proposes that the common good, though superior to individual goods, should return to the persons who constitute the community. His "law of transcendence," in turn, emphasizes that it is not political units but rather persons who are eternal. For this reason, the common good, by its nature, "must favor their progress toward the absolute goods which transcend political society."[14]

From working out an account of community, with an assist from John Wild, we can next turn to W. Norris Clarke's category of "system," a second resource for realist metaphysics. For Clarke, *system* is a category of being, specifically, an irreducible mode of unity. "[I]t is not as strong a unity as a substance, so has no single characteristic action of the whole as such. But it is a stronger mode of unity than just the sum of many different interactions or relations."[15] The members of a system share together in a singular relationship, and we cannot reduce this

---

[12] John F. Crosby, *Personalist Papers* (Washington, D.C.: Catholic University of America Press, 2004), p. 190.

[13] Vatican II presents the common good as "the sum of those conditions of social life which allow social groups and their individual members relatively thorough and ready access to their own fulfillment..." (Pope Paul VI, *Gaudium et spes*, 26, http://www.vatican.va/archive/hist_councils/ii_vatican_council/documents/vat-ii_cons_19651207_gaudium-et spes_en.html).

[14] Jacques Maritain, *The Person and the Common Good* (Notre Dame, Indiana: University of Notre Dame Press, 1966), p. 76.

[15] Clarke, *The One and the Many*, p. 136.

relationship to a mere plurality of accidental relations keyed to their respective *relata*.

The importance of system as a mode of unity is enormous. Clarke notes that systems everywhere order reality and that all real beings participate in multiple systems. Indeed, we are by nature "related to ... other beings and systems of them."[16] Thus, he points out, "we may justly say that both substantiality and relationality are primordial dimensions of reality."[17] To ignore, then, either dimension is to misconstrue badly the structure of being. Given the extraordinary array of possible systems and the range of beings that participate in them, we must pay critical attention to the structure of distinct systems. Thus, for example, theologians from Augustine to Joseph Ratzinger (Benedict XVI) have emphasized the relational structure of the Trinity.[18] At the level of social and political analysis, Clarke himself distinguishes between person-focused systems that tend to develop the individual and totalitarian systems that seek to submerge the individual.[19]

Here, though, I wish to treat marriage, itself a distinctive instance of community, as a unique system. What kind of reality do we find in the *primary* marriage of man and woman? It is a relational, rather than a substantial, reality. It is, most distinctively, both consensual and sexual. As consensual it is deliberate and voluntary; as sexual, it is unitive and procreative. In their mating, man and woman become a single reproductive principle.[20] Thus their marriage can embody a self-giving mutuality that is, literally, the core matrix of the entire human enterprise. Finally, of course, it is always the man and the woman, as persons, who act to form a single reproductive principle and to foster a

---

[16] Ibid.

[17] Ibid.

[18] Tracey Rowland underscores the significance of system and relationality in her *Culture and the Thomist Tradition after Vatican II*, especially pp. 82, 95, 110, and 142.

[19] Clarke, *The One and the Many*, p. 137.

[20] For a development of this proposition, see Robert George, *The Clash of Orthodoxies: Law, Religion, and Morality in Crisis* (Wilmington, Delaware: ISI Books, 2001), pp. 77-80.

self-giving mutuality. A marriage, as such, since it is not a substance, can never function as an agent.

To be sure, we sometimes speak of marriage in other than its primary structure. But in doing so we should distinguish between the insightful and misshapen analogues of the primary structure. Consider some familiar examples of the latter. "He's married to his career." Yes, in a sense; but should he be? No, because a career is not a person. Or, again: "They're wedded to the project." It is better, if possible, that they wed one another. After all, no project can aspire to be a person—and even the best of projects must be put aside if its funding is not renewed.

But let us turn from the perhaps mischievously figurative use of "marriage" to the vigorously sponsored and abruptly commonplace locution "same-sex marriage." Its referent is neither unitive nor procreative. What, then, is the genesis of its referent? What is its purpose? As for its genesis, it is an artifact of the libido and the affections; it is, moreover, driven by economic and social policy concerns. Its purpose is to win social recognition. It demands the civic endorsement of instrumentalized "sex acts" and financial benefits for those who commit to a (relatively) stable engagement therein. Regardless of its genesis and purpose, and more might be said about both, same-sex marriage, as a matter of legal statute, is a *fait accompli*; its widening legal establishment is highly probable. But the philosopher, if not the sociologist, persists: *should* "same-sex marriage" be so endorsed and rewarded?

Perhaps an analogy will sharpen the philosopher's question. In the bell weather State of California, there happens to be a movement to license astrologers. If it succeeds, some astrologers will proclaim themselves to have finally come of age. Money, status, and pride are at stake. But there's also a resistance to the movement. Objectors, quite sensibly, contend that licensing astrologers will lead some people to confuse them with astronomers. Some people, predictably, will be artfully led to think that astrologers are somehow aligned with astronomers--the worthy practitioners of the noble, ancient, and *primary* science of astronomy. Philosophers, I submit, should join, nay, lead the resistance!

But here the reader might cry "foul!" After all, am I not now putting forth an argument by analogy against what I criticize as the fiction of "same-sex marriage?" Given my warnings against the abuse of analogical language, how can I now argue from such an analogy when it suits my own purposes? Such a reader deserves a prompt reply, and I respond as follows. On the one hand, every analogy limps, and some do so from malice. On the other hand, analogy can be illuminating. In diagnosing the inappropriateness of analogizing homosexual partnership to heterosexual marriage, I hope to make matters more, and not less, perspicuous. We might well pause, then, to explore the pair of analogies at issue.

Let's note, to begin, two decidedly relevant points of similarity between the recognizing of "same sex marriage" and the licensing of astrologers. The first point of comparison is the matter of a basic incapacity to achieve a purported goal. Astrologers, as such, cannot effect a science, no matter how long or ardently they might attempt to do so. Neither can same sex partners effect a marriage, no matter how long nor ardently might they attempt to do so. The second point of comparison is the type of incentives that lead some to deny the respective core incapacities to achieve purported goals. Licensing astrologers would bring them both economic and social advantages; practitioners would move from the margins to the mainstream. In like fashion, the statutory recognition of same-sex unions promises economic and social advantages to those who attempt them.

The chief points of *dis*similarity in the analogies at issue are, it happens, also two. The first is that astrology centers on superstition, often marketed as an enlightening *gnosis*. Same-sex unions, in contrast, center on libido, often marketed as a liberating *eros*. But neither superstition nor libido, *a fortiori* as so marketed, merit special legal entitlements. Second, astrology is, and has long been, empirically and irreparably falsified. In contrast, advocates of same-sex unions can still predict that a sterilized sexuality will escape trivialization and publicly project rosy futures for children who are denied, whether by adoptive strategy or reproductive technique, either a father or a mother.

Given the second of this pair of dissimilarities between licensing astrologers and validating same-sex unions, I argue that the case for such unions proves to have even less merit than the manifestly weak case for licensing astrologers. Astrology is a "thinkable" science in that the stars *could* affect our lives other than they in fact do. Same-sex marriage, however, fails to exist in any of the countless possible worlds. Male and female complementarity and a unitive self-donation of a procreative nature are impossible for members of the same sex, unless male is no longer male and female is no longer female.

Given this review of the pair of analogies at issue, the objection that despite my warnings of analogical abuse, I have myself resorted to an abusive analogy fails. But, there is a deeper objection, both logical and metaphysical, to my case against same-sex "marriages" that now demands attention.

3. The Specter of Nominalism

In making my case against counterfeit analogies in general, and same-sex "marriages" in particular, I must acknowledge the ever-lurking specter of nominalism. How, at this juncture, might the nominalist proceed? First, I suspect, our nemesis would favor us with a sigh of regret. Then he would begin his bantering riposte. "Are you done rehearsing your complaints? We've heard it all before. You're no metaphysician. You're a miserable word maven. Language—don't you see?—changes to meet our changing needs. If it suits us, we can call any group whatever we choose to call it. A community, you say? That's the kind of thing we *designate*. Ditto a culture. If you realists want to *discover* something, why not search the sky for a new comet?"

"Popular language communicates and communication," continues the nominalist, "covers a multitude of supposed logical sins. Besides, logic is 'after the fact.' The fact is that we're reshaping our concepts of culture and community, of family and marriage. Philosophers and politicians have reshaped the concepts of truth and freedom, not to mention the American Way. Enough of your realist rant and rhetoric!"

And how should I reply? "It is, sir, because communication counts that language must lay hold of what is real. Make-believe cultures, *ersatz* communities, *faux* families, and "same-sex" marriages only communicate failure. Legal fiction, no doubt, can emulate science fiction. The courts might re-cast marriage as any close sexual relationship that pleases adults, no matter the link between intercourse and procreation. If so, adults would first of all fail their children. But, with so slippery a slope, they would proceed to undermine their own intimacy. Such "close relationships," after all, need not be limited to two persons.[21] For the polyamorous, three is hardly a crowd.

Suitably engaged, I would press on. "Nor is logic 'after the fact.' Logic is 'in the fact.' Absent logic we cannot speak of facts at all, and whatever it is we are speaking of, we are caught in doublespeak. *Sans* logic, everything is what it is and the opposite, and anything else as well. Yet, the truth is that everything is what it is and not another thing. If words mean whatever we want them to mean and if their referents are whatever we take them to be, then the doctrine of non-contradiction fails. But at what cost does it fail? As W. V. O. Quine noted, "when [the deviant logician] tries to deny the doctrine he only changes the subject."[22] And do you speak of truth, freedom, and the American Way? Why, sir, show remorse for the havoc that nominalists have wrecked with them, and then we will speak again."

Yet in so rebuking my nemesis, I might satisfy myself more than a dispassionate reader. Such a reader, perhaps, might ask whether I should not offer a more measured reply; and the question would be legitimate.

Despite the limits of space, I *can* indicate the trajectory of a more fundamental reply to the nominalist. For a reply measured with the deepest of measures, I would turn to the theologian Angelo Scola.[23] He highlights, to contest sharply, what some take to be a formidable, even insurmountable, objection to John Paul II's encyclical *Fides et ratio*. The objection is, indirectly but critically, relevant to my own argument thus far. The charge at issue is that the encyclical, in trying to harmonize faith and reason, assumes too much. It wrongly assumes that, when we

---

[21] For an instructive analysis of the legal model of "close relationship" marriage, see "The Future of Family Law: Law and the Marriage Crisis in North America, a Report from the Council on Family Law," Dan Cere, Principal Investigator, Institute for American Values, 2005. Email: info@americanvalues.org.

[22] W. V. O. Quine, *Philosophy of Logic*, 2nd ed. (Cambridge: Harvard University Press, 1986), p. 81. Robert Hanna recalls this quip in his *Kant and the Foundations of Analytic Philosophy* (New York: Oxford University Press, 2001), p. 283.

[23] Angelo Cardinal Scola is Patriarch of Venice.

come to the heart of things, analogy - any true analogy—*is even possible.* Nor, opine said objectors, need we deny Being in order to sustain this objection. They permit us, rather, to admit Being along with its retinue of attending metaphysicians. It matters not, the critics insist, because Being does not disclose itself. In the beginning, and in the end, there is only and ultimately silence. Nor can Thomists hope for anything from their master. Scola's analysis of the critics' case takes an historical turn. "[T]he majestic intellectual architecture that Thomas brought to completion on the basis of the analogy of being collapsed, they insist, under its own weight when Ockham boldly asserted that everything is a mere *name* because even analogy tells us nothing about the *thing.*"[24]

Keen to their challenge, Scola asks, "How, then, do we respond to this unsparing criticism, which perhaps gives us the key to deciphering a number of contradictory cultural, political, and social phenomena, at least in the West?"[25] Not being a rationalist, his answer makes no appeal to an absolute reason, a Reason that might somehow intimidate Being. Scola's answer is, however, profoundly realist; it is illuminatingly personalist as well. The answer, for the Catholic, is that we are to rediscover Being, to rediscover the One, as *self-revealing.* The human person continually approaches this recovery in a life that freely embraces the real. In Jesus, we find the primary act of abandonment to the One, an act that expresses the primary structure of love. "It is just here," Scola writes, "that we begin to see the import of the gratuitous event of Jesus Christ. For it is Christ who, in his singular person, achieves the *analogia entis* within the *analogia libertatis.*"[26]

In virtue of the Incarnation, one might add, the insight that the best venue for articulating an explanatory metaphysics lies in our interpersonal relationships becomes theologically decisive. No such relationship is more profound than the nuptial relationship that opens

---

[24] Angelo Scola, "The Integrity of Human Experience," in *Restoring Faith in Reason*, edited by Laurence Paul Hemming and Susan Frank Parsons (Notre Dame, Indiana: University of Notre Dame Press, 2003), p. 263. For a fuller context, see Scola's *The Nuptial Mystery* (Grand Rapids, Michigan: Eerdmans, 2005).

[25] Ibid., p. 263.

[26] Ibid., p. 264.

love to life. W. Norris Clarke, indeed, reminds us that Jacques Maritain's thesis, "There is a nuptial relationship between mind and reality," honors the analogical richness of this bond.[27] Indeed, Mary, in her humility, understood this most profoundly of all. For this reason, the Catholic tradition acclaims her, Bride of the Spirit and *Theotokos*, as the Seat of Wisdom.[28]

4. Envoi

This essay has offered only the broad outlines of an argument for its twofold thesis. Still, the thesis is significant. Negatively, I have argued that much of our public discourse muddles the language of analogy and that it sometimes does so with malice aforethought. Positively, I have argued that a realist metaphysics can help put matters right and that John Wild, W. Norris Clarke, and Angelo Scola have given us valuable help for doing so.

But for this thesis to be fully vested and thoroughly developed, we must wait upon more sustained reflection. Indeed, if we are to overcome popular culture, we must also wait upon—to paraphrase Alasdair MacIntrye—both a new George Orwell, for plain speaking, and a new Mark Twain, for comic unmasking. And may both stalwarts come among us as Thomists. Lastly, while we await such estimable allies, let us be cautious. Language has its canny counterfeiters; its referents have their malign mystifiers. Yves Simon dealt with both in times as perilous as ours, and he has put us on alert. "[I]n human affairs, counterfeit is so related to genuine form that it appears, with disquieting frequency, precisely where the genuine form is most earnestly sought."[29]

---

[27] Clarke, *The One and the Many*, p. 39.

[28] *Fides et Ratio* #108 explores this theme.

[29] Yves R. Simon, *A General Theory of Authority* (Notre Dame, Indiana: University of Notre Dame Press, 1962), p. 27.

TRUTH AND SUFFERING

Joseph J. Califano

1. Introduction

Some years ago, while delivering a paper in Nova Scotia, Canada, I made the claim that there can be no attainment of genuine truth without suffering. The vehement reaction of the audience to this claim was surprising. They were angered and insulted by what I regarded as a simple fact that I had learned at eight years of age.[1] Some of them thought that it was absurd to make such a claim. A series of arguments followed, which demonstrated that this assertion touched a very sensitive nerve or sore spot at the very center of their worldviews. Some audience members were blinded by the categories of truth in their contemporary conceptual scheme, which they assumed to be exhaustive and unquestionable, even though some held simultaneously that there were no absolutes truths to be recognized.[2]

The audience's response to this assertion exemplifies a certain modern and post—modern obsession with skepticism and radically empiricist epistemology as the only justifiable account of truth. This obsession has led many to adopt an anti-intellectual and self-

---

[1] Throughout my life, I have had some acquaintance with suffering. Without going into detail, I have lived with some level of pain (from moderate to intense intractable pain) from the time I was eighteen months old, when I contracted polio the first time. When I was eight years old, I was put in a large Quonset building to die with other children, when I contracted polio for the second time. Many of the children in that room died. I have experienced paralyzing pain and spent numerous years in a wheelchair due to injuries to my spine from automobile accidents. I have also had a bout with cancer.

[2] It is not the author's intent to place himself on an equal footing with Jacques Maritain. However the audience's response brings to mind Etienne Gilson's description of the French Society of Philosophy's reaction to Maritain in 1936, as stated by Bouglé: "What is the matter with him. I think he is crazy." Etienne Gilson, *The Philosopher and Theology*, translated by Cécile Gilson (New York: Random House, 1962), p. 203.

destructive *modus operandi* lying at the root of this contemporary epistemological attitude. According to this mindset, when the intellect turns reflexively on itself, it concludes that we are incapable of attaining genuine knowledge pertaining to the truth or goodness of the human person, including moral wisdom and the extra-mental realities of God and the universe. This deflation of truth and goodness leads also to the obscuration of beauty.[3] Following this path has led many persons to the intellectual, moral and personal desert of nihilism, in which a voluntary spiritual death is inescapable. Rhetoric and dialectics on this view[4] take the place of metaphysics and philosophical wisdom. One sees a world that is devoid of saints or sinners—a world devoid of vision[5] or insight. Inhabitants of this world lose an understanding of the meaning of a well-ordered appetite, especially a well-ordered will, and the existential final cause of the acting person is forgotten.

2. Adolescence and the 'isms'—the idols of our time

It is beyond the scope of the present chapter to discuss the preambles to the discovery of the relationship between truth and suffering. We also cannot treat the questions of God's existence, omnipotence, and goodness[6], the nature of the human soul, the

---

[3] The synthesis of truth and goodness in the existential experience of beauty is one of the principal ways the human person can discover God.

[4] To the logician who is only a logician, and thus rejects the possibility of achieving genuine physical and metaphysical truth, what follows would be nonsense. Unfortunately, too many of our contemporaries have chosen this dead-end path. For such persons, it is nonsense to speak of truth and the meaning of suffering. For a further development of the difference between the dialectician and the logician, see the author's article "On the Nature of Being and the Division of the Speculative Sciences," *A Thomistic Tapestry: Essays in Memory of Étienne Gilson,* edited by Peter Redpath (Amsterdam & New York: Value Inquiry Book Series, 2003), pp. 79-93.

[5] "Where there is no vision the people will perish..." (Prov. 29:18).

[6] Cf. Jacques Maritain, *Existence and the Existent,* translated by Lewis Galantiere & Gerald Phelan (Garden City, New York: Double Day Image Books, 1958); *God and the Permission of Evil,* translated by Joseph W. Evans (Milwaukee, Wisconsin: Bruce, 1965). Cf. also Peter Kreeft, *Making Sense out of Suffering* (Ann Arbor, Michigan: Servant Books, 1986); William J. O'Malley, *Redemptive*

facticity of unmerited suffering[7] or the kind of reality attributable to evil. These questions, when they are answered in a way contrary to what follows, are all arguably rooted in a state of spiritual adolescence. Intellectual, spiritual and moral adolescence are at the foundation of atheism, agnosticism, rationalism, deism, relativism, skepticism, and other social and political 'isms' characteristic of contemporary popular culture.[8]

Such views tend to inhibit in varying degrees the intellectual and moral development of the human person beyond the immaturity of youth to a spiritually mature life in God. They are rooted in a perspective that gives precedence to one's own ideas of what God ought to be—the idols of our minds and hearts—over the God who is. Such idols are easily manufactured and more easily put to the torch, since they have no more reality, truth and life than the straw men of materialism or the gods of ancient Egypt.[9] They, each in their own way, proclaim that if they were God, they would have done it all differently. But, since the world has not been created according to their particular plan, the existence of God, His omnipotence and His goodness, which are the foundation of all that exists, must be thrown into doubt. In other words, such views involve a kind of self-deification.

This is why in our contemporary world, where the idols of modernity and post-modernity reign, adolescence is worshiped, exalted and glorified, rather than God. Adolescence is glorified beyond its intrinsic value because of an unwillingness to accept reality and

---

Suffering (New York: Crossword Books, 1997); Harold Kushner, *When Bad Things Happen To Good People* (New York: Schocken Books, 1981).

[7] The unmerited suffering of children may be for many the source of the greatest difficulty with the following argument.

[8] Cf. the author's previous work on suffering: "Human Suffering and Our Post-Civilized Cultured Mind," in *From Twilight to Dawn*, edited by Peter A. Redpath, (Notre Dame: American Maritain Association, 1990), pp. 203-14.

[9] "Their idols are silver and gold; the work of human hands. They have mouths but they cannot speak; they have eyes but they cannot see; they have ears but they cannot hear; they have nostrils but they cannot smell. With their hands they cannot feel; with their feet they cannot walk. No sound comes from their throats. Their makers will come to be like them. And so will all who trust in them" (Ps. 115:4-8).

cultivate the humility required of the human person before God. Personal maturity, on the other hand, requires that one put aside thinking and acting like a child,[10] so that genuine personality can be achieved through self-discovery. Personal maturity is required for the transcendent achievement of an integrated personality and an abundantly meaningful life.[11] In spite of many discussions with so-called 'atheists,' I have never met one who has moved beyond adolescence in thought or temperament. Atheists, too, have their absolutes—the 'gods' or idols that they worship. Whether expressed or implied, they could be the ancient idols of absolute power, wealth, pleasures of the body, or soul for example. In other cases, they worship their own ego as the highest power in existence.

3. A few words on the five ways of understanding the nature of truth

Truth is an analogical reality and there are at least five ways in which we speak of truth, including among others the epistemological notion of truth. We should note that truth is a relationship between an intellect and a being, and that truth or falsity is found in the act of judgment. Speaking epistemically, a judgment is true when it conforms to or is an adequation of what exists independently of the intellect. True judgments unite what is one in reality, and separate what is separated in reality, independent of the intellect. The being of the thing known is therefore the measure of the truth of a judgment.

A second way we speak of truth is the notion of a true friend as opposed to a false friend, who might be a true enemy, or a true love as opposed to a false love (e.g. infatuation), or true gold as opposed to iron pyrite—"fools' gold." Here the judgment concerning a being is rooted in a proper understanding of the essential nature of a thing, and also its excellence, which makes it a being of a certain kind. Intellectual

---

[10] 1 Cor. 13: 11: "When I was a child I used to talk as child, think as child, reason as a child; when I became a man I put aside childish things."

[11] Adolescence may be a stage of development through which we all pass, even though many psychologists believe it is artificial, rooted in the extension of childhood in modern industrial societies. Whether it is necessary or artificial, it is not a stage of life in which one should seek to remain permanently, especially if one seeks the integration of one's personality and one's life, as a good to be achieved.

knowledge of a nature, specifically the identifying activity or characteristics of that nature, is the measure of the truth of the judgment. It is, by analogy, an "acid test" that permits us with certainty to distinguish truth (genuine gold) from falsity (iron pyrite).[12]

A third way in which we speak of truth concerns the identity of a being in and to itself. In Thomistic terms, each and every being, as distinct from God, has its own unique intensity of *esse*, that is its own act of existing, limited by its essence which actualizes it as an *ens habens esse*, a being having it's own act of existing.[13] Thus, God does not create essences as such, but He conveys different intensities of 'to be'—*esse*—that define or limit a being to having a determinate essence.[14]

We can thus speak of natural things as true in so far as they are effects, caused by the Divine intellect and will. We can also speak of natural beings as causes of knowledge in the human intellect and as beings in their own right.[15] The foregoing analogical notions of truth

---

[12] This is similar to the use of sulfuric acid in order to identify genuine gold, and litmus paper to distinguish an acid from a base. All qualitative chemistry operates on this principle, which is related to the principle *operatio sequitur esse*. Thus, we know what a thing is by its operations.

[13] See Califano, "Human Suffering and Our Post-Civilized Cultured Mind."

[14] Reflection on his experience of the gradation of *esse* led Thomas to assert that oneness, truth, goodness, beauty, life and all other pure perfections are identical to the *esse* of finite beings. There is only a logical distinction between the pure perfections of a finite being and its *esse*. The fact that finite beings do not possess pure perfections completely leads to the conclusion that these perfections are not identical to the essence of finite beings. This is evidence that the *esse* of finite beings is received from the one who has these pure perfections perfectly as identical to His essence, namely, God. God is the only being whose essence is His *esse*. Thus, God does not create essences as such, but He conveys different intensities of *esse* that define or limit a being to having a determinate essence.

[15] The truth of natural beings as effects of divine art or causes of knowledge in us is understood via the analogy of attribution, that is *secundum intentionem, sed non secundum esse*. It is only when we view a being as existing in its own right, as an *ens habens esse* that we have an analogy *secundum intentionem et secundum esse* that preserves both the sameness and differences in beings qua beings. The analogy of a genus which is an analogy *secundum esse sed non*

are really distinct from one another, but they cannot be separated without dismantling the nature of truth and falling into nihilism. This is why the unity of these various notions of truth is so important to us. When our intellect is adequated to a natural being, which is the product of Divine intellect or art, it also achieves a proportional adequation to the Divine intellect and will. This, in turn, constitutes one of the many ways in which we are called to unity with God in our very being.

There is a fourth way we can speak of truth when we look at the life of Christ and the lives of the saints and we see how he lived his life and they lived their lives as exemplars or models for us to follow in living our lives. We see that our lives can only be genuinely true insofar as they conform to the way Christ and the saints lived their lives. Speaking of truth in this way delineates a relationship between the various notions of the true cited above and reveals an inseparable connection between truth and the ideas of beauty and moral goodness.

A fifth way of speaking about truth is to identify what may be called certain 'definitive truths'. 'Definitive truths' provide a fully differentiated and developed solution or answer to some difficulty. My contention is that there are definitive truths that can only be discovered with certainty through human suffering. These truths provide a foundation for self-discovery and the dynamic force necessary to achieve the personal integration that renders a life meaningful, even in the face of intense suffering. To speak of the 'meaning of suffering' or the 'meaning of life' presupposes that there are underlying truths that give meaning to life and suffering. Meaning, in other words, is a second intentional notion that requires first intentional discoveries as its foundation.

4. The question suffering poses to us at the center of our hearts

Intense suffering and confrontation with imminent death is unparalleled in posing a concrete, singular, and unique challenge to the human person. This challenge concerns whether such a person possesses a definitive truth that gives meaning to suffering and life. The suffering person needs a definitive truth that will satisfy the

---

secundum intentionem and the poetic analogy of metaphor, *secundum intentionem, sed non secundum esse,* do not apply here.

questions of the human heart in the biblical sense of the 'heart' as the absolute center of our being.[16] Definitive truths fill the human heart—the place of the indwelling of the Holy Spirit—with meaning. Without them, there is a critical absence of the spirit of God in the lives of men and women. This is especially true of the challenge to come to grips with the mystery that God loves us in spite of the fact that He permits evil, while never willing or condoning it. Intractable and intense pain challenges us to recognize God's love for us, and to live the relationship between faith, intelligence, and surrendering lovingly to God that we are called to achieve in this life. Suffering is the two-edged sword that cuts through the Gordian knots of our spiritual struggle and renders the definitive truths of life accessible to us in a concrete personal way.

It is because we are "a stiff-necked"[17] people, "uncircumcised in heart,"[18] and always opposing the Holy Spirit, that suffering can serve as a necessary "wake up call." It leads us to the purity of heart[19] required to attain our existential final cause, which is union with God.[20]

---

[16] The key to understanding the Judaeo-Christian tradition's view of good and evil is the biblical notion of the human heart as the place of the indwelling of the Holy Spirit, or conversely as the absence of the spirit of God in the lives of men and women. The Hebrew word for heart: Lev—Levov, pronounced Lab or Labab, and the New Testament word for heart: Καρδια, refer to the absolute center of a human being, where the knowing and appetitive powers are united to the good by the presence of God or to evil by the absence of God. The absence of God in the heart of men and women leads only to disarray, meaninglessness and the destruction of the person.

[17] Acts 7:51. Cf. Exod. 32:9; 33:3, 9; Deut. 9:6, 13; 10:16.

[18] Ibid. Cf., also "The human heart is deceitful above all things and desperately wicked: Who can know it?" (Jer. 17:9).

[19] "How good is God to Israel to those who are pure of heart" (Ps. 73:1). "Blessed are the clean (pure) of heart for they will see God" (Matt. 5:8).

[20] Maritain quite correctly pointed out that there is no purely natural final cause to the human existent. Cf. Jacques Maritain, *Neuf Leçons Sur Les Notions Premières De La Philosophie Morale* (Paris: Editions Pierre Tequi, 1950); English: *An Introduction To The Basic Problems of Moral Philosophy*, translated by Cornelia N. Borgehoff (Albany New York: Magi Books, 1990).

This attainment must be preceded by the emptying of ourselves in imitation of Christ that is described in Philippians.[21]

C. S. Lewis, who was at one time an atheist, suffered much and was eventually converted to Christianity. He argues that it is precisely because God loves us that suffering is part of His creation. God calls us in this way to respond to His love for the sake of our ultimate fulfillment.[22] Pain reminds us that the pleasures of this life are never intended to possess our hearts.

St. Thomas Aquinas expresses a similar viewpoint when he states that the ills of this life, concomitant with the effects of original sin, may be ordained to help "against future sin, or for progress in virtue, either of him who suffers it or of another.... But the very fact that man is in such a condition that he must be helped, either to avoid sin, or to advance in virtue, by means of these misfortunes or defects pertains to

---

[21] Phil. 2:25-8: "Have among yourselves the same attitude that is also yours in Christ Jesus. Who though he was in the form of God did not regard equality with God something to be grasped. Rather he emptied himself taking on the form of a slave, coming in human likeness, and found human in appearance, he humbled himself becoming obedient to death, even death on a cross."

[22] C.S. Lewis: "The human spirit will not even begin to try to surrender self-will as long as all seems to be well with it... pain insists upon being attended to. God whispers to us in our pleasures, speaks in our conscience but shouts in our pains: it is His megaphone to rouse a deaf world... I remind myself that all these toys were never intended to possess my heart, that my true good is in another world, and my only real treasure is Christ," *Readings for Meditation and Reflection* (Harper, San Francisco, 1996), p. 71. "Christ said it was difficult for the rich to enter the kingdom of Heaven referring, no doubt, to riches in the ordinary sense. But I think it really covers riches in every sense—good fortune, health, popularity and all things one wants to have. All these things tend just as money tends--to make one feel independent from God because if you have them you are happy already and contented in this life. You don't want to turn away to anything more, and so you try to rest in a shadowy happiness, as if it could last forever... But God wants to give you a real eternal happiness. Consequently, he may have to take all these riches away from you: if He doesn't, you will go on relying on them. It sounds cruel doesn't it? But...cruel doctrines are really the kindest of all...think of this world as a.... place of training and it's not so bad" (Ibid., p. 103).

the weakness of human nature... just as the fact that the body of man is so disposed that it needs surgery to cure it pertains to its weakness."[23]

The famous psychiatrist Viktor Frankl similarly describes three psychological stages that prisoners in Nazi concentration camps went through when confronted with indescribable and unavoidable suffering, and impending death. [24] At first they experienced shock, and then they became emotionally numb. Finally, those who were able to survive realized that they must ask what life (and God) was asking of them, not what they should ask of life. We put God to the test when we formulate questions we should ask of Him. The more important questions are those that God—who is life—is putting to us. People who had faith in the camps realized that life—God—was challenging them to bear witness to a truth that helped them to avoid despair. In the same way, Job realized this and persevered in his trust and love of God.[25]

Suffering poses a concrete, singular, unique question that requires self-transcendence, a going beyond oneself to a love of life, God and other persons. The task for each of us is to find the enduring love of the personal God who transcends all of the idols or 'isms'—the straw gods—of our day. The true personal God is the only one who can bring peace within our suffering. Suffering may be the only way we can genuinely find that personal God to whom we are called to surrender in love. Suffering may be the necessary path to experiencing authentically the love of God that enables us to love God, and our neighbor as ourselves. The central issue is not the fact that we suffer, but what we do with our suffering, or more precisely what we let God do with our suffering. The God who loves us loves us enough that He created us, even knowing that we would reject his love and sin. He freely created us out of nothing, giving us the greatest gift of all—our very existence. What is even more overwhelming is the fact that he freely chose to love us,

---

[23] *QDM* q. 5, a.4c, translated by Jean Oesterle (Notre Dame: University of Notre Dame Press, 1995), pp. 223-24.

[24] Viktor Frankl, *Man's Search for Meaning* (New York: Washington Square Press, Pocket Books edition, 1984), pp. 98, 104-05.

[25] Jb 1:21: "Naked I came forth from my mother's womb, and naked I shall go back again. The Lord gave and the Lord has taken away. Blessed be the name of the Lord. We accept good things from God."

suffer for us, and even die for us. These definitive personal truths cannot be captured or comprehended by a merely impersonal deism.

Suffering is a critical existential path to transcendence for the individual, who must move beyond the pleasure principle and the dictates of the sense appetites. The human person must get beyond self-absorption with pain in order to attain spiritual enlightenment, in which one's relationship to God as love becomes concrete in a singular fashion. God desires intimacy with each and every individual soul, created as an object of God's love. Through that intimate love relationship, one discovers the definitive truth that His life is an offertory, and that the spiritual life within God is the final cause of each and every acting person. Suffering calls forth from us transcendence of the limitations of human reason, not by rejecting reason, but by seeing all things in a new and different light that reveals what is genuine in the truths of reason. God is therefore most properly understood as the loving final cause of our being.

In suffering, we are moved of necessity beyond philosophy and theology ordinarily understood. We do not jettison their insights, but they are elevated in the life-giving light of actual grace. We, in turn, must freely accept or reject the concrete union God offers freely and individually to each of us. The suffering human person either turns towards God in love or turns away from God.

We are thus reminded of the three degrees of darkness and separation from God and the three degrees of union with God indicated by the parable of the sower.[26] There are those who hear the word of God with joy and then spend their rest of their lives not understanding it, but explaining it away. These are the proponents of various 'isms' cited above. In the second degree of separation from God, persons become blind to their relationship with God as their end or final cause. Finally, one may lose all contact with the reality of unity, truth, goodness, and beauty, collapsing into nihilism, and even despair and death.

Opposed to the above, we find in the lives of the saints the three degrees of union with God: purgative prayer that empties one's heart of the need to accumulate material things, contemplative prayer that

[26] Cf. Matt. 13, Mark 4.

empties the heart of intellectual self-centeredness, and unitive prayer, which enables us to live in the reality of God's presence. This unity permeates our very being, beyond the depth of emotions or merely intellectual understanding. It involves surrendering our whole being to God's love so that we experience life completely. It is the center of all genuine contemplation and the source of our anticipation of seeing God face to face.[27] It must include a lived experience in which God's word becomes alive in the center of our being: "It strikes to the heart. It pierces more surely than a two edged sword."[28]

What God seeks from us is that we turn to God in our pain, including physical, psychological, and emotional suffering. God seeks a response to His infinite act of love for us, which He manifested by surrendering himself and by becoming one of us in the incarnation, crucifixion, and resurrection of the second person of the Blessed Trinity. He suffers for us and with us in so far as we identify with him and to the degree that we enter into his mystical body the Church as the fulfillment of his loving salvific will.

God's knowledge and love for us is not merely abstract. He knows and loves each of us as an individual. It is in living a person-to-person relationship with God (in three persons) that one discovers the definitive truth that this life is an offertory, and that the spiritual life within God is an offertory.[29] Secularism, and to some degree secular psychology, neglects the integration of one's life and personality that takes place by reason of this recognition. On the other hand, peace while suffering comes to the human heart in unitive offertory prayer,

---

[27] "Set me as a seal on your heart, as a seal on your arm; For stern as death is love, relentless as the nether world is devotion; its flames are a blazing fire. Deep waters cannot quench love, nor floods sweep it away. Were one to offer all he owns to purchase love, he would be roundly mocked" (Sg. 8: 6-7).

[28] *The Liturgy of the Hours* (Catholic Book Publishing Co., 1973), Vol. III, Morning prayer, Common of pastors, Ant. 3., P1751.

[29] Rom. 12:1-2; St. Paul reminds us of how the apostles suffered for the sake of the Gospel and the martyrs offered their very lives for the truth: "Brothers, I beg you through the mercy of God to offer your bodies as a living sacrifice holy and acceptable to God your spiritual worship. Do not conform yourselves to this age but be transformed by the renewal of your mind, so that you may judge what is God's will, what is good, pleasing and perfect."

which demonstrates the shortcomings of the contemporary mindset and the 'isms' noted above. The contemporary world is increasingly devoid of saints or sinners, and so it lacks vision and truth in respect to life and suffering. The truth about suffering is not only that there could be no saints or sinners without suffering, but also that there could be no achievement or failure in the integration of our personalities—no personal transcendence—without suffering. The spiritual level is the only level within which it can be achieved. For many suffering persons, this emerges in the dark night of the soul, when all one has to hang on to is the love of God and there is nothing more than the hope of the unseen of which St. Paul speaks[30] and the sufficiency of God's grace. [31]

Each and every genuine definitive truth I have ever discovered was discovered contemplating the offertory of the Cross of Christ in the Eucharist. Suffering is a gift. It is the key that fits the lock that opens the door to the transcendence that enriches one's heart with the meaning of human existence and the inherent value of life. Look at the saints.[32] They exemplify this truth just as our Lord did: his life was an offertory. That is why He is the head of the Church and why the saints are the Church's successful members. May we all be so successful in our Lord Jesus Christ!

If I discover a fact, I have added data to my data bank. If I discover a truth in the natural order of things, I have gained some limited understanding of some natural phenomena. If I discover a definitive truth that defines my relationship to the one true personal God and my

---

[30] Rom. 8:24-25: "In hope we were saved. But hope is not hope if its object is seen; how is it possible for one to hope for what he sees? And hoping for what we can see means awaiting it with patient endurance."

[31] 2 Cor. 12:7-9: "Therefore that I might not become too elated a thorn in the flesh was given to me, an angel of Satan to beat me, to keep me from being too elated. Three times I begged the Lord about this, that it might leave me, but he said to me, 'My grace is sufficient for you for power is made perfect in weakness.' I will rather boast most gladly of my weakness, in order that the power of Christ may dwell in me."

[32] Heb. 7-8; St. Paul reminds us again of how the apostles, saints, and martyrs suffered for the Gospel: "Remember your leaders who spoke the word of God to you. Consider the outcome of their way of life and imitate their faith. Jesus Christ is the same yesterday, today and forever."

neighbor, a truth that integrates me personally, making me whole, then I have life-giving, heart-enriching, life-sustaining, saving wisdom.

INDEX OF NAMES

A

B

C

D

Q

R

S

T

V

W

X

Z

CONTRIBUTORS

Deacon Joseph Califano, Ph.D., has degrees in Economics and Finance and in Philosophy, done research at the Philosophy of Science Institute, and taught moral philosophy at St. John's University for 47 years. He has given presentations and published in Asia, Europe, Canada, the Third World and the USA. His research in ethics has focused on the areas of social justice, of modernization and applied technologies--both in developed and developing nations--and of medicine and energy. He has served on panels regarding the ethics of stem cell research and other contemporary medical issues, and on the International Commissions on Energy Use Management and Hydrogen Energy, regarding health issues. He has made presentations at hospitals and the American Cancer Society, e.g. on the use of ordinary and extraordinary means in the treatment of children. He has received grants from the National Science Foundation and the De Rance Foundation for his work. Several articles in previous AMA volumes, e.g. "Human Suffering and Our Post-Civilized Cultural Mind" and "The Self, Intersubjectivity, and the Common Good" relate to his article in this volume. He is one of the original founders of the American Maritain Association.

Carlos A. Casanova was born in Caracas, Venezuela, in 1966. He obtained a Law degree from the Universidad Católica Andrés Bello in 1988, and his Ph.D. in Philosophy from the Universidad de Navarra in 1995. After having been the Chair of Graduate Studies in Philosophy at the Universidad Simón Bolívar, he was forced to leave his country for political reasons. He became a visiting scholar at Boston University and then a Senior Research Associate of the Maritain Center at Notre Dame. He has published seven books demonstrating a wide philosophical scope (on metaphysics, natural theology, philosophy of science, philosophical anthropology and political philosophy) and dozens of papers. He also edited an eighth book (the *Festschrift* for Josef Seifert). Presently, he is the Director of Studies of the International Academy of Philosophy in the Principality of Liechtenstein, Chilean campus (at the Pontificia Universidad Católica de Chile). He is married to Laura Ternan and has two children.

Gavin T. Colvert is Associate Professor of Philosophy and Director of the Ecumenical Institute at Assumption College in Worcester,

Massachusetts. He has published articles in the areas of ethics, political philosophy, philosophy of religion, and medieval philosophy. He is currently working on a study of the historical and contemporary importance of virtue and law in Aquinas' ethical and political theory.

J. L. A. Garcia, after his Yale doctorate, was Associate Professor in Notre Dame and Georgetown universities' philosophy departments, Professor in Rutgers's and now Boston College's, and Visiting Professor in MIT's Department of Linguistics & Philosophy. His research won postdoctoral fellowships from Ford Foundation, NEH, and Harvard University, and he was Non-resident Fellow in Harvard's Du Bois Institute. He has published in international journals, collections, and reference works on topics in social philosophy, moral theory, and bioethics, reaching wider readership in *Logos*, *Books & Culture*, *Society*, and *First Things.* Formerly Senior Research Scholar in the Kennedy Institute of Ethics, he has consulted for NIH, U.S. Department of Education, Smithsonian, and ACLS. Past member of Society of Christian Philosophers' and American Catholic Philosophical Associations' Boards, and the APA Eastern Division's Executive Committee, he served on APA's Committee on Hispanics, chaired its Committee on Blacks and was Vice-President of the Society for the Study of Africana Philosophy in New York City.

Marie I. George received her Ph.D. in philosophy from Laval University in 1987, and is currently Professor of Philosophy at St. John's University, New York. An Aristotelian-Thomist, her interests lie primarily in the areas of natural philosophy and philosophy of science. She has received several awards from the John Templeton Foundation for her work in science and religion, and in 2007 she was co-recipient of a grant from the Center for Theology and the Natural Sciences (CTNS) for an interdisciplinary project entitled "The Evolution of Sympathy and Morality." Professor George has authored over 50 peer-reviewed articles and two books: *Christianity and Extraterrestrials? A Catholic Perspective* (2005) and *Stewardship of Creation* (2009). She also co-edited the AMA volume, *Faith, Scholarship, and Culture in the 21st Century* (2002). She is currently working on Aquinas's "Fifth Way," and also on a variety of questions concerning living things (self-motion, consciousness, evolution, etc.).

James G. Hanink is midway in his fourth decade of teaching philosophy. His areas of special interest are Thomism, personalism, and ethics. Essays and reviews of his have appeared in both academic venues and journals of opinion. He is active in University Faculty for Life. With his wife, Elizabeth, he is involved in pro-life work in Los Angeles, California.

James M. Jacobs is Professor of Philosophy at Notre Dame Seminary in New Orleans, Louisiana, where he has taught since 2003. He is also currently Director of the Pre-Theology Program. He holds a BA from Harvard University and a Ph.D. from Fordham University. His major area of research is Thomistic natural law theory, and more generally the need for a philosophical realism as a response to modern nominalism and skepticism. His articles have appeared in such journals as the *American Catholic Philosophical Quarterly*, *International Philosophical Quarterly*, and *Nova et Vetera.*

Patrick Lee holds the John N. and Jamie D. McAleer Chair of Bioethics, and is the Director of the Institute of Bioethics, at Franciscan University of Steubenville. He is known nationally as a speaker and author on contemporary ethics, especially on such hot-button bioethical issues as abortion, embryonic stem-cell research, euthanasia, sexual morality, and same-sex unions. He is the co-author (with Robert P. George) of *Body-Self Dualism in Contemporary Ethics and Politics* (New York: Cambridge University Press, 2008). The second edition of his *Abortion and Unborn Human Life* (Washington, D.C.: Catholic University of America Press) appeared in 2010. He has written numerous articles and reviews in such publications as *Bioethics, Philosophy*, *The Thomist*, and *Theological Studies.*

Alice Ramos is Professor of Philosophy at St. John's University in Queens, New York. She holds a Ph.D. in Philosophy from the University of Navarra in Spain. Her publications include a book, *Signum: De la semiótica universal a la metafísica del signo*, two edited books for the American Maritain Association--*Beauty, Art, and the Polis* (2000) and *Faith, Scholarship, and Culture in the 21st Century* (2002)--and over fifty articles in areas such as Thomistic metaphysics and ethics, Christian anthropology, and aesthetics. She is the recipient of grants and fellowships both in the United States and in Europe. She is a past president of the American Maritain Association and has served twice on the Executive Council of the American Catholic Philosophical Association. Her current research is on the transcendentals in the Thomistic tradition.

James V. Schall, S. J., is a professor in the Government Department at Georgetown University. He has published *Jacques Maritain: A Philosopher in the City*; *The Limits of Political Philosophy*; *The Mind That Is Catholic*; *On the Unseriousness of Human Affairs*; *Another Sort of Learning*; and *The Modern Age*.

Denis A. Scrandis completed a BS in Philosophy at The College of the City of New York, in 1966. After serving in the USAF (1967-71) and having discovered his interest in Thomism from reading Jacques Maritain's *Preface to Metaphysics* and *The Degrees of Knowledge*, he earned a MA at Marquette University, in 1972. He pursued doctoral studies at the University of Toronto and The Catholic University of America and was a founding member of the American Maritain Association. Following a career of government service in New York City, he returned to doctoral studies at Fordham University and contributed to AMA conferences. He is presently teaching introductory courses in philosophy at St. John's University, Jamaica, New York. His article "A Demonstration of the Personhood of the Human Embryo," *National Catholic Bioethics Quarterly* (Winter, 2009) received the Catholic Press Association's 2nd place prize for "Best Essay, Scholarly Magazine," 2010.

Peter L. P. Simpson is Professor of Philosophy and Classics at the City University of New York. He was born and educated in the UK but has lived in the US for over 20 years and is a naturalized US citizen. His main interests are ancient philosophy (especially Aristotle) and moral and political philosophy. He has written books on Aristotle's Politics, on Moral Philosophy, and on Karol Wojtyła, in addition to numerous articles on philosophical topics more generally (for details, see www.aristotelophile.com). He is currently working on translations and explanations of Aristotle's *Magna Moralia* and *Eudemian Ethics*.

Msgr. Robert Sokolowski is the Elizabeth Breckenridge Caldwell Professor of Philosophy at The Catholic University of America, where he has taught since 1963. His most recent publication is *Phenomenology of the Human Person*, published in 2008, and his *Christian Faith and Human Understanding: Studies in the Eucharist, Trinity, and the Human Person* appeared in 2006. He was President of the Academy of Catholic Theology in 2010, the annual meeting of which was devoted to the topic "God's Word and Human Speech." Msgr. Sokolowski gave the keynote address at a conference in Leuven in 2009 commemorating the 150th anniversary of Husserl's birth. The title of his address was "Husserl on First Philosophy."

Fr. Joseph M. de Torre is a University Professor Emeritus of Social and Political Philosophy at the University of Asia and the Pacific. He holds a Ph.D. degree from the Angelicum (Rome, 1953). He is a member of the American Maritain Association, the Fellowship of Catholic Scholars, the American Catholic Philosophical Association, the Society of Catholic Social Scientists, the Carnegie Council on Ethics and International Affairs, the University Faculty of Life, the Atlas Economic Research Foundation, the Acton Institute for the Study of Religion and Liberty, the Royal Institute of Philosophy (UK), the International Society for the Study of European Ideas (Israel), and the Catholic Educator Resource Center (Canada). Several of his books are used as textbooks in many schools in the Philippines and abroad.

Michael D. Torre is an Associate Professor of Philosophy at the University of San Francisco. He edited the American Maritain Association volume *Freedom in the Modern World: Jacques Maritain, Yves R. Simon, Mortimer J. Adler* (1989, second printing: 1990), and has contributed numerous articles to its series, of which he has been the General Editor since 2009. That same year, his *God's Permission of Sin: Negative or Conditioned Decree* was published by Fribourg University Press. He has served as a Vice-President of the Institut International Jacques Maritain.

John G. Trapani, Jr., Ph.D., is a professor of philosophy at Walsh University in North Canton, Ohio. During his 37 years at the University, he has served as Chair of the Philosophy Department and Humanities Division. In addition, he is also the Founder and Director of the University's annual Philosophy-Theology Symposium, now in its 36th year. The current President of the American Maritain Association, John has written extensively on Maritain's philosophy. His book, *Poetry, Beauty, and Contemplation: The Complete Aesthetics of Jacques Maritain*, will be released by Catholic University of America Press in February of 2011. In the AMA book series, he was the editor of *Truth Matters* (2004). John is also a professional musician, and leader of the 17-piece John Trapani Big Band, founded in 1977.

Cornelia A. Tsakiridou is Associate Professor in the Philosophy Department at La Salle University and Director of the Diplomat-In-Residence Program. She is the editor and contributor of a book on Jean Cocteau and has authored numerous articles on the aesthetics of painting, photography, Orthodox and Catholic iconography, and poetry. She is the translator of the Counsels of the Greek ascetic

Elder Paisios the Athonite and has also published in the area of Greek and Turkish nationalism and 19th century Protestant missionary theology. She has just completed a book manuscript on Orthodox theology and the aesthetics of the Christian image.